Muslims in Western Europe

D1610461

The New Edinburgh Islamic Surveys
Series Editor: Carole Hillenbrand

TITLES AVAILABLE OR FORTHCOMING

www.euppublishing.com/series/isur

Muslims in Western Europe

Fourth edition

Jørgen S. Nielsen
and (new edition) Jonas Otterbeck

EDINBURGH
University Press

First edition © Jørgen Nielsen, 1992
Second edition © Jørgen Nielsen, 1995
Third edition © Jørgen Nielsen, 2004
Fourth edition © Jørgen Nielsen and Jonas Otterbeck, 2016

Edinburgh University Press Ltd
The Tun – Holyrood Road
12 (2f) Jackson's Entry
Edinburgh EH8 8PJ
www.euppublishing.com

Typeset in 11/13pt Monotype Baskerville by
Servis Filmsetting Ltd, Stockport, Cheshire,
printed and bound in Great Britain by
CPI Group (UK) Ltd, Croydon CR0 4YY

A CIP record for this book is available from the British Library

ISBN 978 1 4744 0933 9 (paperback)
ISBN 978 1 4744 0934 6 (webready PDF)
ISBN 978 1 4744 0935 3 (epub)

The right of Jørgen S. Nielsen and Jonas Otterbeck to be
identified as authors of this work has been asserted in
accordance with the Copyright, Designs and Patents Act
1988 and the Copyright and Related Rights Regulations
2003 (SI No. 2498).

Contents

Preface

More than twenty years have passed since the first edition of this book. However, its structure and its driving questions have stood the test of time remarkably well. Still, the need for an updated version has become obvious as the field has developed and the legal and political structures of countries have changed. New Islamic organisations have taken the stage, and some old ones have lost influence. Having taught courses on Islam in Europe and benefitting from Jørgen Nielsen's book, I found the need for an update pressing and contacted the author asking if he considered a fourth edition. As it happened, I ended up responsible for the revisions instead, but Nielsen has assisted both with advice and proof reading, possibly becoming more involved than he at first meant to.

The history of an integration process

When Jørgen Nielsen penned the first edition of the book, western Europe was slowly becoming aware of a demographic change that was taking place. The book was timely, up to date, and yet scholarly, written by a historian who was among the first researchers to seriously consider the new Muslim presence in Europe. As time has passed and the new editions have been prepared and published in 1995, 2004, and now in 2015, the original part of the book describing the late 1980s and early 1990s has changed character and is now describing an important, transitional phase in the history of Muslim integration in western Europe. Reading the book today, a pattern emerges that was not there from the beginning. Rather, it has been created by the passing of time and been caught by the updates. If comparing the first faltering steps taken by Islamic organisations in the 1970s with the, at times, highly professionalised, often legally recognised, Muslim organisations of today, the development becomes striking. Muslim organisations have learnt to adapt and make space for themselves through trials and errors, a development that can be observed in all western European countries. Some have received external aid from, for example, the *Diyanet*, the Turkish Department of Religious Affairs, which sends out paid imams and helps out with organising. Others have been built up through local individual initatives when trying to take a stand in a single question – like the possibility of serving halal food at the local school. Later, these initiatives have grown into organisations, increasing the numbers of members, but also taking a political responsibility for integration, representing Muslims locally. For example, the Islamic Centre in Malmö, Sweden, developed just like that, starting in the early 1970s. Some Muslim activists have grown into professional civil society actors with a firm knowledge of legal and administrative matters as well as knowledge of the pragmatic ways of local and national politics.

At the same time, states' politics have developed. The first drowsy and haphazard responses to Muslim activists in the 1970s have led to an increased awareness, legal adaptation, and new administrative strategies. Several countries have developed, or expanded, a category often called something like 'recognised religious communities'. As such, Muslim organisations may gain legal recognition and with it rights on a par with other religious communities that have had a longer presence in western Europe. What these rights consist of differs. It might be the right to organise confessional religious instruction or collect membership fees through governmental taxation systems. The important issue, however, is the signal of integration; that Muslim organisations are legitimate. The process took some 40 years and the present book addresses it in two ways: country by country (chapters 2–7), and thematically with chapters addressing law, transnational and global Muslim organisations and profound political events (chapters 8–10).

The book focuses on the integration of organised Muslim life into western European states, and nowhere is this more visible than when looking at religious education (RE): each country chapter has a part on this. Education is the prime arena for a minority population where state influence is unavoidable. States view RE in numerous different ways. In Sweden, for example, the aim of RE is non-confessional giving pupils a broad introduction to religions as historical, social and ethical phenomena, while in Spain, Islamic organisations are allowed to arrange for confessional RE in public schools, developing their own textbooks for it. Muslim organisations are dependent on the so-called political opportunity structures of society, that is, the existing opportunities given by legal and administrative structures. However, without attempting to mobilise and daring to risk failure, few such structures would have been attainable by Muslims. It is not only the structures in place that matter, the individuals' actions – both the Muslim activists' and the progressive politicians' – are crucial if changes are to come about. Of course, some Muslim activists are also politicians as, over time, some Muslims have taken political office, yet another aspect of integration.

Those who have used the book before will recognise the structure, the one exception being that the bibliographical essay has been taken out due to the ease with which literature can be found today through search engines, and because of the abundance of available literature. For updates on literature, we refer the reader to the many volumes of *The Yearbook of Muslims in Europe* published by Brill and edited by Jørgen Nielsen together with Akgönül, Alibašić, Maréchal, Moe and Račius since 2009. These highly useful handbooks contain country reports covering, for example, the demographic development, the activities of Muslim organisations and legal changes, but also references to new literature.

Jonas Otterbeck
Lund, May 2015

Preface to the first edition

Until the mid-1980s, the documentation of the situation of Muslims in western Europe was sparse and emanated from a very few sources, most of them related either to Muslim or church-based organisations. Until that time, information about this aspect of current Islam had to be sifted out of the literature on immigrants, ethnic minorities and race relations. These were areas of academic study which had their own network of presumptions and disciplinary methods, in which religion and religious identity tended, at most, to be aspects of secondary interest and even then only of interest to those researchers who had a professional interest in the sociology of religion. Indeed, so dominated by the secular assumptions of academic sociology was the field, that well into the 1970s there seemed to be an expectation that communities of immigrant origin would quickly follow a course characterised by the privatisation of religion: one could look forward to the existence of ethnic minority communities who were integrated to the extent that their religion would have a place similar to that of the private Christianity of Protestant northern Europe or laicised Catholic France.

It was partly due to the refusal of a substantial proportion of the Muslim immigrants and their children to adhere to this model that the attitude of parts of the academic community began to alter during the mid-1980s. A few academics began to see valid research possibilities in the issues arising out of the Muslim presence in Europe. The process was helped by the realisation in local and national political structures that there was a growing 'Islamic factor' in the social and political processes associated with immigration and ethnic minority. This was not unconnected with events in the Middle East, where Islam had become a much more explicitly profiled element of some 'disruptive' potential, certainly as perceived from the western European point of view. It is no coincidence that this change took place at a time when the immigration of dependants had virtually ceased, when immigration was becoming a more overtly political question of refugees, and when a racist backlash was threatening the traditional party political systems of France and West Germany. In France and Britain especially, one was also witnessing the growth to maturity' – and therefore to the labour market and into colleges and universities – of the children of immigrants. Finally, the 'Rushdie affair', in Britain, and the 'affair of the headscarves', in France, served to place the subject of Muslims in western Europe towards the top of academic and political agendas. Most recently, of course, the repercussions of the Gulf crisis have again underscored the fact that Muslim communities in western Europe have acquired a political role.

The second half of the 1980s has, in consequence, seen a substantial increase in the number of publications dealing specifically with aspects of the Muslim presence in western Europe. The writings have come, of course, primarily from sociologists and anthropologists, but lawyers, political scientists, planners, geographers, historians, demographers, educationalists, economists and even scholars of Islam have contributed. Publications and papers produced by Christian and Muslim organisations continue to be useful, not only for their intrinsic value, but also because they often provide a helpful general introduction and literature survey, both of which are useful to anyone new to this complex and interdisciplinary field of work.

However, the field remains a largely unexplored one, and the production of research and publication continues to depend on relatively specialised interests and limited funding. This means that any survey of Muslims in western Europe must be uneven – it depends on available research and on the existence of individuals with an active personal interest. It is to be expected that the economic and political circumstances in a particular country will have a major influence on the amount of information and analysis available. It was, for example, only during 1990 that the combination of a debate around new immigration legislation, a large rise in the number of economic migrants across the Mediterranean, moves by the European Community to harmonise internal and external passport controls, and signs of a racist reaction finally focused any kind of serious attention on the substantial Muslim population in Italy – raising the kinds of simple practical questions which many countries further north thought had been solved at least a decade earlier.

All these considerations come together both to justify the purpose of this book and to make its limits quite clear. The number of books which have attempted a survey of Muslims in western Europe overall is small. The best discuss in some depth issues relating to the challenges to both Islam and Europe arising out of this situation. Nowhere, to the best of my knowledge, does one find a reliable description both of the origins, ethnic composition, distribution, and organisational patterns of the Muslim communities, and of the political, legal and cultural context in which they find their way.

I have chosen not to attempt a mainly thematic study of the subject. On the one hand, sufficient comparable research data covering the whole region simply do not exist. On the other hand, the situation is in a constant state of rapid flux, as I was all too aware while this book was being written during 1989, 1990 and early 1991. My purpose has been to provide a reference source which can be used by interested readers of whatever background and for whatever purpose.

I have, however, been particularly concerned to meet my perception of the needs of three categories of readers. One is the researcher working from within a single country who wishes to try to widen his or her horizon towards a comparison with the situation in other countries of Europe – there is a constant danger that those who work with, for example, Turkish Muslims in Germany see Islam and European Muslims solely in the perspective of German Turkish Islam, a phenomenon which is as particular as that of French Algerian or British Pakistani Islam. The other two categories are both within that favourite audience of the serious publisher, namely the interested general reader. Here I have especially been concerned to provide, I hope, a balanced and objective account of the situation of the Muslim communities for those Europeans, Christian or otherwise, who stand outside the Muslim community, as well as an account of the European context and its constraints which may help Muslim observers outside Europe to understand the situation of their fellows inside Europe.

This book therefore concentrates on an encyclopaedic approach to the subject. The main chapters are country surveys which should be read together with the bibliographical essay at the end. The reader thoroughly familiar with the situation in, say, the Netherlands, will obviously find the section on that country highly unsatisfactory in its relative brevity and superficiality but not, I trust, in its general accuracy. For such a reader, I have intended that the chapters on other countries will be a useful beginning for comparative purposes.

Chapters 8 and 9 discuss the main issues which extend across all borders, for which sufficient research exists to make sense of any serious discussion. No excuse is made for including in the chapter on organisations a series of brief introductions to various Islamic movements in their original context; this may seem elementary to the scholar of Islam, but it is absolutely essential to the European sociologist. I have not included a chapter on education, despite the fact that this is probably one of the issues which will be central for some time to come. The reason is simply that the circumstances so differ between countries, that little can be said by way of meaningful generalities. Each country's description reflects this in the weight given to the educational scene.

The concluding chapter builds on the events of 1989 and 1990 in an attempt to define more speculatively the challenges posed by the Muslim presence to the future of Europe.

Apart from the published sources mentioned in the Bibliographical Essay, most of the contextual data as well as much of the direct information in this book are dependent on the information and unpublished accounts and documentation produced from within a small network of people working on the questions created by the recent remarkable emergence of Muslim communities in western Europe. It should come as no surprise, in the light of the initial remarks above, that the core of that network should be a small group of church-related resource people, gathered in the annual 'Journées d'Arras', from most of the countries covered in this book. These people are in very close everyday contact with Muslim leaders and groups and therefore supplement usefully my own contacts and discussions over many years with a variety of Muslim friends and colleagues across the region. The text published here takes into account the reactions, comments and advice of all these people, but the final responsibility for the descriptions and evaluations is mine alone.

My own work over a number of years also entails that some parts of this book reproduce material I have previously published elsewhere. I am therefore especially pleased to acknowledge permission to reproduce in part or in amended form Chapter 1 from the University of Nottingham,[1] the first part of Chapter 9 from the University of Leiden,[2] and parts of Chapter 10 from the Churches' Committee for Migrants in Europe[3] and from my own Centre.[4]

Finally, it should be noted that the completion of this study for the press has taken place under the shadow of the Gulf crisis and the perception of enormous repercussions not only for relations between the Muslim world and the West, or Christendom, in continental terms, but also for those relations within the communities of the industrial cities of western Europe. I can only hope and pray that this survey may contribute to a saner and cooler discussion of our mutually dependent future, a future where both civilisations can benefit and learn from each other, as they have done in the past.

Note to the second edition

I am grateful to the many people who have made comments to me on the first edition of this book. This second edition takes into account many of these suggestions and corrections. It also includes some updating of statistics. More substantially it includes new material on Italy and Spain which has appeared in the last two years. I have decided not to make any major amendment to the chapter on West Germany following the reunification, since the Muslim presence in the East is still not much more than symbolic. However, some of the repercussions of the reunification, such as the rise in racial violence, are dealt with briefly in Chapter 10.

Note to the third edition

In the near decade which has passed since the second edition of this book, our subject has changed almost beyond recognition. While the immigrant generation continues to maintain a significant role in determining the nature and role of Muslim organisations and defining what constitutes Islam, their children are rapidly taking over. This is both beginning to change the character of Islam in Europe and also challenging society, political structures and discourse, and governments sharply. Events abroad, above all the attacks on New York and Washington of 11 September 2001 and subsequent wars, have focused public debate and attention on Muslims in an unprecedented fashion.

The beginnings of serious academic research on this subject, noted above, have been superseded during the 1990s by an explosion of published studies in the form of countless articles, some monographs and a substantial number of collective works arising out of seminars and conferences, a development which is reflected in the mass of new material referred to in the Bibliographical Essay. Islam in Europe has become a subject which research funding agencies now take seriously. It is unfortunately still the case, however, that only a minute number of young Muslim scholars are entering this field.

This growth of activity, both on the ground and in research, means that almost all parts of this book have been subjected to a substantial revision for the third edition. I have decided to maintain the mainly historical approach in the presentation of individual countries, especially since the great majority of the recent studies have been concentrated on the present. Although it is now well over a decade since the fall of the Soviet system, the situation in central and eastern Europe, including what used to be East Germany, remains so notably different from that in the West, that I have felt justified in not adjusting the geographical area defined already in the first edition.

After three editions, it is time that I record my appreciation to the staff of Edinburgh University Press for their continuing interest in this book and, above all, for their care and efforts in nursing it through to publication for the third time.

Notes

1. 'Muslims in Europe', *Renaissance and Modern Studies*, vol. 21 (1987), pp. 58–73.
2. 'Muslim organisations in Europe: integration or isolation?', in P. S. van Koningsveld and W. A. Shadid (eds), *The integration of Muslims and Hindus in Western Europe* (Kampen: Kok Pharos, 1991).
3. 'Islamic law and its significance for the situation of Muslim minorities in Europe: report of a study project', *Research Papers: Muslims in Europe*, no. 35 (September 1987).
4. 'Co-existence of cultures – the European experience', *Newsletter: Centre for the Study of Islam and Christian-Muslim Relations*, no. 16 (November 1986), pp.18–27; German original: 'Zusammenleben verschiedener Kulturen – Erfahrungen in Europe', in J. Lähnemann (ed.), *Erziehung zur Kulturbegegnung* (Hamburg: EBV-Rissen, 1986), pp. 135–47.

CHAPTER 1

A brief history

The presence of Muslims in one or another part of continental Europe probably goes as far back in time as historical Islam. Traders and diplomats have over the centuries been a continuous feature of many places in especially central and southern Europe. But it is also possible to identify three distinct periods of established Muslim communities. The first of these has passed into history, namely the period of Islamic Spain and Muslim rule in Sicily and southern Italy. The Normans put an end to the latter in the eleventh century, and the Spanish *reconquista* finally put an end to the last Muslim foothold in Spain in 1492. All that remains today of that phase is the rich contribution it made to all aspects of European culture.

The two following phases have, however, left permanent communities. The second was the result of the spread of Mongol armies during the thirteenth century. After only a few generations, their successor states became Muslim, and one of these, the Khanate of the Golden Horde, centred on the Volga river basin north of the Caspian and Black seas, left a permanent Muslim population of various Tatar groups stretching from the Volga down to the Caucasus and Crimea. As itinerant traders and soldiers, many of these groups later travelled around the Russian empire and established colonies in places such as Finland and the area which today straddles the border between Poland and the Ukraine.

The third phase was the period of Ottoman expansion into the Balkans and central Europe. This was the context for the settlement of Turkish populations which still survive today in parts of Bulgaria, former Yugoslavia, Romania, the republic of Macedonia and Greece. Many of the Ottoman subject populations also became Muslim, to the extent that Albania became a country with a Muslim majority, and Slav groups in Bosnia-Herzegovina and parts of Bulgaria also became Muslim.

The period with which this book deals is a relatively new, fourth phase, namely the establishment of Muslim communities in western Europe. This is generally regarded as a feature of the great period of immigration after the Second World War, but in fact the foundations were laid long before then.

Situated as they were in the centre of Europe, the German states had a very particular experience of Islam, in the form of Ottoman Turkish expansion through the Balkans during the sixteenth and seventeenth centuries. This was a history very much characterised by conflict culminating in the two sieges of

Vienna, in 1529 and 1683, events which helped to instil into German thinking the idea of the 'Turkish peril'. The second of the two sieges, especially, also provided the circumstances in which people of Muslim origin first became permanent residents in Germany. The relief of Vienna and the Ottoman retreat left behind large numbers of Ottoman soldiers and camp followers, either as stragglers or prisoners. There are numerous accounts of such individuals entering court service or taking up trades and professions, mainly in the south, but also elsewhere. Several are recorded as having converted and become priests or pastors. One was raised to the Hanoverian nobility.

A new phase commenced with the expansion of Prussia in the mid-eighteenth century. In 1731, the Duke of Kurland presented twenty Turkish guardsmen to King Frederick William I. Ten years later, King Frederick I (the Great) formed the first Prussian lancer unit from Tatars who had deserted from the Russian army. Further desertions led to other units being created, and at one time about 1,000 Muslim soldiers are said to have served in the Prussian cavalry. The Prussian kings' fascination with the Enlightenment was reflected in their consideration for the religious concerns of their Muslim troops. Already the first contingent of Turkish guardsmen had been given the use of a prayer room – on Sundays!

It soon became necessary to establish a Muslim cemetery in Berlin, in which a mosque was finally built in 1866. Diplomatic relations had been established between Berlin and Istanbul in the eighteenth century. These were being slowly expanded a century later, when the Sultan extended his patronage to this mosque. Trading treaties had been concluded between the Ottoman empire and the Hanseatic cities in 1839 and the Customs Union in 1840. The German states remained preoccupied with central European problems until the unification in 1870–1, after which Bismarck refrained from challenging the great powers in the Middle East. However, after Bismarck was dismissed, the Emperor embarked on a more ambitious approach to the Ottomans, expanding trade and diplomatic relations and building up German economic interests, especially in modernising the Ottoman infrastructure.

As a consequence of these developments, the Muslim community in Germany, and particularly in Berlin, grew significantly in the years before the First World War. During the war itself, when the two countries were allies, the German government and the Turkish ambassador in Berlin worked together in providing a mosque and imams for the Muslim prisoners taken from opposing armies: Tatars, Caucasians and Turks from Russia, Indians from Britain, and Senegalese and Algerians from France.

The German and Turkish defeats ended an era. After the war, a small Muslim community remained in Berlin and was able to build a mosque in the Wilmersdorf district, where it still stands today. A new era started with the next war, when perhaps as many as a quarter of a million captured Soviet troops chose to serve the Third Reich, either in the *Ostlegionen* or in Wehrmacht and SS units. A large proportion of these troops were from Soviet Muslim nationalities. They were served by a corps of Muslim 'chaplains', some of whom were trained at the faculty of Islamic studies at the University of Göttingen.

In one of the more shameful episodes of the Second World War, the Allies sent many of these troops back to the Soviet Union at the end of the war. Some, however, were able to remain in Germany and were joined by others fleeing from eastern Europe and Soviet control. Several thousand Muslims of different Balkan and east European nationalities thus settled all over Germany after the war. By 1958, they had succeeded in organising themselves into the *Geistliche Verwaltung der Muslimflüchtlinge in der Bundesrepublik Deutschland* (spiritual administration for Muslim refugees in the Federal Republic of Germany). This grouping still exists today but under another name (*Islamische Gemeinschaft in Deutschland*).

In central Europe, attention has been concentrated on the early settlement of Muslims in the territory today encompassed by Germany, necessarily so because of the importance of the Muslim communities in that area since the 1960s. But this should not allow one to forget that, in a sense, the modern state of Austria has inherited a much more institutional history of relations with an indigenous Muslim community. Until the defeat of the First World War, the Habsburg empire, which became the Austro-Hungarian empire during the nineteenth century, with its capital in Vienna, had been one of the two European powers which had faced the Ottoman empire – the other was Russia – for a period of centuries. Some of the effects of this have already been described above, but, during the late nineteenth century, Austria entered into a new experience with Islam which sets it apart from any other western European country of immigration.

In 1878, this dual monarchy of Austria-Hungary acquired a substantial Muslim population with the occupation of Ottoman Bosnia-Herzegovina. Already accustomed to a multicultural and multireligious state, it was not long before Vienna had a resident mufti. Four years before that occupation, a law had already been passed giving certain concessions to Muslim law regarding the family. In 1909, the Vienna government abolished the separate status of Bosnia-Herzegovina, incorporating the province into the main realm. Three years later, an act was passed 'relating to the recognition of the followers of Islam of the Hanafite rite as a religious community' within the terms of the 1867 constitution. This extended the recognition of Muslims to the whole realm, and it was to become the legal basis of the renewed recognition of Muslims in 1979. One result of this particular history was that the Austrian legal system was for a time required to apply Islamic family law within its courts for Muslims in Bosnia-Herzegovina. To help the courts, a German translation of a Hanafi code of Islamic family law was published in Vienna in 1883.

The early history of Islam in Britain is closely associated with the expansion of British and colonial involvement in India. During the second half of the eighteenth century, the East India Company was recruiting to a significant extent in Indian ports. These men were laid off and left to fend for themselves while their ships were docked in Britain. In 1822, following an investigation by the anti-slavery campaigner Thomas Clarkson, the East India Company was obliged to arrange for the establishment of boarding-houses. Further campaigns to improve the men's situation culminated in the opening in 1857 of a home for 'Asiatics, Africans and South Sea Islanders' in the Limehouse district of London.

Some of these Indian seamen were Muslims, but the Muslim element increased substantially after the opening of the Suez Canal in 1869. Through Aden, large numbers of Yemeni Arabs and Somalis were recruited. Yemeni boarding-houses started appearing in a number of ports, in particular Cardiff and South Shields. Based on these, Yemeni communities started settling, the men often marrying British women. At the end of the century, the stability and cohesion of these communities was strengthened with the arrival of a shaykh of the 'Alawi Sufi order. Soon centres, or *zawiyahs*, of this order were to be found also in inland cities to which Yemenis were moving. These *zawiyahs* were centres of social and religious life, providing basic Islamic instruction and facilities for worship and, in the larger ones, teaching of Arabic and the Islamic religious sciences. They also provided a focal point for the British wives, who had usually become Muslim.

London and Liverpool were centres for a wide mix of people of Muslim background. Seamen from West Africa were common in Liverpool, where traders also sponsored the education of West African notables. In general, there was a growing population of Muslims coming for higher education, as well as a number of Indian aristocrats. The post of personal physician to Queen Victoria was for a long time occupied by an Indian Muslim. It was for these cosmopolitan communities that the first mosques were established in Britain. The foundation of the mosque in Liverpool at the beginning of the 1890s is associated with one of the most singular characters in the history of British Islam. Shaykh Abdullah (Henry William) Quilliam had become a Muslim in 1887 while travelling around the Ottoman empire and Morocco. The Ottoman sultan had appointed him Shaykh al-Islam of the United Kingdom, and the Shah of Persia made him consul in Liverpool. The congregation which gathered around Quilliam found permanent premises in a group of terraced houses in 1891. There he organised regular prayers, festivals, weddings and funerals as well as a boys' day school, evening classes, a hostel, a library and a printing press. For potential British converts, he arranged Sunday morning and evening services on the pattern of church services, so that they might 'feel more at home at our missionary meetings...'. His activities sometimes aroused opposition, especially when he advocated the cause of Islam. His protests against the British expedition against

Mahdist Sudan had some people talking of treason, as did his continuing loyalty to the caliphate of the Ottoman sultan. In 1908 he left Liverpool for good, and with his departure the work that he had started withered away.

In London, it was the activities of a Hungarian Orientalist, Dr Leitner, who had been registrar at the University of Punjab, which led to the building of the Shahjehan Mosque in Woking in 1889. Funded primarily by the ruler of Bhopal, the mosque was envisaged as the centrepiece of an Islamic centre, with a library, a hostel for Indian students, and ultimately its own teaching facilities culminating in the establishment of an Islamic university. Of these dreams, only the hostel materialised. When Dr Leitner died in 1899, his sponsors lost interest, and the mosque became the property of his heirs. In 1913, the mosque was again taken into use, when one Khwaja Kamal-ud-Din sponsored by an English convert, Lord Headley, bought it and made it a centre of missionary work for the Ahmadi movement. During the Second World War, the people around the Woking Muslim Mission preserved an apolitical profile and concentrated on welfare work, in particular for the widows and orphans of Indian soldiers. They also sponsored a Muslim Literary Society, of which both the Qur'an translators Marmeduke Pickthall and Abdullah Yusuf Ali were members. The Woking Muslim Mission was linked to the Lahori branch of the Ahmadi movement and had always rejected the claims of the Qadiani branch that Mirza Ghulam Ahmad was a prophet. But this was not sufficient at a time when Indian Sunni opposition to the Ahmadis was mounting. Khwaja Kamal-ud-Din and Lord Headley died in 1932 and 1933 respectively, and two years later a new management committee rejected all further ties to the Ahmadis.

After the First World War, Lord Headley and his Muslim acquaintances at the Woking Muslim Mission had started talking of a central mosque for London. Initially received as an unrealistic dream, it was given a boost when a central mosque was opened in Paris in 1926. Soon afterwards, Lord Headley succeeded in interesting the Nizam of Hyderabad in the project, and in 1928 the London Nizamiah Mosque Trust was established. After this initial impetus little further happened until the Second World War when the Saudi Arabian ambassador, Shaykh Hafiz Wahba, became interested. A site became available when King George VI donated a plot in Regent's Park by Hanover Gate at about the same time as a site in Cairo was donated by King Faruq for a new Anglican cathedral. In November 1944, the Islamic Cultural Centre was opened by King George VI. Three years later, the ambassadors and high commissioners of some thirteen Muslim countries formed the Central London Mosque Trust to raise the money to build a mosque. Starting with the funds of the now defunct Nizamiah Trust, other donations were solicited. A foundation stone was laid in 1954, but the Suez war, plus funding problems and disagreements over design, served to delay the project through the 1960s. After an architectural competition in 1969, it was possible again to start construction, and the new mosque was finally opened in 1977. Then, however, the character of the Muslim community that it served had undergone a radical change.

While the history of Muslim immigration into France is about as old as that of Britain, it is characterised by much greater continuity. There were, certainly, students and businessmen as well as political exiles during the nineteenth century – the most famous exiles being Muhammad Abduh and Jamal al-Din al-Afghani. However, even before the First World War, there was a significant element of labour migration. The largest number came from Algeria, and during the first few decades of migration, the Kabyles were the single most numerous group. In 1912, half of the 4,000 to 5,000 Algerians worked in olive oil refining and related industries around Marseilles. The rest were spread around the factories and mines in the east and north of the country. The initial reaction to the outbreak of war in 1914 was characterised by a sharp drop in population, but quickly the need for men in both civilian and military work tempted tens of thousands of Algerians and many more Tunisians and Moroccans. In addition, the government adopted a policy of requisitioning men. During the war, nearly 200,000 Algerians came to France, two-thirds of them requisitioned. The French government, in recognition of this involvement in the war effort, allocated a grant for the purpose of building a mosque in Paris. Under the direction of a trust run by representatives of Algeria, Tunisia, Morocco and Senegal, this mosque was opened in 1926.

During the 1920s, North African immigration was erratic because of constantly changing government policy, and, after the 1929 economic crisis, people returning to Algeria regularly outnumbered immigrants. In 1942, after German occupation of part of France, the Vichy government contracted to supply 16,000 Kabyles to the Todt Organisation to build the Atlantic Wall for the Germans. The allied invasion of North Africa in November of the same year both put a stop to further such deals and forced these workers to stay in France for the duration of the war. By 1946, there were only 22,000 Algerians in France and so few Tunisians and Moroccans as to escape the net of the census. But, with peace, migration resumed, and by 1954 the census registered 212,000 Algerians.

Some of these immigrants were beginning to bring over their families and to look at their migration as a permanent move. This did not mean that their links with Algeria were necessarily weakening. It was in this immigrant community that the early steps were taken towards Algerian independence. The 1920s had seen the first political agitation and publication of journals and tracts going much further in their demands than was possible among groups in Algeria. When the war of independence commenced in the mid-1950s, the Algerians in France were effectively the financiers of the rebellion – at great cost to themselves. A curfew was imposed on them in Paris and many were arrested when they marched in protest. During 1957 alone, about 40,000 were imprisoned.

The early Muslim presence in Nordic countries developed rather differently. The first Muslim immigrants came from Russia. Already, by 1830, Finland (then part of Russia) had become the home of Tatar and Kazakh soldiers with a Muslim background. But it was with the arrival of Tatar Muslim businessmen and their families from 1870 onwards that the first permanently settled Muslim community took form in a Nordic country. After Finnish independence in 1917, these were granted citizenship and eventually, after the Freedom of Religion Act took effect in 1923, they were officially recognised as a religious community. During the Second World War, additional families of Tatar Muslims fled the Baltic countries to Finland. A few made their way to Sweden and ended up in Stockholm. In the late 1940s, the Tatar community consisted of six or seven small households, all together thirteen individuals. Together with a few Turkish and Arabic men working at embassies in Sweden, the Tatars organised in 1949 the first Muslim association in Sweden called The Turk–Islamic Association in Sweden for the Promotion of Religion and Culture.

CHAPTER 2

France

Muslim immigration after 1962

Until the beginning of the 1960s, North African immigration into France had been overwhelmingly Algerian. Despite consistently higher unemployment rates among Algerian workers in France, and despite employers' continued preference for workers from southern Europe (mainly Portugal and Italy), Algerians continued to cross the Mediterranean. In the decade up to 1957, over 190,000 Algerians had arrived, mostly from the regions around Tizi Ouzou, Setif and Constantine in the north-eastern parts of Algeria. In the following decade the figure rose to almost quarter of a million.

The traditional lack of a coordinated and consistent foreign labour policy continued, until the rise in immigration became remarkable in the early 1960s. The major contribution to this change came, in fact, not from the Algerians but from Morocco and, to a lesser extent, from Tunisia. Migration from the Tunis conurbation and the border regions with Algeria started in the late 1950s, and settlement in France reached a total of close to 48,000 by 1964. This total jumped to 161,000 a decade later and then slowed down considerably. The Moroccan population of France had reached about 50,000 by 1962, but the next decade saw a massive growth to over 400,000. Algerian growth also took off, reaching a total of about 830,000 in 1977. These increases continued in different proportions until the mid-1980s (see Table 2.1).

The reaction of the French government was finally to try to adopt some form of immigration policy, which very quickly became a policy for control and limitation, as distinct from the earlier policies of facilitating labour immigration. To begin with, the policy was haphazard, consisting mainly of an accord with Algeria agreed in 1964. In a revision four years later, a limit of 35,000 annual immigrants was agreed, subsequently reduced to 25,000. In practice, these accords were virtually impossible to enforce, and the government was reduced to policing clandestine immigration. In response to the economic recession of 1974, controls were very rapidly tightened. This culminated in the period 1977–81 with a policy of subsidising migrants to return to their countries of origin. The aim was to achieve the return of 1 million people. However, the policy met with little success, and the legalisation of 130,000 clandestine settlers in 1981–2 amounted to an admission of failure.

Table 2.1 Maghrib settlers in France, 1957–90

	Algeria	Morocco	Tunisia
1957	313,000		
1962	350,484*	50,000*	
1967	562,000		
1975	710,690*	260,025*	139,735*
1980	792,000	299,900	147,100
1982	805,100*	441,300*	190,800*
1985	820,900	516,400	202,600
1990	614,207*	572,652*	206,336*

Source: Ministries of Interior and Labour figures, except for census figures, marked *

By this time, two further substantial sources of Muslim immigration had developed. Workers from sub-Saharan West Africa had started to come in larger numbers in the late 1960s. By 1982, they numbered possibly 80,000, mainly from Senegal and Mali. Most were members of the Soninké people, who lived along the Senegal river, and to a lesser extent from the Toucouleur district. In 1966, a labour accord was signed between France and Turkey, but it was not until the early 1970s that the immigration took off. By 1983, there were nearly 150,000 Turks resident in France. On the whole, they came from central Anatolia and the eastern provinces ranging from the Black Sea to the Syrian border. Almost half of these Turkish citizens were probably Kurds, in addition to a large number of both Kurdish and Turkish Alevis, some Arabs from the area of Antioch and Alexandretta, and smaller numbers of Chaldean Christians from the Mardin area.

As in most of the rest of Europe, the first phase of the immigration of people of Muslim culture was dominated by men seeking work. It was a small proportion of the Algerians who first started to bring their families over in the 1950s, attracted by the improving welfare system and availability of public housing – it must be remembered that Algerians had a degree of citizenship of France. By early 1953, about 100 Algerian families were reported to be arriving in France every month. As the immigration momentum gathered pace in the late 1960s, data show that 60 per cent of male immigrants were arriving with their wives and children. This pattern was not necessarily repeated with other groups. Thus family migration remained much lower among Tunisians partly, it is suggested, because by the early 1970s family welfare benefits were payable to dependents living outside France. The results of the 1982 census show clearly how the various population groups are no longer so overwhelmingly male-dominated. They also show how, despite different migration patterns in earlier phases, all the main population groups concerned had reached roughly the same gender distribution by 1982.

This overall picture disguises the fact that the age distribution of the relevant groups is very uneven. Thus, for Algerians in 1982, there was a virtual balance between men and women in the age groups up to 35; it was the preponderance of men in the group above the age of 35 which produced the imbalance in the total. On the other hand, the under-representation of women among Tunisians and Moroccans was spread evenly across all the age ranges, partly because there were many fewer in the over-35 age group and partly because many families preferred to leave their daughters with the extended family in the countries of origin.

A rather different group, at least in their origins and, therefore, in the self-perception of the first generation, are the so-called 'Harkis' or '*Français musulmans*' (French Muslims). The official term more recently has been '*Rapatriés d'Origine Nord-Africaine*' or RONA, meaning those of North African origin repatriated to France at the end of the Algerian war of independence in 1962. These people were of Algerian origin but had in one way or another been associated with French rule: police, military, civil service, judiciary and professional middle classes. Their social backgrounds were very diverse, and all they had in common was the need to leave Algeria because they had been associated with the colonial regime. In France, they registered as a distinct category in the census until 1968, when they numbered 140,000. Various estimates since then bear witness to the gradual growth of this population until it reached about 400,000–450,000 in 1988.

Initially, the Harkis were kept in camps under a special government agency. As these camps acquired permanence, they became increasingly embarrassing, until riots in several of them in 1975 forced the government into a reorganisation. Further reorganisations culminated in responsibilities being handed over to the mainstream welfare authorities of the departments in 1986. As a result of all this, some parts of the Harkis population have been assimilated while others have remained isolated.

Of all the countries in Europe, France has probably the highest number of converts to Islam. It is virtually impossible to arrive at a reliable and agreed figure. A former rector of the Paris Mosque reported that he witnessed 12,000 conversions from various nationalities between 1957 and 1982, while Dr Hamidullah, the widely respected Indian scholar who was for a long time the imam of the Da'wa mosque (commonly known as Stalingrad from the Paris

Table 2.2 Estimate of Muslims in France by origin, 1989	
Algerians	850,000
Musulmans français ('Harkis')	400,000
Moroccans	450,000
Tunisians	200,000
Turks	200,000
West Africans	100,000
Others	?

district in which it is situated), cites 22,000 conversions of various nationalities for the decade to 1982. Some observers have suggested about 10,000 converts annually during the 1990s. More recent studies suggest a total of French converts to Islam in the region of 70,000 to 110,000.

By the end of the 1980s, using a combination of official statistics and research reports, it was possible to arrive at a total of over 3 million Muslims in France, or at least people who are of Muslim cultural background (see Table 2.2). As in most other European countries, the definition of Muslim for statistical purposes must be a cultural one, since official data have ignored religious affiliation, especially after a law of 1978 prohibited any reference to religious adherence in any government statistics.

In addition, there were an estimated 450,000 young people of North African parentage with French citizenship, the so-called 'Beurs'. The 1990 census (see Table 2.1) showed some marked changes among Algerians and Moroccans, but as indicators of the Muslim population they are unreliable due to the relatively high proportion of Algerians becoming French citizens. Estimates by social scientists, using a variety of sources, suggest that by the year 2000 the total number of people of Muslim origins may have been as many as 5 million. Of these, about 1.5 million were of Algerian origin, 1 million Moroccans, 350,000 each of Tunisians and Turks, 250,000 West Africans and 450,000 Harkis. The proportion which holds French citizenship by birth or by naturalisation increased substantially during the 1990s to reach a total of about one-third by the end of the decade. Later estimations from 2003, 2009 and 2010 have repeated the figures 4–5 million.

We have already briefly hinted at the unevenness in age distribution among the different Maghrib nationals. Analysis of regional distribution in France suggests that, in addition, among Algerians in 1982, the older men were more widely spread around the French industrial scene. The family-based Algerians appear to have been more concentrated in the great urban centres. Immigrant families of Moroccan and Tunisian origin, having arrived later and therefore still mobile with the labour market, tended to be more evenly spread than the Algerians.

The large concentrations of all Muslim nationalities in 1982 were to be found in the regions of Marseilles, Lyons, Lille and, above all, Paris. This picture has hardly changed in the three decades since. Within this general situation it is, however, interesting to note that Moroccans are much more widely spread outside those centres than either Algerians or Tunisians. The black Africans were concentrated in the Paris region, with smaller communities in all areas of industry, especially around Lille and up to the Channel coast. Age and gender distribution figures showed a sharp preference among families for settlement in Paris. Turks were to be found mainly in the greater Paris region and the eastern regions centred on Lille, Alsace and Lorraine.

It should be remembered in this context that foreigners of a 'Muslim' nationality were not the only immigrants. Before the Second World War and for the first decade after it, southern Europeans were the preferred foreign labour in French industry: Italians, Spaniards and, above all, Portuguese. In the years immediately after 1945, there was also a mainly temporary influx of several tens of thousands of Germans seeking work. The 1982 census indicated that as many as 1.5 million foreign residents came from the three southern European countries.

As elsewhere, the large majority of people of Muslim background in France are employed in unskilled and semiskilled occupations in industry. However, a significant minority, relatively higher than in most other western European countries, are in the professions. Among the young, there is a high proportion going into further education and skilled labour. Again, as elsewhere, unemployment during the 1980s hit immigrant men and the young particularly hard. As the economy picked up towards the end of the decade, job expansion favoured the employment of women. Among the Muslim populations, Turkish women have shown particular readiness to seize this opportunity. On the other hand, the children of especially North African immigrants have continuously been vulnerable to the effects of economic slowdown. Persistent high unemployment during the 1990s hit a much higher proportion of young Arabs than in the general population. The majority which had not found educational success, concentrated in the large housing estates, were through the mid-1990s additionally often subjected to police harassment and public suspicion for being somehow associated with Islamist extremism in the violent civil war going on in Algeria, especially after two bomb attacks on the Paris Métro. Unemployment has remained high, especially among foreign citizens. While 7.5 per cent of

French nationals were unemployed in 2007, as many as 19.6 per cent of male foreigners from outside the EU and 26.1 per cent of females of the same group were outside the labour market according to *Institut national de la statistique et des etudes économiques.*

Mosques and organisations

The position of Islam and Muslims, as a religious community, within the French system is centrally conditioned by the laicist character of the French state. This is determined in a law of 9 December 1905 concerning the separation of church and state. In its article 1 this law says that, 'The Republic guarantees liberty of conscience. It guarantees the free exercise of religion limited only by the following restrictions in the interests of public order.' Article 2 goes on to say that, 'The Republic does not grant recognition to, pay the salaries of, or provide subsidies for any religion.' As part of the arrangement, which this law represented, places of worship and chaplaincies were left in the control of the existing churches. However, the state is still responsible for the maintenance of churches which existed prior to 1905. In the area of Alsace-Lorraine, a separate concordat rules by which the state recognised the existing religions, a recognition which includes the obligation of the state to pay the salaries of the recognised clergy, much like the Belgian model.

In neither Alsace-Lorraine nor in the rest of France do the Muslim communities gain anything from this system. Islam cannot be given recognition in the concordat regions. Elsewhere, as a newly arrived religious community, Muslims do not own inherited property or status. However, as is clear from article 1 of the law of 1905, Muslims do have freedom of worship within the law of France, a freedom which is further guaranteed today by the right of appeal to the European Convention on Human Rights, which has been ratified by France.

The process of organisation and association of foreigners and immigrants, whether by religious or ethnic criteria, is governed by the law on association, which has had a mixed history. Chapter IV of the 1905 law confirmed the freedom of religious association within the framework of the law of association of 1 July 1901. This granted the freedom to form associations to all residents of France, whether French citizens or foreigners, but such associations had to be registered with the authorities, including the names of their officials and their constitutions. During the late 1930s, there was a growth in fascist organisations with links to Germany and Italy, and to counteract this a government decree made the formation of associations of foreign citizens subject to the approval of the Ministry of the Interior. This decree was cancelled on 9 October 1981 and the legal situation reverted to the position it had been in before 1939.

The consequence of this liberalisation was an enormous growth in the number of associations founded by foreign residents, especially those of Muslim backgrounds. It seems that many associations already existed informally – extra-legally – which were now registered. Others, not many because in 1976 only twenty-one were officially registered, had had a legal existence using French sympathisers as the official front or working in tandem with French solidarity groups. All of these types were now registered legally, and many more came into existence because the legal regime had been opened up.

One exception to this situation is the status of the Paris Mosque. After the First World War, a law was passed on 19 August 1920 extending a line of credit to the *Institut musulman*, which had been established in Algeria in 1917 in recognition of the many North and West Africans who had fought on the Somme and elsewhere. A society was established in Paris in December 1921, which proceeded to collect subscriptions for a new mosque. The building was completed and inaugurated by the Sultan of Morocco in 1926. The directorship was in the hands of the French government for a long time, which in 1957 appointed an Algerian, Si Hamza Boubakeur. When he retired in 1982, he ensured that control passed to the Algerian government against the protests of the French and, less outspokenly, the Moroccans and Tunisians. While the mosque has sought to attain recognition as the general representative of Islam in France, through activities such as determining dates for festivals and networking provincial mosques, recognition by North Africans other than Algerians has been ambivalent, while Turkish groups have tended to ignore it completely.

Major demographic changes took place during the 1950s, 60s and 70s which meant, in purely French terms, that new suburbs developed around all cities and that new towns appeared in the vicinity of major industrial regions. It was recognised that the religious life of these new communities, in the early stages mainly Catholic, had to be an integral part of community development. Thus it was accepted that local authorities (departments and communes) could supply plots of land for places of worship in exchange for a nominal rent. The finance law of July 1961 allowed local authorities to guarantee the loans taken out by local cultural and religious associations to construct their facilities. The central government was authorised to guarantee such loans taken out by associations of a national character. Under the heading 'developing towns and suburbs' it has often been possible to extend the benefits of this legislation to Muslim associations.

Such a flexible interpretation was confirmed and encouraged in a government circular issued in September 1976 by the Secretary of State for Immigrant Workers. The purpose of the circular was to improve immigrants' social conditions and to preserve their roots and cultural identity. The financial assistance, which was to be made available for this purpose, was to be granted recognising that for Muslims – the circular was quite explicit on this point – Islam was an integral part of the culture. It was therefore legitimate to grant financial assistance to projects which had a religious character. Unfortunately, there appears to be no statistical information as to how far this principle, enunciated by central government, was carried out in practice. Anecdotal evidence does, however, suggest that some financial aid did materialise as the government had intended, and there is certainly a good deal of evidence that, at the local level, social programming and assistance by the departments and the communes included provisions for meeting the religious needs of Muslim immigrants.

The terminology used in France for Muslim places of worship creates some difficulty in making comparisons with other European countries. In one way, the creation in 1926 of the Paris Mosque helped to set the tone, since it was for many years the only building in French usage to carry the term *mosquée*. There were at various times short-lived *salles de prière*, or 'prayer rooms'. Not until the late 1960s do we witness the beginnings of the new phenomenon of publicly identifiable places of Muslim worship. This change was linked not only to the growth in numbers mentioned earlier but also, perhaps more significantly, to the beginnings of unofficial organisation, the reunification of families, the weakening of the expectation of migrants returning, and the availability of financial support from the government and from charitable organisations, often church-related. From the early 1970s, the support – or expectations of support – from international Muslim organisations such as the Muslim World League were an added incentive. All of this accumulated pressure broke out into the open after the change in the law of association of 1981.

France does not have any particular administrative procedure by which it is possible to identify Muslim places of worship, so statistics are by definition approximations. A 1986 survey by Legrain took into account surveys conducted by a variety of church, governmental and Muslim organisations. Thus, for example, the Minister of the Interior in November 1985 gave a written answer to a question in the National Assembly indicating that there were at that time seventy-two mosques functioning in terms of article 25 of the law of 9 December 1905; in other words, the worship was taking place in locations belonging to the religion in question and 'open to inspection by the authorities in the interests of public order'. This is clearly a very narrow definition of a Muslim place of worship, a fact underlined when one refers to the figures held by the police and published in *Le Monde* in early April 1985: at that time the police authorities knew of 438 Muslim places of worship distributed across sixty of the ninety or so departments in the country. On the other hand, questionnaires distributed by the Muslim World League recorded a growth from seventy-two places of worship in 1978 to 456 in 1985. Using such and other sources, Legrain arrives at a total of 941 Muslim places of worship at the end of 1985 (see Table 2.3).

The early 1990s saw a further major expansion in the number of places of worship, still mostly small locations in apartment blocks on housing estates, known as *foyers*. By the beginning of the new century, the Ministry of the Interior recorded 1,600 prayer houses and, in 2006, a specialist on Islam in France

Table 2.3 Muslim places of worship founded, 1976–85

	Total	foyers	other
1976	131	93	38
1978	197	125	72
1980	322	178	144
1982	451	212	239
1984	578	234	344
1985	619	238	381
undated	322	187	135
Total	941	425	516, end-1985

counted 2,150 places of worship of which twenty could host more than 1,000 people. Only a few, less than a dozen, were purpose-built. Establishing a mosque can still be very difficult as, despite any national policy guidance which may be issued, it is usually the local mayor who has the final word. This has tended to politicise the founding of mosques, whose fortunes have then depended very closely on the local electoral strength of, on the one hand, the *Front National*, or, on the other, on the size of the Muslim electorate. Still, in 2011, a report from the French National Muslim Council estimated the number of mosques under construction to be between 100 and 150.

Mosques are one outward sign of the existence of an organisation, but it is by no means all organisations which have been created for the purpose of supporting a mosque: in fact, the number of registered associations of Muslim character has generally been almost twice that of the number of mosques. In reality, it appears that the vast majority of organisations in France have an often explicit national orientation, even when their leaders proclaim the unity of all Muslims.

As in other European countries, immigrants of Muslim cultural background have often been grouped into organisations which have no explicit reference to Islam. This is particularly the case in France among the Algerians. Here, the *Amicale des Algériens* has operated primarily as a political force linking the FLN (*Front de la Libération Nationale*) structures of Algeria with the communist-linked trades union federation, the CGT (*Confédération générale du travail unitaire*). However, there is some evidence that the *Amicale* has become involved in the establishment of mosques in the Lyons area, while elsewhere the Paris Mosque has been left to get on with things. Among the Turks, the Turkish government has sponsored the presence of nearly 200 Turkish teachers, authorised by the French Ministry of Education to teach mother tongue and culture. These teachers form the bulwark of Kemalist laicism. They have been supported by *L'Association culture et entraide des travailleurs turques*, formed in 1976 and widely regarded as being supported by the Turkish government.

Apart from these two particular situations, most other organisational tendencies incorporate an explicit reference to Islam, either in their titles or in their constitutions, while at the same time affirming national or ethnic identities.

Among the Algerians, on the political front, a network opposing the FLN *Amicale* was set up by Ben Bella after he broke with the FLN and sought exile in France. Part of the programme of this group was a revived role for Islam in the political life of Algeria. This link between Islam and factional Algerian politics was perceived by Ben Bella's enemies and other observers to be behind the establishment in Paris in 1984 of a General Secretariat of Muslim Workers in Europe, at the initiative of the London-based Islamic Council of Europe.

The majority of Moroccan organisations express a Muslim identity at one level or another. In contrast to the Algerian organisation of similar name, the *Amicales des travailleurs et commerçants marocains*, with its close links to the Moroccan monarchy, supports numerous mosques across France and is engaged regularly at the level of popular culture and celebration. Political opposition groups are splintered.

The Tunisian community is the least structured. While Habib Bourghiba was still in power in Tunisia, the main opposition group established a French branch in 1980 under the title *Groupement Islamique en France* (GIF). It organised summer camps and conferences but above all made itself noticed through its literature work, which confirmed its Muslim Brotherhood heritage. This particular background may explain why the GIF has appeared to be more ready to enter into alliances with other Muslim groups and federations.

Among the Turks, generally isolated from the North and Sub-Saharan African communities, movements from Turkey itself have become established. The National Salvation Party of Erbakan was initially represented in France by *L'Union islamique en France*, founded in 1983. Reflecting developments in Turkey, its association with the *Milli Görüş* has become more visible and openly acknowledged during the 1990s until, in 2001, it changed its name to *Communauté Islamique Milli Görüş en France*. The more radical movement of the rightwing politician Türkes, represented in *L'Association des travailleurs turcs idéalistes de Paris*, founded as early as 1978, has since declined in importance. Outside Paris, these national Turkish Muslim tendencies appear to have less of a hold and have a more explicitly Islamic identity, often centred on sports programmes. The most influential Turkish organisation in 2015 is coordinated by the Turkish *Diyanet* and is called *Comité de Coordination des Musulmans Turcs de France*. As will become clear when reading the coming chapters, the Turkish *Diyanet* – the Department of Religious Affairs (*Diyanet Isleri Baskanligi*) of the Prime Minister's Office – is probably the most successful and skilled transnational actor when it comes to organising Muslim life in Europe.

France has probably the most lively and extensive Sufi activity among Muslims of all western European countries. Certainly, the organisational activity of the Muslims from West Africa is dominated by the Sufi tradition as expressed in the characteristics of the Mourides and *tariqas* of Senegal and Mali. The Senegalese Mourides, with origins in the Qadiriyya tradition, are the most widespread, partly through small itinerant trading networks among the immigrants and partly through student links. Other groups have well-established presences in France, such as the 'Hamalistes' devoted to a shaykh of a Tijaniyya branch of Mali. Several other West African 'marabout' organisations have been founded since 1981.

The Algerian Alawiyya order, which has come out of the Moroccan Darqawi tradition, established its first *zawiyah* in Paris in 1924 and is popular among Algerians. Descendants of the founder (Ahmad ibn Mustafa al-Alawi, died 1934) are based in France and seek a revival of classical mystical disciplines cleansed of the accretions of popular superstition while opposing the legalistic reformism of the Muslim Brotherhood and figures such as Ibn Badis. It is unclear to what extent widespread Darqawi traditions are active in France.

The Naqshbandi tradition is most active among Turks, both directly in the form of orders, and indirectly through its connections into the *Süleymançis* and other groups such as the *Milli Görüş*. On the other hand, the Alevi movement and its closely associated Bektashiyya are also very active, especially among the many Kurds, although they are not as visible in the form of mosques as other more orthodox tendencies.

Shi'ite tendencies of Ja'fari allegiance are to be found primarily among Iranians and, to a lesser extent, Lebanese students, refugees and immigrants. Support for Iran since the revolution of 1979 has extended beyond Shi'ite circles into some Sunni quarters. Adherents of the smaller Shi'ite sects, in particular the Isma'ilis, are also present. The Aga Khan, leader of the Isma'ilis, has his world community headquarters in Paris, where there is also a Society for Isma'ili Studies. Small Khoja and Bohra communities are based around Paris and tend to originate in Indian migrant communities from the Indian Ocean, in Mauritius and Madagascar.

It is really only at the elite level and in relation to international organisations that Muslim groups have seemed able to surmount the divisive effects of national and ethnic origin. This has been the case with associations of Muslim doctors and students, and with associations of converts such as *Terre d'Europe*, formerly *Les amis de l'Islam*, associated with the North African Alawiyya, and

Vivre l'Islam en Occident. The latter is involved in producing a weekly Sunday television programme broadcast on the public channel France 2. Similarly, the Muslim World League office in Paris, since its opening in 1976, has had some effect in achieving cooperation, mainly through the resources at its disposal. According to the League's own information, it distributed 4.5 million francs for the building and repair of mosques in the years from 1979 to 1983.

As elsewhere, it has been difficult to achieve a fully representative federation of Muslim groups. A proposal in 1981 by Si Hamza Boubakeur of the Paris Mosque to create a *Conseil Supérieur des Affaires Islamiques* foundered on differences among various tendencies, as did the more personally based attempt in 1984 to create a *Consistoire Islamique en France* by an opponent of the Paris Mosque. In 1983, a number of mosques and associations of tendencies based in the Muslim Brotherhood formed the *Union des Organisations Islamiques en France* (UOIF). During 1985, two new rival initiatives were taken. One, involving the Paris bureau of the Muslim World League, was a *Fédération Nationale des Musulmans de France* (FNMF) established at a large meeting in Paris in October; West African groups stayed out, and Algerians boycotted it. The other initiative, instigated by the Paris Mosque, was the establishment in December of the same year of a *Rassemblement Islamique*, bringing together mostly Algerian groups. In 1986, the *Fédération* claimed to have the membership of about 500 organisations across France, while the *Rassemblement* claimed about 300. Organising themselves separately, groups of sub-Saharan and Comoran origin formed *La Fédération Française des Associations Islamiques d'Afrique des Comores et des Antilles* (FFAIACA) in 1989. In early 1990, a broad-based meeting of representatives of the Harkis succeeded for the first time in establishing their own generally recognised Representative Council. Younger people, women and men, have become increasingly active in these organisations and have also established their own, the *Jeunes Musulmans de France*.

Completely separate from either of these two attempts at federation is the movement *Foi et Pratique* (Faith and Practice). Established in Paris in September 1972, this is a branch of the world-wide movement *Jama'at-al-Tabligh*. It controls a few mosques in the Paris region but has its effect through the visits of its itinerant preachers to the many small prayer houses spread around the country. While the leadership is overwhelmingly Algerian, *Foi et Pratique* has attracted adherents from all ethnic communities. Particularly during the mid- and late 1980s, the movement experienced an enormous growth, especially among the younger artisan and student population. During the 1990s, *Foi et Pratique* led the establishment of places of worship in the Paris region in particular.

A number of attempts to establish nationally representative organisations have been initiated by government, wishing to have only one dialogue partner. A first major attempt was the setting-up of a *Conseil de Réflexion sur l'Islam en France* (CORIF) in 1989 after the 'headscarves affair' (see Chapter 10). It lacked legitimacy in most Muslim quarters, and further attempts to achieve such a national body through the 1990s were complicated by the Algerian civil war, internal Muslim rivalries and the reluctance of the government to deal with groupings which it considered 'fundamentalist', above all the UOIF. A new initiative was taken by the socialist interior minister Jean-Pierre Chevènement in October 1999, when he set up a consultation on Islam in France, commonly called by its Arabic term *Istichara*. After some delay, caused both by change of government and by the difficulty of getting all parties involved, elections took place in April 2003 to create a new *Conseil Français du Culte Musulman* (CFCM) which could perform the role of denominational representative envisaged in Chapter IV of the 1905 law separating church and state. Consisting of a general assembly and twenty-five regional councils, the new CFCM is the most representative body of its kind yet achieved, but at the same time the election process exposed the internal divisions of French Islam. The Paris Mosque and its regional representations received only 12 per cent of the vote, seriously weakening the position of its director, Dalil Boubakeur, who had by prior agreement been appointed president. The two major winners were the FNMF with 39 per cent and the UOIF with 27 per cent of the vote, forcing the authorities finally to accept their significance. As with any governmentally established Muslim organisation in any European country – and there are quite a few – CFCM will have to earn its legitimacy over time. Some new national organisations have emerged in recent years. The first national Shi'ite organisation, *Fédération Chiite de France*, was set up in 2007 following the Twelver Shi'a creed. A new association, promoting French Islam and encouraging acculturation, was set up in 2011, *Fils de France* (Sons of France). *Fils de France* is active in civil society arranging debates and lectures.

At a superficial level, there has been little activity by the churches in France to register the Muslim presence. The Catholic Bishops' Conference created a *Secretariat pour les Relations avec l'Islam* (SRI) at the end of the 1970s. Its function has been to help educate the church itself about Islam, and to help individuals and local groups seeking to establish some form of cooperation with Muslims. The SRI has had the support of some bishops, while most of the church has tended to devote more of its energies to combating the growing racist tendencies during the 1980s. In the small Protestant church, the few individuals who have been concerned were able to form a working group in cooperation with the French-speaking Protestant church in Belgium and Switzerland. But behind this lies an enormous amount of activity in organisations – research, information and publishing projects, social work, political lobbying and so on – which have been founded with substantial church involvement shared with other concerned groups. Clearly, the division of France between public laicism and the sphere of the church has meant that many Christians felt that it was necessary to refrain from explicitly Christian organisation to be able to work together with other groups for a common social or political goal.

In recent years, a number of surveys have been conducted giving an impression of the degree to which people of Muslim cultural origin in France are also practising Muslims. In this, France is unique among the countries surveyed in this study. Surveys of this kind have been carried out elsewhere in western Europe, but only at a local level or within limited fields of concern. Only in France have detailed national surveys been carried out.

One of the earliest of these surveys, from the beginning of the 1980s, indicated a major decline in religious adherence from immigrant parents to their children. Virtually all fathers of North African origin declared themselves to be Muslim, while over a quarter of their children refused to identify themselves with Islam. Almost half of the parents said they continued to perform the daily prayers as against only 3 per cent of the children. Only 13 per cent of the children read the Qur'an regularly as against 45 per cent of the parents. On the other hand, this same survey suggested that three-quarters of the young continued to celebrate the main feasts, but that less than half observed the fast of Ramadan. A study published in 1983 suggested that only about 10 per cent of adult men attended the Friday noon prayer. Since 1989, the newspaper *Le Monde* has published a regular series of surveys of the extent of religious practice among Muslims. These record a marked reversal of the earlier trend away from religious practice. Based on a survey conducted in the week after 11 September 2001, more than one-third declared themselves to be practising believers, while a further two-fifths considered themselves believers. The number of people claiming to attend Friday noon prayer had doubled since the 1983 survey. A recent poll (2011) suggested a further increase in ritual behaviour: 39 per cent claimed to pray daily prayers, 23 per cent attended mosques for prayer and 71 per cent fasted during Ramadan. Especially among Muslim youth from all over Europe, fasting is among the most popular of religious rites.

Respect for dietary rules has been upheld rather more than most other Islamic practices. Thus the survey from the early 1980s showed that 69 per cent of young people continued to respect the prohibition of alcohol and pork. The main problem in this area in France has been the inability of Muslim groups to meet the strict requirements of French law. A government decree of October 1980, regulating the slaughter of animals for food, allowed an exemption for religious reasons from the requirement of rendering an animal unconscious before killing it. However, a further decree the following year required that such slaughter could only be carried out by persons named to the Ministry of Agriculture by religious authorities approved by the Ministry of the Interior. The lack of agreement among Muslim organisations has meant that no such body has obtained approval by the Ministry of the Interior. In the absence of such national authorisation, the Prefect of a Department is empowered to issue the necessary permission to named individuals, but this still indirectly requires some degree of local consensus among the Muslims. Despite these obstacles, a number of butchers exist, wherever there is a Muslim population, offering halal meat. To counter suspicions that some of these are not completely trustworthy, organisations have come into existence to inspect and provide guarantees, as have several associations of halal butchers and retailers. In the mid-1990s, when the interior minister Charles Pasqua attempted to promulgate the Paris Mosque, whose director by this time was Dalil Boubakeur, as the officially recognised representative of Islam, the Mosque was given the sole right to certify halal food products for the whole of France. However, protests from a broad span of Muslim interests temporarily put paid to this project. As of 2015, three main mosques in France, including the Paris Mosque, have the right to name slaughterers.

Seventy Muslim sectors of communal cemeteries have been opened, mostly in major cities, to provide for Muslim needs. The Muslim section of the cemetery at Bobigny served the Paris region for a long time but is now full. Its place has been taken by three or four smaller cemeteries. Strasbourg opened an all-Muslim public cemetery in 2012. It is the first and, so far, only one in France. For some people, the preference still remains to be buried in the country of origin, in Islamic land.

Education

In 1980, statistics showed that almost 9 per cent of children up to the age of fourteen were foreign. This was reflected in the fact that almost that proportion of children in school were of foreign origin, and two-thirds of them, totalling over 650,000, were in nursery and primary schools. Slightly over half of the foreign children at that time were North African or Turkish. The proportion of children of Muslim background in the various categories of secondary school was lower, rather less than half, in a total of foreign children which itself was lower. The total number of children of Muslim background will thus have been nearly half a million. By 1988, the total number of children in French schools had hardly changed, and the total number of foreign children had only slightly increased. In view of the major shift towards a resident foreign population of Muslim origin and of the fast-increasing numbers of French-born children of Muslim parents, described earlier in this chapter, it can be assumed that a fast-growing proportion of the children in French schools are of Muslim background.

Given the uneven distribution of the Muslim communities across France, it is inevitable that Muslim children are concentrated in the schools of some districts. France is organised into twenty-six educational regions, and two-thirds of the children of foreign origin are concentrated in eight of those regions. In Paris in 1980–1, 40 per cent of children of foreign origin were concentrated in only twenty schools in four of the twenty *arrondissements* in the city.

As part of the agreement between church and state reached at the beginning of the twentieth century, religious communities are entitled to run their own schools with public funding covering some of the costs. Consequently, there are a large number of Catholic 'free schools' and a smaller number of Protestant and Jewish ones, which cater for almost one-fifth of the population of school age. Up to a tenth of school costs are covered, but more importantly, the school's curriculum and diplomas are officially recognised. In 2003, the first Muslim publically subsidised school was opened in Lille called Lycée Averroès. By 2014, an additional three schools had been initiated. France also has some forty-five privately funded Muslim schools.

Muslim children tend to be sent to state schools rather than free schools partly because of the expense of school fees, but also because the free schools are less common in the urban areas where Muslims are concentrated. This means, however, that they get no access to religious education within the school, because the state school system is firmly laicist in its ideology, to the extent that the wearing of symbols which can be considered of a religious nature may be forbidden. On the other hand, a factual introduction to Islam is included in the official history syllabus, and some state schools include aspects of Islam as part of intercultural education programmes. In the Catholic free schools, each school has its own approach to dealing with the presence of Muslim pupils, and some do provide for Islamic instruction in parallel with Catholic catechesis; this tends to be done in conjunction with a local imam. Primary schools with a substantial proportion of North African pupils often provide some Arabic instruction as part of a general policy of mother-tongue teaching. The few existing private schools offer their pupils in-depth studies in Arabic and Islamic ethics. If a school has a contract with the state and is financed through public means, regulations demand religious instructions to be optional.

After the 'headscarves affair' of 1989 (see Chapter 10), there has been a gradual opening of traditional, ideologically constrained attitudes to secular education. It is now common in state schools to find provision for religious festivals and access to halal menus, although not to halal meat. But the teaching of religion remained, and remains, in dispute. A poll conducted in 2000 suggested that public opinion on this point had hardened with a decline in those in favour from two-thirds to 57 per cent since a similar poll in 1988 and an increase from 28 per cent to 41 per cent of those against over the same period. This may, it has been suggested, reflect the fact that some ground had already been conceded in the 1996 reform of the history curriculum to include more reference to Islamic history and culture, and that many felt that this was sufficient. However, in early 2002, a commission chaired by the former socialist prime minister Regis Debray recommended that the state school should include education about religions in its curriculum, a proposal which was welcomed later in the year by the minister of education and by President Chirac but nothing concrete has come out of it as of now.

By the end of the 1980s, most mosques were providing some form of Islamic instruction for a growing proportion of Muslim children. Especially in the case of North Africans, this is related to the teaching of Arabic as the language both of the Qur'an and of their culture. At a quite early stage, a number of both Muslim and national organisations established Arabic courses. Thus by the end of the 1970s, the mosque of Paris as well as the Algerian *Amicales* were running regular Arabic courses, often with the cooperation of public authorities, which were encouraging the teaching of the mother tongue to children. In the early 1990s, the mosque of Paris expanded this activity in the form of an Islamic theological institute which, despite initial ambitions, remains a framework for adult evening classes. Separately, the Moroccan consulates were running their own Arabic courses for Moroccans.

The training of imams has continued to be a significant issue both for the Muslim communities and for the French authorities, given that many imams still lack sufficient Islamic education and often have little understanding of the society their communities inhabit. The major initiative to deal with this problem was taken in 1992 by the UOIF with the opening of the *Institut européen des sciences humaines* in the Nièvre, commonly known as Château-Chinon or the Bouteloin Institute. It has the capacity to house 150 resident students, male and female (more than 40 per cent of students are female), and also offers courses by distance learning that are followed by around 200 students according to the institute. In fact, most students seem to use it to become familiar with Islamic sciences, and only about thirty graduates have completed imam training.

Founded in 1993 and closed in 2002, the *Institut d'études islamiques de Paris*, located at Saint-Denis, for a time met a demand for evening and weekend further education in Islam, but only about ten students appear to have completed the full course. A completely different approach has been suggested since 1996 by a retired professor at the Protestant faculty of theology at Strasbourg University. Located in the Alsace-Moselle region, where the 1905 law on church-state separation does not apply as it has retained the German system introduced while under German rule 1871–1918, Strasbourg University has both a Protestant and a Catholic theological faculty. The proposal has been simply to establish a parallel Islamic faculty. For a long time the idea was opposed from both secular and Catholic quarters, but during 2002, President Chirac expressed his interest in the proposal, which has therefore attracted renewed interest. Since 2012, Strasbourg University has organised a Diplôme Universitaire course in imam training centred on law, history and sociology. In 2014, the decision was taken to expand this program to three more public universities. Parallel to this development, Muslim private institutions have taken new initiatives, the most ambitious being the Turkish *Diyanet* initiative to start a five-year Islamic theological training programme in Strasbourg, hoping to eventually be acknowledged on a par with the Catholic and Protestant faculties of theology at Strasbourg University. Although large sums have been invested, the *Diyanet* programme has not yet materialised.

CHAPTER 3

Germany

Immigration and growth

The settlement in what was West Germany of a substantial Muslim population, the second-largest in Western Europe, is dominated by Turkish immigration. During the 1950s, there were a number of private and regional initiatives to recruit workers from Turkey to meet the beginnings of a shortage of industrial labour. An agreement between the Ministry of Labour of Schleswig-Holstein and the Turkish Ministry of Foreign Affairs led to the arrival of a dozen Turkish craftsmen in Kiel in April 1957. A programme was sponsored by the Hamburg Chamber of Craftsmen. In Bavaria, a private 'Research Institute for Turkish-German Economic Relations' was in fact a recruitment agency, while a number of 'translation bureaux' sprang up for the same purpose. The best of these programmes provided some training, but most were simply looking for cheap labour. The experience of many of these early 'guest workers' (*Gastarbeiter*) was disappointing, as they learned that their Turkish craft qualifications were not recognised, that they had to do unskilled or semiskilled work below their qualifications, and that only a few of them were given the opportunity to train further.

These early settlers were concentrated in the industrial cities of the north, particularly Hamburg, Bremen and Kiel. The rules governing immigration at the time were liberal compared to later stages, and the immigrants were able to bring their families with them and to settle in quite quickly. As a result, despite their early disappointments, they were later to express quite a high level of satisfaction with the results of their move.

The federal government soon came to the view that the process of recruitment should be regularised while also being expanded. The move towards making recruitment of Turkish – and other foreign – workers a government monopoly was completed with a bilateral recruitment agreement between Turkey and Germany in 1962. The date was not coincidental. This was only a year after the Berlin Wall was erected, blocking the inflow of East Germans. It was also the year which saw the beginning of Turkey's first five-year plan, in which the export of labour was a major element.

The effect of the agreement was that German companies seeking Turkish workers had to operate through official recruitment offices set up by the German and Turkish authorities in Turkey. People looking to find work in Germany had to go through medical checks and job interviews in Turkey and were issued with work permits and entry papers. The assumption throughout was that the period of employment was for a limited number of years, after which the worker would return home, so the men were discouraged from bringing their wives and children with them.

As a result of the growth of the German economy, the employment of foreign workers more than trebled between 1960 and 1963, and an increasing proportion of them were Turks. The number of Turks entering Germany over the same period increased tenfold.

Having established recruitment as a government monopoly, the authorities proceeded to regularise most aspects of the Turkish workers' circumstances. The social welfare of foreign workers had previously been placed in the hands of the social work arms of the two main churches: the Protestants had been charged with looking after Greek workers, and the Catholics had been given responsibility for Italian and Spanish workers. The care of Turkish workers was given to the *Arbeiterwohlfahrt*, the social welfare arm of the Social Democratic Party and the labour movement. Workers' earnings were converted to Turkish currency at a special rate to avoid a black market. Government funds were made available to support the establishment of cultural associations, and regular broadcasting in Turkish started. The German government also encouraged the opening of Turkish consulates in the main cities where the new immigrants were settling.

The first crisis in this development came with the short economic recession of 1966–7. Somewhere in the region of 70,000 Turkish workers lost their jobs, but against expectations most did not return home. Although virtually all these people had found work again by the middle of 1967, the event had raised questions about Germany's foreign labour policy. Was foreign labour simply a reserve which could be drawn on or discarded according to need? What about the social and cultural problems which the brief period of unemployment had brought to the surface?

During the following half-dozen years or so, Germany saw its greatest influx yet of Turkish workers, over 100,000 in 1973 alone. The immigration was no longer overwhelmingly male. On the one hand, women workers were being recruited – they made up almost a quarter of the 1973 influx. On the other hand, wives were beginning to join their husbands. There was the first public awareness of particular city districts becoming Turkish 'ghettos', and the German health, social and educational services were beginning to feel the pressure. There was also an increase in irregular immigration.

As a result, in 1973 the federal government introduced a new policy of integration. Employers were required to provide housing to acceptable standards and to pay a much higher rate for the recruitment service of the government. The funds thus acquired were to be used for the education and integration of new arrivals. However, almost as soon as this new policy was in place, the economic recession following the 'oil crisis' struck, and Germany put in place severe restrictions on the recruitment of industrial workers, leaving the gates open only for family reunion and for particular specified professions and crafts.

Throughout, the basic German policy remained to benefit the labour market within limits of political acceptability. Germany has always insisted that it is not a country of immigration, so the term 'guest worker' remains in common use. At various times, measures have been taken to encourage the return home of foreign workers, such as the Turks. These measures have either been positive, such as paying them lump sums, or they have been negative, such as restricting access to welfare benefits on an equal basis with German citizens. On the same principle, basic civil rights have often been withheld from foreigners, and suggestions that they should be allowed to participate somehow in the political process through, for example, a local vote have been strongly resisted by the authorities.

While such restrictive measures changed the nature of Turkish immigration, they did not put an end to it. The total Turkish population in Germany did not level off until the beginning of the 1980s. In 1973, the figure had been 616,000. By 1980, it had reached 1.46 million and continued upwards to 1.58 million two years later. It then started falling, to reach 1.4 million in 1985.

In that same year, there were 47,500 Moroccans, 23,300 Tunisians, and smaller numbers of other Muslim nationalities in Germany. There were also nearly 600,000 Yugoslavs, 20 per cent of whom according to some estimates may have been Muslim. In addition, several agencies estimated that there might be as many as 200,000 undocumented Turkish migrants. By the beginning of 1989, the number of Turks had again risen to over 1.5 million. The number of Moroccans had also risen, to over 50,000, while Tunisians had decreased slightly. At this time, there were also over 17,000 Pakistanis resident in Germany.

During the mid-1980s, the pattern of immigration into Germany had begun to change character again. Very few people were coming for work. Instead, there were growing numbers of refugees from various parts of the world, including Turkey, Iran and the Arab countries. Many of these had been entering via East Berlin, where the East German authorities were allowing people without valid papers to land and then sending them across to the western half of the city. An agreement between the two governments succeeded in putting a stop to this practice in August 1986, but the arrival of refugees continued, albeit in smaller numbers, and German policy towards the status of foreigners was, by the end of the decade, dominated by its attitude towards refugees. By the beginning of 1989, this change was reflected in the presence of 73,000 Iranians, over 22,000 Lebanese and more than 9,000 each of Syrians and Jordanians, many of the latter being Palestinian.

The number of Turks cannot necessarily be taken to equate with the number of Muslims in the way that can be applied to, for example, Moroccans and

Tunisians. A significant minority of Turkish immigrants are Christian, either Armenian or Syrian Orthodox. In addition, a number of Turks of what might be called Muslim cultural background would not call themselves Muslim, rather secularist or even, in the case of a few, atheist. The national census which took place in May 1987 included a question on religion. There were almost 100,000 Turks who did not declare themselves to be Muslim. The other interesting figure to come out of that census was the almost 48,000 Muslims with German citizenship. Most of these are people who have changed citizenship, but over 5,000 of them are German converts to Islam. The total number of Muslims registered in the census was 1,650,952. A later survey from 2008 confirms it being a mistake to think everyone from predominantly Muslim country self-identifies as Muslim. In fact, 26 per cent of immigrants from these countries claim to be Christian. Regarding immigrants from Afghanistan, 20.4 per cent tick the box 'No religious affiliation' and 10.2 'other religious affiliation'. The figures for those with an Iranian background are 38.4 and 12.9 per cent. Only 48.7 per cent self-identify as Muslim.

Otherwise, the 1987 census also confirmed the regional distribution of Muslims, which one could derive from previously published data on the location of foreigners. Over a third were concentrated in the state of North Rhine-Westphalia, especially in the massive industrial conurbation stretching from Cologne through Düsseldorf and Duisburg to Essen. The city state of Hamburg had over 50,000, while Baden-Württemberg had over 250,000 concentrated in cities like Stuttgart and Karlsruhe. There were nearly 250,000 in Bavaria, the largest number of them in and around Munich, while Hessen had 170,000, mainly in Frankfurt. German unification took place in 1990 but did not affect the number of Muslims much; few Muslims lived in the East. In 2009, less than 2 per cent of German Muslims lived in the territory of the former GDR.

In 2000, the Federal Statistical Office gave a figure of just short of 2 million Turks, of which just over one-third had been born in Germany. By then the impact of the wars in former Yugoslavia had also become visible, with 156,300 Bosnians and 51,800 Macedonians recorded, many of whom were Muslims, especially in the former case. At this time, new laws introducing dual citizenship and the possibility of acquiring citizenship by birth in Germany were already having their impact. The official statistics for Turks showed the number falling to 1,912,200 by 2002, a decline of almost 90,000 in just two years. An independent research institution, basing itself on Muslim sources, gave a total of 3.2 million Muslims in 2001. Of these, some 2.2 million were estimated to be Sunnis, 340,000 Alevis, 170,000 Shi'ites, and 310,000 German passport-holders, of which some 11,000 were of German descent.

From 2007 onwards, a few larger statistical studies focusing on Muslims in Germany have been published. The Federal Ministry of Interior Affairs produced a report, *Muslims in Germany*, the first larger quantitative study, followed by *Religion monitor 2008* and the *Muslim Life in Germany* report in 2009. The latter report put the number of Muslims in Germany at a total of 3.8–4.3 million, Turkish immigrants being the most prominent group (2.5 million). Sunni Muslims were still the largest group (74.1 per cent) followed by Alevi (12.7) and Shi'ites (7.1). Ahmadis were few (1.7) but accounted for 28 per cent of those from South and South-East Asia. Seventy per cent of the Muslims were born abroad. The report states that 45 per cent of the interviewed were German nationals. Muslims make up, approximately, one-quarter of those with an immigrant background in Germany.

Law and organisations

Germany's constitution, called the Basic Law, guarantees freedom of religious worship, organisation and teaching. The state is regarded not as being laicist in the French or Dutch form, rather it is *religionsneutral*. In other words, it does not take a position on religious affairs. The distinction is important, because the state and religious institutions are not rigidly separated as in France. The Jewish community, the Catholic dioceses and the regional Protestant churches all have the status of a publicly recognised corporation (*Körperschaft des öffentlichen Rechts*). In practice, this means that the state collects a church tax from the members of the churches on their behalf and hands the tax over to the churches after deducting an agreed administration charge. The regional states and the churches cooperate very closely in areas of education, and 80 per cent of the publicly funded nursery schools are run by the churches, as are a number of hospitals and other welfare institutions. The state has also, as we have seen, delegated to the churches' welfare agencies the oversight of the social care of southern European immigrants. The specific questions relating to education will be dealt with below.

Religious communities which have not been granted such recognition can operate freely under the laws of association. There are two such categories which have been used by Muslim organisations, namely that of registered association (*eingetragener Verein* or e.V.) and that of a foundation (*Stiftung*). The status of registered association has been by far the most common form to be sought, and a 2001 estimate suggests that there were then about 2000 such associations. To satisfy the requirements for this, the association must have a democratic structure with a recognisable membership list. The structure of a foundation is controlled by a group of trustees with strict rules as to the administration of and responsibility for properties.

In these two forms of association, Muslim groups have been able to put into practice most of the activities they have wanted to set up. First and foremost, of course, this has meant the opening of places of worship. The earliest mosques to be established in Germany after the Second World War were in Frankfurt and

Hamburg by the Ahmadi movement during the 1950s. Mosques arising out of the immigration only started to appear in the late 1960s, usually in converted flats, rooms, outhouses and garages. Occasionally, with time, resources were found to purchase larger properties such as warehouses, small factories, shop premises and, in one case, a former four-storey public bath-house. By the mid-1980s, a few new mosques had been constructed, of which probably the most notable is the Islamic Cultural Centre built in Iranian style on the shore of the Alster Lake in Hamburg, where it has become something of a tourist attraction. In Berlin, the old mosque in Wilmersdorf was restored to use, and in Aachen and Munich mosques and Islamic centres have been built with particular encouragement from groups of German converts to Islam. By 2000, there were over sixty mosques, many of them purpose-built, and over 2,000 other spaces in regular use for worship. Fourteen years later, approximately 2,700 facilities for Friday prayers existed and, in addition, several hundred Alevi *Cem evi*, gathering houses. Two hundred mosques had been renovated or purpose-built to resemble traditional mosques and scholars estimate another 150 to be under construction.

When the Turks started arriving in large numbers, there was already a small network of Muslim associations bringing together people of various nationalities, including Germans. There were a number of Sufi groups which tended to be international in their recruitment among young intellectuals. The ideas of the Indian Sufi Inayat Khan are said to have been influential in attracting young Germans during the 1950s and 1960s. In Berlin, the scene was long dominated by the charismatic figure of Salah Eid, who brought together a variety of Sufi groups and others in an attempt to present a unified Islam to the city authorities. Since his death, the grouping has mainly dispersed. The early Sufi tendencies were, in any case, being overtaken by the growth of Turkish Muslim organisations. Here, the Naqshbandis were prominent for a time, but as an organisation they also had to give way, and their influence in more recent years has tended to be more through the Naqshbandi links of officials within the main Turkish associations.

In the years until the late 1970s, the most active Turkish Muslim groups were those linked to movements which were either banned or disapproved of by the Turkish government. The most prominent of these was the *Avrupa Islam Kültür Merkezleri Birligi*, the association of Islamic Cultural Centres in Europe, known in German as *Verband islamischer Kulturzentren e.V.* With its headquarters in Cologne, this represented the European branch of the *Süleymançi* movement which, as an organisation, was banned in Turkey at the time. From Cologne, it controlled at its high point in 1981, 185 mosque associations and a further twenty-four 'fraternal groupings'. Although the member mosques were all constituted with e.V. status, the central control of the 'Chief Imam' in Cologne was considerable. During the 1970s, the Chief Imam represented an assertive form of Turkish Islam which laid great stress on the Qur'an school model which the founder of the movement in Turkey had emphasised. At times, the Chief Imam wrote in Turkish in the newspaper *Anadolu* aggressively against the churches and the German order, and this led to a campaign by the German trade unions supported by the Turkish federation of workers in Germany, FIDEF, to have the Islamic Cultural Centres banned. The Imam finally received instructions from the *Süleymançi* leadership in Turkey to tone down his statements. Soon afterwards, he was recalled, and the leadership during the 1980s took a much more constructive approach to working with German institutions. But it soon resumed its more public activities in opposition to official Islam in Turkey, stressing more openly its Sufi character, and therefore has remained suspect also by the German authorities. It has also started training imams at the head-quarters in Cologne. After a change in leadership in Turkey in 2000, *Süleymançi* in Germany was ordered to interact less with German society and engage in opening boarding schools to protect the Muslim youth from bad influences. The order has not been popular among adherents, and it has not lessened suspicions against the group.

A slightly smaller but also very active group is the *Islamische Gemeinschaft Milli Görüş* (IGMG), first known as *Avrupa Milli Görüş Teşkilati*, which in the early 1980s claimed to have the support of about half of the Muslim population of Berlin. In many ways, it was more militant in its attitude to German society and Turkish politics, and during the 1970s the movement was perceived as being very close to the Turkish National Salvation Party (MSP) of Necmettin Erbakan. During the 1980s, a section of the movement broke away to form a separate section sympathetic to the trend of the revolutionary leadership in Iran. Commonly identified with its leader Cemalettin Kaplan, it began to dissipate after his disappearance in the mid-1990s and was finally banned by the authorities in the aftermath of the events of 11 September 2001 (see Chapter 10). In the meantime, the main movement has grown to become one of the most important among Turks across Europe, not just in Germany. The growth in its support reflected the growth of the Refah Partisi in Turkey, also led by Erbakan, for a time prime minister (in 1996) until the military forced him out and had the party banned in 1997. IGMG experienced severe setbacks due to this, especially when economic investments in Turkey connected to Refah Partisi failed. Many in Germany lost their savings and blamed the IGMG leadership who had encouraged the investments.

In Germany, the IGMG did not develop local political ambitions and restricted itself to providing cultural, educational and religious services to the community, but this has not stopped the internal security services from retaining an interest in its activities. A new, younger leadership emerged after the loss of legitimacy of the older. Under the leadership of Mehmet Sabri Erbakan, nephew of the famous Turkish politician, especially with support from younger, educated members, the organisation moved its attention away from purely

Turkish concerns to an activist involvement in German society, encouraging members to apply for German citizenship and claim space. In so doing, they are also showing a tendency to relate more closely with like-minded groups across ethnic and national borders. This is also reflected in the proliferation of youth and women's sections in the local branches of the IGMG.

Mehmet Sabri Erbakan resigned in 2002 and a new leadership emerged stressing cooperation with German institutions instead of confrontation. By acknowledging that German secularism had actually created space for Islam, a new understanding of the Muslim presence in Germany grew. As a result, IGMG has since tried to develop a progressive minority *fiqh* (Islamic jurisprudence).

During the 1980s, the Nurçuluk movement claimed about twenty-eight local associations, which they called *medreses*. Early supporters of this movement could be found in Germany long before the Turkish immigration – in fact, the movement's founder had spent some time in Berlin after being released from a Russian prisoner-of-war camp after the First World War. However, not until the 1970s did Nurçu activity take an organised form. Apart from education of the Muslim community, often organised in *dershanes* (reading houses) of which there were fifty-seven in 2003, they have been particularly active in publishing. Politically, they have kept a low profile and seem not to have engaged actively in the Turkish political conflicts of the late 1970s, although they did use their German base to extend their educational and religious activities in Turkey. During the 1980s, trained followers of the movement appeared to have some success among Turks who had returned to Turkey.

A completely different picture emerges from observation of the Turkish Alevi community (which must not be confused with the Alawis, or Nusayris, of Syria). According to statistics from 2008, they make up as much as a fifth of the Turkish migrant population. The community's organisation rests overwhelmingly on family and clan structures. They distinguish themselves by taking a more relaxed view of religious ethical requirements than do strictly orthodox Sunnis. The women are allowed more freedom of movement and have greater disposition over how they arrange their lives. As the religious life of the Alevi tradition hardly requires mosques (their worship is based on a form of the Bektashi *dhikr*) or Qur'an schools, they are hardly visible in the organised Muslim life of Germany. A study of the community in Berlin published in 1988 could only identify one Alevi organisation. An additional factor in this 'invisibility' is the distrust expressed towards them both by Sunni movements, who regard them as heretical, and by the Turkish authorities, who regard them as perhaps not quite loyal Turks. The latter feeling is strengthened because many Alevis are Kurds.

For a long time, this meant that the Alevis themselves preferred to keep a low profile. However, in 1986, Alevis established a national organisation called *Alevitische Gemeinde Deutschland* in Cologne. It coordinates 125 local associations.

During the 1990s, the growing self-assertion of the Alevis in public in Turkey was reflected also in a much more visible representation of Alevism in Germany. By expressing and explaining Alevi uniqueness to the authorities, Alevi parents and organisations have gained the right to have Alevi religion taught in several schools with the start in 2006 in Baden-Württemberg. In fact, the Alevi organisation is the only one who, this far, has been fully recognised by the state in accordance with article 7, section 3 of the German Constitution regulating religious communities.

As the 1970s progressed, tensions within the Turkish communities increased in line with tensions in Turkey itself. Besides the Muslim organisations, Turkish trade union activity was also great. Turkish teachers employed to teach mother tongue and culture to Turkish children in German schools joined the trade unions in campaigning for the secularist traditions of the Kemalist lay republic. There were small but active groups on the Marxist left, in addition to radical Kurdish groups. As the movement in Turkey itself for a more conscious reislamisation of the country moved ahead and met with the secularist response, so the Turkish émigré communities in Germany became a base for all the various parties to the growing conflict, and it was not unusual for the conflict to spread into Germany.

The year 1980 was a crucial one. Among the Muslim movements, the success of the Islamic revolution in Iran was an encouragement to further campaigning. In September, the Turkish armed forces took power. As part of the consolidation of the influence of the new regime, control over the émigré communities was essential. A variety of methods was used, among which the organisation of Islam was an important one. It helped that it suited both the German and the Turkish governments to cooperate in this field. The central arm of the Turkish religious policy was the *Diyanet*.

It has been suggested that the religious policy of the military government and its successor in reality represents a continuation of the policy of moving towards a compromise between strict laicism and Islam which started during the 1940s. What has happened in Germany since 1980 has hence been merely an extension of that policy from Turkey to Germany. In 1972, the *Diyanet* had established a branch for overseas affairs. By 1981, it had only eighty religious officials placed throughout Europe at a time when the total number of Turkish mosques may have been as high as 1,000. During the late 1970s, a few mosques had come into existence in Germany linked to the *Diyanet*.

Soon after the military coup of September 1980, *Diyanet* officials in Ankara were moving towards a policy requiring that only imams and religious teachers approved by the *Diyanet* should be allowed to service the Turkish community abroad. Of all the European countries concerned, Germany was the easiest with which to reach such an arrangement. The *Diyanet* established a German branch in 1982, headquartered in Cologne (*Diyanet Isleri Türk-Islam Birligi* or DITIB), which proceeded to expand its influence among the Turkish mosques in the country.

There is little doubt that the move was welcome among the ordinary Turkish community. A survey in the early 1980s had shown that nearly two-thirds of the Turks in Berlin were uninterested in links with organisations such as the *Süleymançi* or the *Milli Görüş*. Another survey at the same time had shown that the same proportion of Turks attended prayers in the mosques with some degree of regularity and that they regarded the religious education of their children as important. The possibility of being related to mosques and finding Qur'an schools which were not so closely identified with movements involved in anti-government activity was clearly attractive.

By the end of the decade, a number of mosques linked to DITIB had been established. Some of them were new, but in others the membership had elected leaders who were sympathetic to DITIB. It was not unusual as a next step for the new leadership to have the status of the mosque association changed from e.V. to that of a foundation, the trustees of which would overlap with the trustees of the DITIB head office in Cologne. In this manner, DITIB not only expanded its influence but also made it irreversible. By 1984, it was estimated that 200 to 250 mosques in Germany had become linked to the *Diyanet*, and by the end of the decade, between half and two-thirds of the Turkish mosques had thus fallen into line with DITIB. Ten years later, registered membership of DITIB associations far outnumbered the combined membership of all other Muslim associations. In 2014, DITIB organised nearly 900 mosques and was still the largest organisation by far. Given the formal link with the Turkish state and popular suspicion of both the IGMG and the *Süleymançis*, German public opinion tends to regard DITIB as the natural partner for the German authorities.

At various times, the leaderships of these various organisations have been involved in serious mutual conflict. This has occasionally expressed itself in public, and it has often been difficult to arrange meetings even at national level, where rival leaderships were prepared to share the same platform. At the local level it has often been different. It was not unusual for local mosque committees to include members from a variety of organisations, even when the particular mosque association was publicly identified as being linked to one of the rival movements. It was even possible to find committee members from both the *Diyanet* and the movements banned in Turkey sharing work on a committee.

Since the 1980s, this phenomenon of crossing boundaries has, if anything, increased. At the Turkish end, the theological training, which is a prerequisite for employment by the *Diyanet*, tends to attract young men – and women – who are Islamically conscious and often consider themselves supporters of one or other of the Islamic movements, especially the *Süleymançi* and the *Milli Görüş*. Such imams, once stationed in Germany or other European countries with

Turkish communities, find it not too difficult to establish personal relations with fellow sympathisers, relations which can be difficult to control by the officials in Cologne or Ankara. Ultimately, the only form of control is the requirement that these officials return home after four to six years according to the agreement between Ankara and Berlin. At the same time, the official German policy of only allowing entry to imams approved by the Turkish government has been an incentive to activists in the Muslim movements to get their people through the official Turkish training system and into Germany through the official channels – essentially a form of infiltration.

Besides the Turkish movements, there are a number of active groupings in other circles. Perhaps the most influential has been the association of German-speaking Muslims, which also includes German converts and their children. Their activities are ubiquitous but centre in particular around the Islamic Centres in Aachen and Munich. These centres were founded by groups of students and converts who sympathised with the ideas of the Egyptian and Syrian Muslim Brotherhoods. Each group has regular conferences and assemblies, while its individual members take an active part in local Muslim affairs, regardless of the particular political, ideological or ethnic pattern.

Native German Muslims deserve a particular mention in this context. More than in any other European country, German Muslims played a crucial role in the establishment of Islam. For many years, Turks who sought to live according to Islam found that they had to turn to German Muslims for help. The laicist history of the Turkish republic meant that the educated Turks who came to Germany were unwilling to identify themselves with Islam. They were therefore not available as a leadership resource which could mediate with German society. This role was taken by countless German Muslims, and it is a role which continues even as the Turkish Muslim groups are beginning to build up their own competent leaderships.

In view of the tensions among groups over the years, tensions which were only exacerbated by the rival demands for religious education to be given in Turkish or German, to be discussed later, it should come as no surprise that efforts towards overall Muslim federation have shown few results. At various times different attempts at union have failed, both nationally and locally. The most recent attempt was the foundation in 1987 of the Islamic Council of West Germany and Berlin, which brought together several of the independent Turkish groups, the Alevis, the Muslim World Congress and the Muslim Refugees Spiritual Administration. However, this fell apart over disagreements concerning what attitude to take towards the North Rhine-Westphalia Islamic religious education syllabus.

Perhaps the greatest success has been the Islamic Federation of Berlin. Founded in 1980, much of the initiative lay with the *Milli Görüş* in association with a number of German Muslims, but the Federation also includes a number

of women's groups and individual mosques and associations independent of the
Milli Görüş, as well as students' associations.

The lack of unity is one reason for the failure of any Muslim organisation to
achieve recognition as a public law corporation. The first application for such
recognition came from the Islamic Cultural Centre of the *Süleymançi* in Cologne
in 1979. This was made to the regional state of North Rhine-Westphalia. One
response to this application was an informal agreement among the federal states
that they would coordinate their responses to such applications. This one was
turned down, as was one a few years later from the Islamic Federation of Berlin.
A reason for such negative responses has clearly been the lack of unity among
Muslim groups. The German law on recognition requires that recognition is
granted to an institution or organisation which is broadly representative, both
in its following and its internal structure, of the faith-community which it claims
to represent. The organisation must also have a character of permanence and
accept the provisions of the Basic Law. The last two requirements have also
created problems. Permanence is a difficult quality to prove, given the relatively
short life of the organisations in question. The fact that Germany, for a long
time, also officially denied the fact of immigration and permanent settlement
allowed the authorities to question the permanence of Muslim organisations.
One suspects that the suggestions made by some constitutional lawyers that
recognition may be unwise, given also that Islam might be in conflict with the
Basic Law, may themselves be unwise: reference is made to the inequality of the
sexes and to a potential loyalty to authorities other than the Basic Law, both
points which could legitimately be raised in relation to, for example, the Roman
Catholic dioceses, which do have recognition.

Being excluded, until the end of the 1990s, from German citizenship, Turks
have had to find other ways of influencing the German political process. They
have been only marginally successful. During the 1980s, an at times quite
heated debate took place over whether foreigners should be allowed to vote in
local elections. This possibility seems to have been finally stopped by a decision
of the constitutional court in 1990 that such a voting right would be unconstitutional. It has been mainly through their own organisations that Turks have been
able to achieve some influence, and this almost exclusively from the Kemalist
side. Turkish labour unions have been active in Germany and have developed
a close collaboration with their German counterparts. This link was exploited
successfully in the years around the military coup in September 1980 in Turkey,
when the Turkish unions were successful in mobilising their German partners
against Muslim organisations and their activities centred around the *Süleymançi*
mosques and Qur'an schools.

Following a reform of the nationality law (2000), German federal politics
changed towards a more inclusive understanding of the Muslim presence.
Since then, some very prominent politicians have symbolically expressed that

Islam belongs in Germany, or is domestic to it, for example German President Christian Wulff (in 2010) and Chancellor Angela Merkel (in 2015). Educational politics especially have changed to be more inclusive (see below).

The Gülen movement is active in Germany, organising intercultural dialogue associations (there were fifteen in 2012), engaging in social work and education (more than 100 educational facilities were associated with Gülen in 2012). The movement has a remarkable ability to arouse enthusiasm in people, but also to provoke and attract harsh criticism.

Both the Protestant and Roman Catholic churches established structures to educate their congregations and to establish relations with Muslim organisations. The Federation of Protestant Churches (EKD) appointed an official specifically for this purpose at the end of the 1970s, and by the end of the following decade all the regional churches had a counterpart. The order of the White Fathers set up a documentation and information centre, CIBEDO, in 1979, which a decade later was officially taken over by the Bishops' Conference. Throughout the same period, a Muslim–Christian Working Group (ICA) met regularly, involving representatives from the churches and the main Muslim groups. The Protestant churches involved Muslims in programmes in the biannual popular church gathering, the *Kirchentag*, throughout the 1980s, and by the end of the decade the Catholic equivalent was following suit. The Catholic church started the practice of issuing official greetings to Muslims at the time of Ramadan and 'Id al-Adha, following the pattern set by the Vatican. By the end of the 1980s, the EKD was also doing this, although not without opposition from among its members. In 2014, interreligious relations have become a part of the everyday work of Muslim organisations. Several organisations promoting meetings, dialogues and information exist, for example *Koordinierungsrat des christlisch-islamischen Dialogs e.V.* in Buseck.

Education

In the context of Germany, education has to be considered in at least four different spheres, namely nursery schools, the teaching of mother tongue and culture, religious education in both state and Qur'an schools, and religious education at universities. In addition, it must constantly be remembered that education is the responsibility of the regional states, not the federal government. Certainly, the ministers of education of the various states have their standing conference in which they meet regularly to coordinate matters. But that has not prevented significant differences of policy from developing, quite apart from the differences in religious education imposed sometimes by the differences in the constitutions of the states.

Ever-growing numbers of nursery schools in all the major cities of Germany, including Berlin, have been finding that they have a majority of Muslim, especially Turkish children. Eighty per cent of nursery schools are run by the Protestant and Catholic churches on behalf of and funded by the state authorities. This Turkish and Muslim presence has placed demands on the staff and the system which correspond to some degree with the general school situation. Thus teachers have been undergoing training, and educational policies have in some places been adapted. However, one of the main problems with the church-sponsored nurseries has been that, while they are funded by the governments, the staff are actually recruited and employed by the responsible church agency.

These agencies usually have the aim of providing a Christian upbringing for the children who attend. On the one hand, this has meant that nurseries have had to deal with a distinct change of emphasis in their practice, a change which some have coped with better than others. On the other hand, the church lawyers have tended to take the view that the nurseries cannot, therefore, employ staff from other religions on a full-time permanent basis. This is a view which has succeeded in blocking any significant appointment of, for example, Turkish nursery teachers. Although the leaderships of both the Protestant and Catholic churches have officially taken the view that their nurseries must respect Turkish and other Muslim children in their home culture, it was not until the 1990s that they were able to find legal ways around the problem.

A few Muslim nurseries have been established but as part of one or other Muslim association. They therefore are regarded as private initiatives and excluded from public funding. In addition, there were seven public Muslim kindergartens receiving public subsidy in 2009.

In the schools, the emphasis has been on establishing support structures for Turkish children. This has tended to be arranged by the states in conjunction with the Turkish authorities, but different patterns of such cooperation have developed. All the states provide complementary mother-tongue teaching, which is provided by Turkish teachers usually trained and qualified in Turkey. In the states of Bavaria, Hessen, Lower Saxony, North Rhine-Westphalia and Rhineland-Palatinate, this complementary teaching is run by the ministries of education. They employ the Turkish teachers, often recruiting them from Turkey, usually on a time-limited contract. The other states, that is, Baden-Württemberg, Berlin, Bremen, Hamburg, Saarland and Schleswig-Holstein, have an arrangement with the Turkish authorities whereby the Turks are responsible for mother-tongue teaching, employ the teachers, and fix the curriculum.

Up until the first decade of the twenty-first century, Islamic religious education was, if it was to be found in schools at all, part of this complementary teaching. Only in Bavaria was there in the early 1980s a regular period of two hours per week specifically devoted to Islamic religious instruction. This was taught by Turkish teachers with Turkish qualifications in religious instruction and according to the syllabus and with the textbooks designed for Turkish schools.

All the regional states have some form of arrangement whereby Christian religious instruction is offered within normal school hours, usually by normal teachers, although in some places by priests or ministers with some educational training. While the educational standard of the teachers and the syllabus has to be approved by the regional state's education authority, as do the textbooks used, the content of the syllabus and the religious standing of the teacher have to be approved by the recognised church authority.

The question of introducing Islamic religious instruction as a separate subject for Muslim children has exercised German educationists and Muslim leaderships since the mid-1970s. The issue reached something approaching a crisis at the end of the decade. The education authorities had resisted Muslim demands for facilities similar to those of the churches. At the same time, the independent, mosque-related Qur'an schools had experienced an enormous growth. As the political crisis in Turkey spilled over into demonstrations and odd incidents of violence in Germany, the call was raised from many German and secularist Turkish quarters for the banning of such schools, especially those connected with the *Süleymançi*. Motions were placed before regional parliaments as late as 1983 demanding their closure on the grounds that they were in conflict with the German Basic Law.

In response, the introduction of some Islamic religious instruction within the complementary hours for Turkish children was speeded up by some states which had not already adopted the pattern. However, this was clearly not a satisfactory solution for those Turkish Muslim groups which were independent of the Turkish government, and it was certainly of no use to Muslims who were not Turkish. Even the minimal intentions of the model were often not met, as many of the Turkish teachers tended towards secularism in the Kemalist tradition and were thus not trusted by many Muslim parents. The city state of Bremen was not even able to move forward this short step, because its constitution contains a paragraph stating that only a non-denominational Christian biblical study may be offered in the state school.

Two regional states attempted, however, to adopt a more constructive approach to providing a form of Islamic religious instruction which might break the near-monopoly of the Qur'an schools. In Hamburg, separately from any Islamic instruction which might be given within the mother-tongue teaching supervised by the Turkish consulate-general, the education authority for some years in the mid-1980s offered, on an experimental basis, two hours per week of Islamic religious education for Turkish children. The syllabus had been developed under the auspices of the education authority itself, and the textbooks for it were developed in the light of experience. The course was taught by Turkish teachers employed by the Hamburg education authority and given a special training course. The course was voluntary, and in 1987 there were 2,000 pupils enrolled.

The major reaction to the crisis was sponsored by North Rhine-Westphalia, the state with the largest Muslim population in the Federal Republic and the one in which both the *Süleymançi* and the *Diyanet* had their European headquarters. The state authorities, and not just the Ministry of Education, had clearly been worried about the increasing political activism associated with the mosques and Qur'an schools. It had also been the first to have to deal with a request for recognition of a Muslim organisation as a public law corporation.

In a major report on the policy of the state towards foreigners, which was published in June 1980, the government of North Rhine-Westphalia decided to counter the 'inadequate' and 'negative' forms of Qur'an instruction in a mainly 'positive and constructive' manner. This was to be achieved, in the context of a stronger reference to the cultural and religious characteristics of the Muslim community, by offering a suitable Islamic religious instruction within the school curriculum and thus 'move Qur'an instruction into the school'. In other words, the independent Qur'an schools were to be driven out of business by competition.

The task of producing this official Islamic instruction was not simple. The law of the state required that religious instruction be implemented in consultation with the appropriate religious institutional leadership. This did not exist, so far as Islam was concerned, or rather competing claims to this status existed, and the state had refused to entertain the request for recognition by one of the major groupings. The state was advised that by calling the subject *religiöse Unterweisung* rather than the legal terminology *Religionsunterricht*, it should be safe. A curriculum task force was established consisting of German experts in education, including religious education, as well as Islamic scholars and representatives of the Turkish religious authorities represented in Germany, mainly DITIB.

In 1984, the first units of the new syllabus were being implemented on a trial basis, and by 1987 the first four years of a primary-school syllabus were ready, including the associated teaching materials and the teachers trained to deliver the syllabus in schools. These teachers were employed by the state of North Rhine-Westphalia.

The syllabus commission had sought to obtain the support of a variety of Muslim organisations, Turkish and otherwise, but it soon found that this was impossible. Most of the independent Turkish Muslim organisations withdrew their support, mainly because *Diyanet* representatives had been closely involved. Groups representing Germans and other non-Turkish nationalities remained sceptical because the syllabus was explicitly to be taught in Turkish. A number of the German Muslim representatives attacked the syllabus on educational and methodological grounds. These arguments contributed to the demise of the Islamic Council for Germany only a few years after it had been founded. The syllabus itself had a mixed reception, with many Turkish parents welcoming it, partly because the teaching was perceived as being independent of the intra-Turkish rivalries.

With the reunification of Germany, the new eastern states were reluctant to adopt the western model of cooperation between state and church in the design and delivery of religious education. In 1996, the state of Brandenburg passed a law introducing the subject 'Life Stances, Ethics and Religious Knowledge' to much heated public debate, and in Baden-Württemberg and Lower Saxony experiments were conducted with an (intra-Christian) ecumenical approach to the religious education syllabus. In the meantime the North Rhine-Westphalia experience had reached the point that the University of Münster had appointed a professor for training teachers of Islamic religious education. The events of 11 September 2001 brought the debate about Islamic religious education into the open across the country, and in several states political moves were made to make the subject available, taught in German, within the mainstream curriculum in cooperation with Muslim community organisations. During the last fifteen years, a tremendous change has taken place. In 2015, most states have acknowledged Islamic collaboration partners, established, tested and approved curriculum and textbooks in *Islamischer Religionsunterricht*, and have at least some years of experience of teaching. Baden-Württemberg is widely acknowledged as a model and a pioneer in this, already starting Islamic religious instruction in German in 2006. In the state, in 2015, thirty-one schools arrange Islamic religious education for some 2,000 pupils. In Bayern, 261 schools give 11,500 pupils Islamic religious education, engaging sixty-five registered teachers specialised in the field. Some courses are obligatory, others voluntary, depending on the state. Courses are not offered at all schools in a state. In Bayern, approximately one in eight pupils with a Muslim background takes the subject.

The introduction of Islamic religious education in schools has created a demand for trained teachers. In 2010, the German Council of Science and Humanities recommended the establishment of centres for Islamic theology at German universities, especially in regions where a large number of Muslims lived. Soon after, the federal minister responsible for universities announced federal funding for up to fifteen chairs in Islamic theology spread over a limited number of universities. As of 2015, four such centres have been established in Erlangen-Nürnberg, Frankfurt/Gießen, Münster/Osnabrück and Tübingen. The aim is to provide education relevant to teachers, but also to community workers and theologians.

It has been possible in a couple of instances to establish Muslim schools, namely a publicly funded primary school in Berlin, opened in 1989, and a combined primary-secondary school in Munich. In both cases some public funding is involved, although the methods differ according to the practices of the distinct federal states. At least six colleges for women are in operation in various parts of the country, mostly at the initiative of the *Milli Görüş*, and in 1995 a King Fahd

Academy opened in Bonn. The *Verband islamischer Kulturzentren* runs an imam training school in Cologne, and a few independent associations run others.

When the Gülen movement started to operate in Germany it quickly established private schools, which is its policy. In 2013 there were more than twenty of them, including six upper secondary schools.

CHAPTER 4

United Kingdom

Immigration and settlement

The immigration of people of Muslim background in the period after the Second World War has tended to be subsumed under the general heading of 'coloured', 'immigrant', New Commonwealth and similar all-embracing terms. This disguises not only the fact that these general definitions include Afro-Caribbean, South Asian and other origins, but also the significant differences of origin, culture, religion, class and education which are to be found within the main subcategories. I shall concentrate on those groups which come from a wholly or mainly Muslim background.

Until 1962, entry into Britain by citizens of British colonies and member countries of the Commonwealth was unrestricted. The first major wave of immigrants after the end of the Second World War came from the various islands of the West Indies, starting in the late 1940s. The migration from the Indian subcontinent took off much more slowly, and was based very much on those hundreds of men who had worked on British ships during the war, as well as on the smaller number of professionals. During the 1950s, 'travel agents' from these communities were active in setting up business alongside the family networks. Together, they facilitated an annual gross immigration of about 10,000 men from the Indian subcontinent. Economic decline reduced this rate in the last couple of years before 1960, but the existence of the networks meant that when the time was ripe, there was the capacity for a very sharp rise in the rate of immigration from the Indian subcontinent.

The one immediate cause of the sudden rise in entries during 1961 and 1962 was the prospect of legislation restricting entry. The Commonwealth Immigrants Act 1962 was a response to a growing public debate over the desirability of large-scale immigration of 'coloureds'. There were clear elements of racism in the debate, linked to a perception of Britain moving out of its imperial mode. The debate had been fuelled by 'race riots', in particular those in Notting Hill (London) and Nottingham in 1958. Over the eighteen months during which policy and then legislation were discussed, there was a massive increase in immigration from all regions, particularly from the Indian subcontinent. In addition, the controls were ineffective. The networks had developed sophisticated methods of circumventing the exit controls of their home countries, which were now put to use to get into Britain. Almost half of the more than 130,000 Pakistanis who had arrived in Britain by the end of 1967 had arrived after the introduction of controls on 1 July 1962; the majority of the rest had arrived in the eighteen months before that date. Less than one-fifth of Indians arriving before the end of 1967 had arrived by the end of 1960, before the big debate started. This unintended effect of the immigration act was particularly ironic, since a number of studies have shown that the rates of immigration during the 1950s were very directly related to the swings in employment in the general labour market in Britain.

The regions of origin of settlers from the Indian subcontinent were quite limited. Muslim Gujaratis have come from the well-educated trading and professional families of the three adjoining districts of Baroda, Surat and Broach, and often had relatives among the Gujaratis of East Africa.

However, the largest groups of Muslims from the Indian subcontinent have come from Pakistan, both West and East (the latter Bangladesh since 1971), but here also from a few very defined areas. In Pakistan (the western part before 1971), major impetuses to emigrate came from the poorer agricultural areas of the Mirpur district in southern Kashmir and in the Cambellpur district of the north-eastern Punjab. Smaller numbers left limited areas of the North-West Frontier Province next to the Afghani border. In the case of Mirpur, a further factor was the disruption caused by the Mangla Dam project which started in 1960 and was ultimately to flood about 250 villages. In East Pakistan (later Bangladesh), the two main sources of immigration were in the Sylhet district in the north-east and the maritime region around Chittagong.

The Muslim population of Indian subcontinental origin did not all come directly from India and Pakistan. In 1968, a further restriction on immigration was introduced, primarily by withdrawing the automatic right of entry from British passport-holders who could not show a family connection with Britain. The purpose of the Act was to control immigration of East African Asians who were experiencing pressure from the Africanisation policies of especially Kenya and Uganda. These people had originated in India in the nineteenth century, when most of them had been brought over as indentured labour by the British, but they also included traders usually of Gujarati origin.

A completely different group of Muslim background to settle in Britain was the Turkish Cypriots. The number of immigrants from Cyprus started to rise in the mid-1950s and speeded up in the aftermath of the 1957 troubles. It then peaked in the two years before the implementation of the 1962 immigration act. Other groups to have arrived in smaller numbers have come from Malaysia, West Africa, Morocco and Yemen. The attraction of London as a political and commercial centre has ensured that substantial numbers have arrived and settled from Iran and the Arab world.

As with most European countries, Britain has not generally kept religious statistics. Census and other figures are mostly analysed by place of birth rather than nationality, and as the vast majority of Commonwealth immigrants have almost automatically become UK citizens, place of birth was for a long time a more useful indicator. However, such figures include British people who were born in the colonies and have since returned home, so there has been a degree of unreliability attached to using the figures from the censuses before 1981. By 1981, however, this ageing population had virtually ceased to influence the census figures, while at the same time it was still possible to identify the children of immigrants, born in Britain, as they were listed in one analysis by the place of birth of the head of household. On this basis, it was possible to reach the following estimate of Muslims in Britain for 1981:

Pakistanis-Bangladeshis	360,000
Indians	130,000
East Africans	27,000
Malaysians	23,000
Nigerians	15,000
Turks	5,000
Turkish Cypriots	40,000
Arabs	50,000
Iranians	20,000
	690,000

Corrections, in particular for underenumeration, would allow a total estimate of the number of people of Muslim background in 1981 of about 750,000.

Ten years later, the 1991 census suggested the following results:

Bangladeshis	160,000
Pakistanis	476,000
Indians	134,000
Malaysians	43,000
Arabs	134,000
Turks	26,000
Turkish Cypriots	45,000
Sub-Saharan Africans	115,000
	1,133,000

Corrections indicate that the total 1991 population of Muslim background was possibly about 1.25 million.

Behind some of the increases lay new factors encouraging immigration to Britain. The increase in Iranians and Arabs reflects the unrest in those regions during the early 1980s, in particular the revolution in Iran, the war between Iran and Iraq, and the civil war in Lebanon.

In 2001, the census included, for the first time, a question on religious adherence. It had been introduced comparatively late in the planning process in response to significant lobbying and was one of the few questions in the census which it was voluntary to answer. The total number of people who identified themselves as Muslim in 2001 was just short of 1.6 million in England and Wales and just over 42,000 in Scotland. The underenumeration, which a number of studies has suggested affects the 2001 census results, is likely to have led to the Muslim figures being particularly low, although it is not certain that this justifies a total of 2 million Muslims as some have suggested. The most recent census, of 2011, stated that 2,822,095 Muslims lived in the UK.

As elsewhere, the immigration ban of 1962 moved the emphasis in immigration towards family reunion. In the 1961 census, only 15 per cent of Pakistani-born people were women. By 1981, almost half of the Pakistani-born population were women. Having come latest, the Bangladeshi population in 1981 was still only one-third women. The nature of the migration has also ensured that the population was young. Again using the Pakistani figures, the age group 25–44 dominated. In the 1961 census, 52 per cent of Pakistanis were in this group, a figure which rose slightly in the 1971 census, compared to 26 per cent for the British population as a whole. A 1974 survey showed that 71 per cent of the Pakistani-born population had arrived when they were between fifteen and thirty-four years old.

A consequence of this age distribution is, of course, a relatively high birth rate compared to the size of the population. At the same time, the peaking of the immigration during the 1960s means that by the 1980s a fast-growing proportion of Muslims have been born in Britain. Again the Pakistani figures are a good indicator of this (including Bangladesh):

	total	of which UK-born	as %
1951	5,000	—	
1961	24,900	300	1.2
1971	170,000	40,000	23.5
1981	360,000	135,000	37.5
1991	636,000	299,000	47.0

By 2001, the census showed that almost 55 per cent of Pakistanis and over 46 per cent of Bangladeshis had been born in the UK. Overall the Muslim population was among the youngest in the country with one-third aged fifteen and under, and a further nearly 20 per cent aged 16–24.

Settlement in Britain has been geographically very uneven. On the one hand, one sees the common phenomenon of settlement in the large cities and towns. Almost 40 per cent, slightly more than a million, of the Muslims in

Britain live in and around London. The West Midlands, Yorkshire, and the region around Manchester account for almost two-thirds of the rest. Within the West Midlands, three-quarters of the Pakistani and Bangladeshi community live in Birmingham, forming a major part of the 14 per cent of the city's total population declaring itself to be Muslim in 2001. Three-quarters of this community are concentrated in just eight of the city's forty-two wards (local electoral districts). In Yorkshire, almost half of the Pakistani and Bangladeshi community live in the city of Bradford, while in Scotland, nearly half the Muslim population lives in Glasgow. The ethnic distribution around the country is also uneven. Turkish Cypriots live almost exclusively in the inner-city areas of East London, where more than half of the Bangladeshis are also concentrated. London accommodates most of the Arabs and Iranians, with the exception of Yemenis, who have significant communities in Cardiff, Liverpool, Birmingham and some north-eastern ports. Outside London, the only major Indian concentration is the West Midlands, while less than a third of Pakistanis live in London. So the impression is one of a large and varied, cosmopolitan Muslim community in London and the south-east, while outside that region the Muslims are almost synonymous with communities of Indian subcontinental origin. Altogether, the 2001 census indicated that there were nineteen local authority districts with more than 10 per cent Muslim population and a further twenty-five with more than 5 per cent. By far the largest concentrations were to be found in the two London boroughs of Tower Hamlets (36.4 per cent) and Newham (24.3 per cent). In the census of 2011, Tower Hamlets was the one borough of London where the percentage of Muslims (34.5) was higher than that of Christians (27.1).

In Britain, conversion to Islam is not of the magnitude or significance seen in some other countries. It is almost impossible to arrive at any even remotely reliable figure. Using the 2001 census for Scotland that included questions on religion of birth as well as on current religious affiliation to create a model for calculation, researcher Sopie Gilliat-Ray reached an estimation of 20,000–21,000 converts for 2010. As distinct from many other countries, very little conversion takes place through marriage – the small numbers of cases are usually university and college students. During the late 1980s and the early 1990s, the largest single source of converts to Islam appears to be people of Afro-Caribbean origin, who were particularly attracted into various Sufi-oriented groups. Certain smaller Sufi groups have also shown some success in attracting white converts, particularly marked during the 1990s in the case of the Naqshbandi group led by Shaykh Nazim al-Haqqani. There has also been a noticeable group of young white students and professionals who have become Muslim through individual independent choice and only subsequently linked themselves, sometimes only loosely, to an organised form of Islam. Because the immigrated Muslim community has had a relatively high and active professionally educated component, converts have not been asked to play the kind of mediatory role characteristic of their position in, for example, Germany.

Mosques and organisations

Britain has no generally applicable legal framework for religious communities. In England, the Anglican Church of England has established status and the monarch is the head of the church. In Scotland, the monarch is Presbyterian, but the church is not established. Other churches are governed by their own legislation passed by the Houses of Parliament, the most recent significant case being the 1972 Act of Parliament which enabled the amalgamation of the Congregational and Presbyterian churches in England and Wales into the United Reformed Church. On the one hand, this means that the traditional religious communities, including the main churches and the Jewish community, have historical privileges, which in many fields have more to do with status than with material advantages. On the other hand, it means that there are statutory limits to their freedom of action, which many of their members would prefer to be without. A status of recognition, such as that which can be achieved in Austria, Belgium and Germany, does not exist in Britain.

The law which regulates charitable organisations provides the form under which most Muslim organisations and mosques operate. There is no legal requirement that a group register with the Charity Commissioners under this law. Technically, organisations can set themselves up without registering anywhere. So long as they have some agreed internal rules, they have a juridical existence, although the bank manager may require some conditions to be satisfied before the bank will open an account and accept signatures on cheques. Registration under charity law provides, however, some material advantages, especially company tax exemption and reduced local property taxation. Two of the three categories of organisation which qualify for charitable status are religion and education, so virtually all mosques and Muslim organisations are registered charities.

The growth of mosques in Britain has been closely related to the phases of immigration. In 1963, there was a total of thirteen mosques registered with the Registrar-General; the first opened its doors in Cardiff back in 1860. From 1966, new mosques began to register at an annual rate of nearly seven. This new activity was the direct result of the reunion of families brought about by the immigration policies earlier in the decade.

A new phase started in 1975, when eighteen new mosques registered within one year. This was, at least in part, an effect of the new oil wealth of certain Muslim states. Most anecdotal evidence suggests that only a few mosque projects have in fact benefited from infusions of oil money, and most of these have been purpose-built, prestige projects in city centres. But a number of house purchases were clearly made for conversion to mosque use, where the organisers proceeded in the hope or expectation of receiving such support. But this phase also coincided with the immigrants' increasing acquaintance with local political and administrative power structures and preparedness to make use of them. In the years following 1975, registrations never fell below an annual seventeen and in several years reached more than twenty (see Table 4.1). By June 1985, a total of 314 mosques had been registered, a figure which by 1990 had reached 452. A number of local planning departments know of more mosques than those registered within their districts, but it is unlikely that this would increase the total by more than a few dozen. In England and Wales, there were 870 officially registered mosques in 2009, but estimations including unregistered mosques or mosques constructed without full planning permission might be as high as 2,000. In Scotland and Ireland there are at least sixty additional mosques as of 2015.

A variety of organisations and their activities are centred on these mosques. Among the Sunni communities, they fall into three basic categories, none of which can really be said to be earlier than any other. Most mosques and organisations have arisen out of local initiatives, and are community mosques in the sense that they have been set up by processes familiar to the community and to serve a particular community, however defined. Simultaneously – and not seldom overlapping – has been the process whereby Islamic movements with origins in the Indian subcontinent in particular have established branches in Britain.

It is out of this background that the Deobandi and Barelwi movements appear in Britain in a number of guises. It is clear that among the mass of ordinary members of the community, it is these two traditions which have the widest support. This support has been so deep-rooted that conflicts over control of mosques and associated resources are almost stereotypically presented as Deobandi–Barelwi conflicts. Even where there are evidently clan and caste reasons for the conflict, its presentation in Deobandi–Barelwi terms has served to legitimise it and to mobilise support from wider circles. Neither network is structured directly in a formal way. Among the Barelwis, various competing *pir* loyalty groups serve to prevent common action except in the most unusual circumstances. Deobandi mosques are held together by the personal links of their imams and other religious functionaries, links established through the 'old school tie' of the Deobandi colleges and kept alive through the Dar al-Ulum in Dewsbury. The *Jama'at-al-Tabligh* serves to keep the network alive at the more popular level. Neither of these networks has a formal organisational structure, at least not in terms recognisable by British forms of organisational structure.

Two other movements fit more clearly into the second category, that of movements of Indian subcontinent origin. The *Ahl-i-Hadith* movement controls some dozen mosques around the country, with its main centre of operations

Table 4.1 Annual registration of mosques, 1966–90

Year	No.	Total
1966	5	18
1967	4	22
1968	9	31
1969	7	38
1970	11	49
1971	8	57
1972	8	65
1973	8	73
1974	8	81
1975	18	99
1976	20	119
1977	17	136
1978	21	157
1979	17	174
1980	19	193
1981	30	223
1982	23	246
1983	22	268
1984	22	290
1985	24	314
—	—	—
1990		452

in Birmingham. Apart from providing the common services expected from mosques, mainly Qur'an school facilities for the young, the *Ahl-i-Hadith* have made themselves particularly noted for their distribution of literature and audio- and video-cassettes propagating a policy of separation from non-Muslim society. They have on several occasions sponsored speaking tours by the South African preacher Ahmad Deedat and are the main European distribution centre for his materials.

The *Jama'at-i-Islami* have, in Britain, adopted a quite deliberate form of organisation based on an analysis of perceived needs and priorities. The *Jama'at* exists as a movement, but not as an organisation. Its four organisations are held together by overlapping personnel and cooperation in programmes. The Islamic Foundation, in Markfield outside Leicester, was established as a centre of research and publishing, and has taken the lead in publishing materials for children, as well as a growing list of translations of the writings of Mawdudi. It also has a special interest in Islamic economics. Its interest in research led to the creation in 2000 of the Markfield Institute of Higher Education, which offers postgraduate degree programmes with formal university validation. The Muslim Educational Trust specialises in making arrangements with schools for the provision of Islamic instruction to Muslim pupils outside the regular timetable. The Trust usually has contacts with over fifty schools at any one time. The UK Islamic Mission works primarily through a network of mosques centred in Birmingham, although the national main office is in London. In 1976, recognising the tensions between Pakistanis and Bangladeshis, a Bangladeshi parallel was created in the Da'watul Islam. The Mission provides Qur'an school facilities for hundreds of children every day, but it is perhaps more remarkable for the role it has taken upon itself of linking with local authority structures. On the one hand, its mosques welcome visiting groups of professionals who wish to familiarise themselves with Muslim perspectives and concerns. On the other hand, the Mission makes itself available to local officials in government, law, school and church, and it invites them to open celebrations of the major festivals. The Mission is thus able to play a mediating role which gains it public standing and dependants in the Muslim community which far outstrip what sympathy the *Jama'at-i-Islami* may have as a movement.

The third category is that of 'elite' organisations founded on a national basis, or at least aspiring to that status. This began with the increasingly international organisation of Islam during the 1970s, especially around the Mecca-based Muslim World League (the *Rabita*), but also the Libya-based World Islamic Call Society. Several small institutions started as 'one-man operations', some with more success than others. The Muslim Institute achieved prominence by identifying with Iran during the 1980s, but it attracted more attention in the press than it found support within the Muslim communities of Britain. Others, like the International Centre for Islamic Studies in London, have no link with the wider community as such, nor do they appear to be particularly interested in such links.

All these categories have overlapped. National elite structures have been inspired by movements with some history in the Muslim world. This is clearly the case with such as the Islamic Foundation and the UK Islamic Mission. Likewise, the Federation of Students' Islamic Societies (FOSIS), which until recently recruited mainly among Muslim students from abroad, has had a close association with the ideas of the Muslim Brotherhood of Egypt. At the same time, there is clearly an overlap between these and the community-based mosques, when one looks at the work of the UK Islamic Mission in some of its main centres: Birmingham, Manchester and Glasgow.

A further dimension is that of national umbrella organisations, or federations of organisations. In 1970, the Union of Muslim Organisations of the UK and Eire (UMO) was established. It was the first attempt of its kind, and visionary in so far as it recognised the importance of establishing a Muslim presence in the national structures. The annual conferences of the UMO and its lobbying of party and government figures have been a preview of the direction in which the Muslim community might go if it takes seriously the constructive involvement in British social and political life about which its leaders so often talk. The problem of the UMO has been two-fold. On the one hand, it failed to recognise that most of the decisions and policies affecting Muslims in everyday life are taken at local, not national, political level. On the other hand, the UMO was essentially premature. The major Islamic movements, as they established themselves, found that their concerns were more limited and internal to their constituencies and immediate tasks.

By the mid-1980s, when the main groupings had begun to feel need for some kind of country-wide coordination, the UMO had come to be regarded as just another grouping among several, and very much identified with the person of its general secretary, Syed Aziz Pasha. At this point, two attempts at establishing national federations were made. The Council of Mosques in the UK and Eire was set up with the encouragement of the London office of the Muslim World League, where it has its head office. This has been used as a channel for joint action on several occasions, particularly in coordinating a Muslim reaction towards the major multicultural education report of 1985 (see below). The Council has also been the network through which the League has arranged various kinds of courses and conferences for mosque functionaries. At the same time, and with much public fanfare, a Council of Imams and Mosques was established at the initiative of a former director of the Islamic Cultural Centre in London, Dr Zaki Badawi. He had established a Muslim College in West London in cooperation with the Call of Islam Society of Libya, and the new Council operated from there. For some years, this Council particularly succeeded in linking together mosques from the Barelwi network, which had no sympathy with the rival Council of Mosques and its perceived Saudi connections. However, one of the immediate effects of the 'Rushdie affair' was a serious weakening of the link between the mosques and the leadership of the Council (see Chapter 10).

The most successful attempt to create a national umbrella organisation arose out of the organised response to the Rushdie affair. In 1997, a number of the individuals and organisations which had joined together in the UK Action Committee on Islamic Affairs established the Muslim Council of Britain (MCB). The MCB brought together a broad spread of Sunni groups but did not succeed in including Shi'ite or Barelwi associations. Its internal structures were arranged so as to maximise the Council's impact on public policy, with subcommittees on, for example, education, social affairs, employment and foreign affairs. For several years, the Council met with some success in representing Muslim interests to government and, indeed, on a couple of occasions was able to get draft legislation changed to reflect Muslim concerns. The MCB became a prominent partner in the policy of widespread consultation introduced by the Labour government elected in 1997, but it was also accused of wanting to be the only partner, creating resentment among those Muslim groups not represented in the Council. However, the MCB was to fall from grace because of its criticism of British engagement in the US-directed so-called 'war on terror'. Later, in the years following the London bombings of 7 July 2005, the MCB was increasingly drawn into a web of suspicion and accusations of political extremism. Instead the government turned its ear to the newly established British Muslim Forum (2005) and the Sufi Muslim Council (2006), both considered to be less politicised and therefore more suitable collaboration partners. Neither the Forum nor the Sufi Council have been very successful or high-profiled as lobby organisations. The latter has not been active at all since 2012–13.

The Islamic Cultural Centre and mosque in Regent's Park in London has to be treated separately from these categories. As already indicated in Chapter 1, its history is peculiar. As it became increasingly active in the 1950s and 60s, it served mainly the expatriate, business and professional communities in London, so it made eminent sense for it to be run by a board of trustees consisting of the ambassadors of Muslim countries. Two developments served to change the role and perception of the mosque and Centre, as well as the pressures to which its management had to respond. Firstly, the construction of a new, prestigious building created its own pressures. There were disputes over design and orientation of the building while plans were being made. The construction itself was expensive, and continuing maintenance since has placed financial pressures on the management. Secondly, the growth of the immigrant Muslim community raised questions about the role of the Centre. While it continued to serve its old clientele, the Centre also felt encouraged to take a lead in representing the Muslim community. For a time, this meant a policy of activity with a public profile, seeking to guide the Muslim community in directions considered appropriate by the leadership of the Centre. This almost inevitably provoked negative reactions in some parts of the community, leading to disputes which were picked up in the British press. Subsequently, a much lower profile was adopted, in which the Centre sought to serve the whole community by placing itself at the disposal of all major groups which wanted an Islamic location from which to address wider constituencies. It also started, during the 1990s, to adopt individual causes. Thus, the Home Office's introduction in 1999 of official Muslim 'chaplains' within the Prison Service was the result, at least in part, of a long campaign of lobbying by the Islamic Cultural Centre.

These various organised expressions of Islam, including others at the local level and single-issue groups, are the ones which are, so to speak, visible to the world outside the Muslim communities. They represent that part of the search for a new way of life which needs to relate to the wider society for Muslim reasons. This represents an acceptance that there are areas of life which affect Muslims significantly but which are generally outside their control; they therefore need to organise themselves visibly to gain at least some influence on these external circumstances.

Such an attitude of relating to the wider society cannot necessarily be taken for granted. For many years, there was in Norwich a small Muslim community of varied ethnic background, including a number of British converts. This community had specifically decided that it did not need the structures of British society. It educated its own children, organised its own family relations without reference to civil registries or English family law, spurned the health service in favour of traditional 'Islamic' medicine, and so on. When it split up in the early 1980s, much personal bitterness as well as ideological conflict was involved. The question must be raised whether such an 'isolationist' mode of expressing a Muslim way of life does not produce such pressures on its participants that bitter fragmentation is the almost inevitable outcome.

In the early 1990s, a new phenomenon was the growth of small but highly profiled groups which particularly attracted the disaffected young. The most notable among these was *Hizb al-Tahrir*, notable for its call for the reestablishment of the Caliphate, for which reason one of its symbols is the date 1924, representing the year in which the Ottoman Caliphate was abolished. The movement initially made itself most noticed on university campuses, where it was occasionally successful in winning temporary control of the local Islamic students' society, until a number of universities banned its activities. In the mid-1990s the movement split, with one group forming the movement known as *Al-Muhajirun*, whose policy was both more radical and hard-line against non-Muslim institutions.

There are other ways of expressing Islam in British urban society which are almost invisible to the outsider. The orders, or *tariqas*, of the Sufi tradition have moved to Britain with immigration, just as well as other more visible movements. But both their structures and aims have contributed to keeping them out of sight for a long time. Their structures are usually informal, with a leadership, charismatic in style, which gains a following by appointment rather than by merit. As their purposes are usually centred around the development of individual piety and devotion, they hardly impinge on the wider society. Most of these groups have come into Britain as branches of orders with centuries-long traditions in the Indian subcontinent, especially out of the Naqshbandi and Chisti traditions. However, the geographical distance of the community from its roots has also given space for individuals to establish their own small followings in Britain, a case of leadership by merit rather than by appointment, especially if recruitment could take place on the fringes of the social networks, for example among converted Afro-Caribbeans. It is notable that some of these Sufi groups have become more 'visible' over the years, often because they have seen advantages in giving themselves a formal structure recognisable in the wider society. This has enabled them to apply for public funding and has given them a degree of legitimacy in social networks which otherwise would not have taken notice of them. The already mentioned Sufi Muslim Council (SMC), with headquarters in London, was set up in 2006 with government funding. The strongest organisational part of the SMC was the Naqshbandi-Haqqani led by Shaykh Hisham Qabbani. Its goal was to provide British Muslims with advice about how to live based on traditional Islamic legal rulings and spiritual guidance. In its webpages, the SMC strongly proclaimed its repudiation of extremist violence. General support for the SMC was marginal among other Muslims groups; much criticism was directed towards the council for its pliability.

Britain, among all western European countries, is unique in the extent to which political participation is possible for immigrant ethnic minorities. Residents in the United Kingdom with Irish or Commonwealth nationalities have the right to vote and to stand for election in local and national elections. In fact, for the vast majority of Muslim immigrants, this right soon became of marginal significance. Until the introduction of the new Nationality Act 1983, Commonwealth citizens resident in Britain could acquire full UK citizenship by a simple process of registration, rather than through the longer, more complicated process of naturalisation. By the mid-1970s, the vast majority of immigrants had done this. Today, most Muslims are UK citizens, the exception being refugees from outside the Commonwealth who arrived after 1983. When, in 1973, Parliament made special transition arrangements for Pakistani citizens following Pakistan's departure from the Commonwealth (the country rejoined in 1990), the majority of Pakistani citizens in Britain registered as UK citizens under special provisions.

Traditionally, the votes of 'New Commonwealth' immigrants have gone to the Labour Party, often in a proportion of over 90 per cent, primarily due to the perception that the Labour Party was more sympathetic to their interests. This held true also of those groups which came from a Muslim background. But during the 1980s, Muslim support for Labour appeared to begin to weaken. This was due partly to the internal disputes within the party and the contradictions between the views, especially in the field of sexual ethics, of Muslims and their leaders and Labour politicians, especially those to the left of the party. At the same time, the pronouncements of the Conservative government (not necessarily matched by policy) on family values were attractive to Muslims. The weakening appears to have shown itself only marginally in voting patterns; it has rather tended to find expression in more vocal criticism of certain Labour policies and actions, and pressure for them to be changed. In particular, the Labour Party's readiness to support 'the war on terror' has damaged its reputation among Muslim supporters. But as long as the Conservative Party remains identified as being against immigrants and ethnic minorities and soft on racism, and as long as the upcoming populist and nationalist UKIP has a hard-line anti-Muslim agenda, it is not likely that conservative or nationalist politics will gain votes from a more critical Muslim stance vis-à-vis Labour.

The accession to power in 1997 of the Labour Party, which had by then drawn back into the centre of the political spectrum, provided opportunities for pushing forward a number of Muslim interests in the political arena. The election itself had seen the arrival in the House of Commons of the first Muslim member since the period of major immigration, namely Mohammed Sarwar representing Glasgow Govan; a further Muslim member joined the Commons from Birmingham in the 2002 election. The new prime minister soon appointed three Muslim personalities to the House of Lords, to which more were added in subsequent years. In 2014, there were thirteen Muslims. As already mentioned earlier, regular consultations now took place between government ministries and Muslim representatives, including the Muslim Council of Britain, sometimes with specific policy results, in particular in education. At the same time, however, there was a growing resentment in some places at the persistent hold over local Labour Party structures by its traditional, especially trade union, elements which were often successful in preventing South Asian or Afro-Caribbean activists from furthering their political ambitions. In Birmingham, this resentment led to the creation of a 'Justice Party', whose ostensible purpose was to raise the profile of Kashmiri concerns, but which became the conduit for such resentment. It succeeded in taking a number of city council seats from Labour and also in finding some following in a number of other cities. The twenty-first century has seen the rise of several Muslim politicians. In 2005, there were 230 Muslim local government councillors and, after the election in 2010, Parliament had eight Muslim MPs in the House of Commons (out of 646). Still, if the number were to reflect the proportion of Muslims in the country, there ought to be twenty!

Sections within the churches were among the earliest to react seriously to the religious dimension of the ethnic minority communities. The immediate spur to action was the large cultural World of Islam Festival, which took place in 1976. In advance of that, the then British Council of Churches (BCC) set up a small group to consider the relationship of the churches to Islam and Muslims in Britain. A few years later, this developed into a Committee for Relations with People of Other Faiths, dealing with all the major religions that had settled in Britain. At an early stage, the United Reformed Church had established a subcommittee on other faiths within its Committee on Mission and Unity. This pattern was adopted by most of the other mainstream churches through the 1980s, working in close cooperation with the BCC's committee. The work of these groups has been addressed primarily to the churches themselves in a programme of informing and raising awareness. Individual members of the various groups were all in different ways in close contact and local cooperation with Muslim and other groups. It was this kind of experience and the related informal network which facilitated the creation in 1987 of the Interfaith Network for the UK. This encompassed the main organisations of all the major religious communities in Britain, including the Muslims. It was this same experience and network which meant that the churches were the only major British institution where Muslims found some degree of understanding for their concerns during the affair over Salman Rushdie's *The Satanic Verses*. Interfaith dialogue played a significant role in civil society and in local politics in Britain years, if not decades, before it became of importance in other European countries.

Particular issues

Many of the practical problems faced by Muslims in living as Muslims in Britain have had to be sorted out at the local level, since much of government administration is decentralised, as are decisions on the details of policy implementation.

Establishment of mosques is subject to local planning permission for a place of worship. For many years, Muslim communities experienced serious problems in obtaining such permission for the buildings they wanted. The planning authorities were reluctant to allow scarce housing to be converted to use as a mosque. They were also reluctant to accept that mosques had different functions from churches, so it took a long time before many authorities accepted that mosques would also be used for education and that the need for car-parking space was not so important as it has tended to become for churches. On the whole, Muslim communities have been reluctant to take over redundant churches, as distinct from Sikhs in particular, for whom traditional English church architecture appears to be more easily adaptable. During the late 1970s and early 1980s, a change of attitude took place, led by cities such as Leicester and Birmingham. In 1981, the latter adopted guidelines for religious communities such as the

Muslims, whose requirements differed from those of the churches. It became possible to convert houses, and it was accepted that teaching might take place, that an official, usually the imam, might be living in part of the house, and that the usual car-parking requirements could be eased. A few years later, Birmingham City Council gave permission to the Central Mosque to call to the noon prayer over an external loudspeaker, a facility granted to only very few other mosques in the country, for example in Bradford, Blackburn, Bolton, Coventry and Manchester.

Most mosques, once they have achieved planning permission, have sought registration as a place of worship with the Registrar-General of England and Wales, although this is not a legal requirement. It does have the advantage of further legitimising an application for local tax reduction. It is, however, also a prerequisite if the mosque is to be used for the performance of marriages with validity in civil law. About a quarter of mosques in Britain are recognised as buildings where valid marriages may take place – the figure is not higher because traditionally the community has tended not to want to celebrate marriages in the mosque. In these instances, an official of the civil registry must be present. A few individual mosques have gone one step further and sought recognition of one of their officials to act on behalf of the civil registry. In such cases, a fully valid marriage can be performed in the mosque by a Muslim official. It remains the case, however, that the vast majority of Muslim marriages are performed in the offices of the civil registry, and the associated celebrations take place in a rented hall where the Muslim formalities usually take place as well, unless they have already been done in a private home.

No general survey has been undertaken to indicate the extent to which Muslims in Britain practise aspects of their religious duties. Anecdotal evidence and personal observation suggest that mosque attendance is far from including the majority of the adult community. However, it is also apparent that during the 1980s there was a rising participation, in the Friday noon prayer in particular, of the younger and more educated. The purpose-built mosques usually have a very small women's section or balcony – small because of a traditional expectation among Indian subcontinent Muslims that women do not attend mosque prayers. Almost without exception, these sections are proving too small, as especially the younger educated women are beginning to participate in congregational prayers in growing numbers.

Observation of Ramadan and the great festivals is more widespread – but therefore also raises more acutely the question of time off work or school. As in other spheres, there are enormous varieties of practice among employers and schools, ranging from those who make no allowances, through those which seek to deal flexibly with individual cases, to such as Leicester City Council which allows Muslim employees time off for the two main festivals as part of statutory leave provided annual advance notice is given. But with the passage of time, more and more employers, especially in the public sector and among the larger private-sector companies, have adopted permissive personnel policies. From December 2003, in response to a European Union directive, all employers are required to adopt policies which outlaw discrimination among employees on religious grounds. This has led to a distinct increase in the number of private and public employers that consider it fair that Muslim employees take time off for larger Islamic holidays. However, the differences between Muslim denominations and the multitude of Islamic holidays they celebrate cause confusion at times, not least when the same celebration has different names and celebrations furthermore start on different days.

Britain has one of the most liberal regimes in Europe as regards the provision of halal meat. The law provides that exceptions may be made to the requirement of stunning before slaughter on religious grounds. Resistance to proposals to abandon this exception has been so strong from both Jewish and Muslim quarters that the government has left the law alone. The decision as to granting such permission to individual slaughter-houses rests again with the local authority. As a result, some half-dozen Muslim slaughter-houses operate around the country providing halal meat from cattle and sheep. Poultry slaughter has been more difficult to control, as many small grocery shops have tended to keep live poultry in their back yards and, despite health hazards, have resisted attempts by the authorities to concentrate the provision of poultry into fewer, larger centres. Still, the acceptance of pre-stunning at slaughter has grown in Muslim circles. In 2012 it was estimated that 75–90 per cent of halal meat is pre-stunned.

As elsewhere in Europe, for a long time Muslim families preferred to send the bodies of deceased relatives back to the country of origin for burial. But this preference has been declining, and more and more Muslims are now being buried in Britain. In most cities with significant Muslim populations, burial areas have been set aside allowing for the correct alignment of graves. But problems have remained over the wish to bury the deceased within twenty-four hours of death and whether to bury in a coffin or a shroud, even though the former is quite permissible by strict Islamic law. Some local councils have insisted on having forty-eight hours' notice, and, with a few exceptions, all have insisted on burial in a coffin. It was reported in 2009 that a general disapproval of autopsies from the Muslim side has caused coroners – wanting to be faith-sensitive – to use, when possible, Magnetic Resonance Imaging (MRI) instead.

The practice of Islamic family law as a Muslim right has been raised in Britain. It was first raised in 1975 by the UMO, and has regularly been raised by that organisation since. Other groups have expressed sympathy, although without the effort and enthusiasm of the UMO. Soundings among ordinary Muslims seem to suggest little active support for the idea. While the reaction of the British authorities and legal circles was for a long time uncritically negative, some legal experts suggested during the 1980s that the concept should not be dismissed out of hand. They were not suggesting a separate system of family law for Muslims, but they were suggesting that the legal system should develop some degree of flexibility to accommodate varying cultural traditions within a consensus framework of common law. To meet demands from British Muslims, but also to apply control, Muslim arbitration tribunals (or Shari'a councils), some licensed in accordance with the Arbitration Act of 1996, have been set up. A BBC programme broadcast in 2013 claimed that eighty-five such tribunals were active, but there are certainly not that many licensed. The tribunals take it upon themselves to advise British Muslims how to solve conflicts taking both British and Islamic law into account. If all parties agree, an arbitration can become final if put down in writing and registered. Voices have been raised about the need to protect women's rights and about the alleged claims of tribunals to be courts with the right, not only the possibility, to enforce Islamic law. A bill with the aim of outlawing any court conflicting with the British legal system was presented in 2011 and is still under discussion.

Education

For the first part of the period under consideration, the education system in England and Wales was determined by the 1944 Education Act. In 1988, a new education act was adopted which is having far-reaching effects, but this will be discussed later in this section. Under both acts, responsibility for providing education is in the hands of local education authorities, which are the counties or, in the major conurbations, the district councils. Within the general framework set by the local council, the individual head teacher has had substantial autonomy. Implementation of curriculum, choice of textbooks in a free market, entry criteria for pupils, and selection of teaching staff have all been substantially in the hands of head teachers.

The 1944 Act was the result in part of a compromise between the state and the churches, and Jewish and private foundations which had for a long time been the main providers of education – it should be noted that compulsory primary education was only introduced in Britain in 1870. The compromise involved the churches handing over a major part of the responsibility for education to the state in exchange for a continuing commitment to religious education within the general state system. Thus, religious 'instruction' and daily collective acts of worship within school were the only part of the school day which were required by law. All other parts of the curriculum were governed by regulations, government inspection of schools, examination requirements, local education authority decisions and the policy of the individual head teacher.

Muslim pupils came into this system slowly at first and could, in effect, be assimilated into classrooms in which they appeared in ones and twos. This no longer applied after the burst of immigration in the early 1960s. In the second half of that decade, the numbers of Pakistani children in schools doubled, on top of an already major growth earlier in the decade. By the end of the 1980s, there were numerous schools right across the country with a majority – sometimes more than 90 per cent – of Muslim pupils.

The initial reaction of the authorities to increasing numbers of ethnic minority children in schools was to concentrate on provision of English-language teaching and, in some places, policies of transporting children around to even out the proportion of ethnic minority children in different schools. The 1970s saw major advances in recognising that some practical concessions had to be made by schools for Muslim children to feel at home to some degree. In 1971, a national report on schools' reactions to immigrant pupils listed matters relating to religious education, school worship, uniform dress, dress for physical education and swimming, and diet under the heading 'miscellaneous provisions'. No authority had been approached regarding single-sex education, and most approaches on the other matters had been made to individual schools, which made their own decisions. Most advance had been achieved in the provision of variety in school meals, though always by providing vegetarian alternatives rather than halal meat. Some authorities had made special provisions for religious education and assembly. A survey conducted fifteen years later showed that most authorities had relaxed school uniform rules to allow Muslim girls to wear acceptable dress, and the same had been widely achieved for physical education and swimming. By the end of the 1980s, some authorities were providing halal meat and were cooperating with local Muslim organisations over religious education.

At the same time, however, continuing disappointing academic progress by ethnic minority children led to a widening of educational policy options and the introduction of concepts such as multicultural and anti-racist education. This process reached its high point of official acceptance with the publication in 1985 of the report of a government commission, chaired by Lord Swann, and entitled *Education for All*.

Reaction to the so-called Swann Report was evidence of the significant changes which had taken place over the previous two decades. On the one hand, there were signs of a growing reaction among English parents and communities against perceptions that the ethnic minorities' concerns had increasingly been taking precedence over those of the 'white' majority. On the other hand, the reaction of Muslim bodies, while generally welcoming, was sharply critical of the report's attitude to religion and Muslim concerns.

What had happened over the intervening period was not only that Muslim organisations had come into being to campaign for what they saw as their concerns. Major changes had also been taking place in the education system. During the 1960s and early 1970s, a major restructuring had been attempted towards non-selective secondary education. Part of this policy was a massive reduction in the number of single-sex schools just at the time when growing numbers of Muslim parents were looking to send their teenage children to them. These changes were taking place at a time when research and policy-making in relation to the new ethnic minorities was increasingly being expressed in terms of the 'black' minorities living among a 'white' majority, an analysis which was strongly influenced by the US civil rights movement. This analysis was one which ignored the significant differences among the various ethnic minority groups, and which tended to ignore the inherited potentials for tension between Muslims, Hindus and Sikhs among the 'Asians' as well as signs of new tensions between Asians and Afro-Caribbeans. Additionally, it was an analysis which ignored religion as a symbol of communal identity of increasing strength through the 1980s.

Equally significant was the change of the nature of religious education (RE), which had traditionally been Christian and Bible-based according to the understanding underlying the 1944 Education Act. But new research and theories on children's comprehension of religious concepts were coinciding with the realisation that growing communities of world religions other than Christianity were now present in the schools. In the decade following 1975, the majority of education authorities introduced new RE syllabuses of a multifaith nature. Related to this was a growing debate over the role and nature of the legally required collective worship at the start of each school day. How was the traditional pattern of hymn, prayer and Bible reading to be justified in a multifaith school – and what was to replace it? While much solidly professional work was being done, arguably much more was being done incompetently and without understanding of the fundamental principles and problems by a teaching profession which, with a few exceptions, had little conception of the backgrounds from which their pupils came. With little in the way of credible practice replacing what white parents had known from their own school days, or offering the new communities something satisfactory, a reaction from both sides should not have been a surprise.

The late 1980s saw the process come to a head as various trends combined. In RE, the continuing difficulties experienced by the education authorities in convincing a wider public of the legitimacy of multifaith curricula met a growing disquiet among Muslim leaders. The example of the Inner London Education Authority (disbanded in 1990) may serve to illustrate the point. During the early 1980s, an actively anti-racist policy was being implemented which at times brushed off RE as mere tokenism, and at times simply ignored RE. At the same time, another group within the authority was developing a new RE syllabus. When it was published in 1984, it was condemned by teachers because it included within its objectives 'to help young people to achieve a knowledge and understanding ... so that they are able to continue in, or come to, their own beliefs ...' For many teachers, this was too close to being an educationally unacceptable nurturing of faith. On the other hand, a wide spectrum of Muslim leaders objected to what they regarded as the secular foundations of the syllabus and to the implication that all religions were equally valid.

This Muslim hesitation was expressed more strongly in reaction to the Swann Report the following year. The good intention of the commission was acknowledged, but its perceived misunderstanding of the Muslim concerns and Islam was sharply criticised. The report, reflecting the general attitudes of the educational and race-relations establishments, dealt with Muslims in terms of culture and ethnic groups rather than in terms of religious principles and priorities. The uncritical acceptance of educationists that one of the purposes of education is to create an autonomous and critical individual was decried as being a refusal to accept the absolute of the divine. Here was an expression of a common element in Muslim concern about education both in Britain and else-where, namely a fundamental disagreement about purpose. From some quarters, this was expressed as being a refusal by educationists to accept the authority of 'revealed truth'. Other quarters put forward the view that if the education system produced good Muslims, it would thereby have produced good citizens.

The two specific points on which Swann and Muslim leaders clashed were religious education and Muslim schools. The report had praised RE as one of the few subject areas which had taken the multicultural nature of British society seriously, and strongly recommended that it be supported to continue to do so. Muslim reactions again expressed disquiet over the underlying secular implications in the theory and practice of RE as they saw it.

The Muslim schools issue went deeper and further because it had serious political implications at both local and national level. Three years before the Swann Report was published, the Muslim Parents' Association in Bradford had applied unsuccessfully for five local schools with a large majority of Muslim pupils to be made into voluntary aided schools under Muslim control. This status had been invented in the 1944 Education Act to allow mostly church schools to remain in church control but receive the bulk of the running costs from public funds. In the mid-1980s, the Church of England and the Roman Catholic church each had over 2,000 such schools, while the Jewish community and the Methodist church each had a few dozen. There was no reason in law why other communities should not be able to establish their own schools with voluntary aided status, and certainly during the decade a number of new voluntary aided Church of England schools were created.

The arguments against the Bradford applications were primarily in terms of the danger of such schools leading to social segregation and the probable poor quality of the education likely to be provided. The latter argument was based on observation of the dozen or so private Muslim schools which had been set up, schools which were usually chronically underfunded and badly staffed because of the poverty of the community and the unreliability of foreign donors. The former argument, although much more substantial, ignored other forms of social segregation in the British school system: segregation based on class or wealth, or on academic ability. It also ignored the fact that numerous schools were already ethnically and religiously segregated simply because of the geographical distribution of the school population.

At about the same time as the Bradford applications were being rejected, the Islamiah Primary School, set up in the London Borough of Brent by the former pop singer Cat Stevens, now Yusuf Islam, was seeking similar recognition. After several years of negotiations and bureaucratic delays, the borough council first accepted it; then when political control changed hands, new obstacles were raised in the form of planning, health and hygiene regulations. In 1990, the government rejected the application, but the school governors asked for a judicial review in the High Court. Two years later the court ruled that the government's decision had not been properly considered. In the spring of 1993, the minister again rejected the application, much to the anger of parts of the Muslim community.

In Bradford, the relationship between the city council and the Muslim community now began moving to a more confrontational stance. The Bradford Council of Mosques started a campaign against a local head teacher who had written an article in a noted right-wing journal attacking established educational views on multicultural and anti-racist education. In the following controversy, which attracted national attention for several months, the Muslim leadership had the support and cooperation of anti-racist groups within and to the left of the Labour Party. The campaign was ultimately successful in leading to a negotiated early retirement for the head teacher.

This was the first major public campaigning victory of any Muslim community in Britain, but it had also frightened significant parts of white society. Not long after the Muslim success in Bradford, one began to witness groups of white parents taking measures to prevent 'Asian takeovers' of traditionally white schools. For purely demographic reasons, this was a process which had obviously been going on for years, but now it suddenly became critical, symbolised in the campaign during 1988 of a group of parents in Dewsbury to insist that their children were allocated places in a 'white' school rather than an 'Asian' school.

Inevitably, the national debate was strongly influenced by the preference of the media for stories with excitement and controversy. As a result, the comparative success of the Muslim leadership and city council in Birmingham in reaching a form of cooperation has largely escaped attention. After starting with one of the worst reputations in dealing with ethnic minorities in Britain, the city entered into a major change of course during the 1970s. In 1983, the newly founded Muslim Liaison Committee presented a set of concerns regarding how schools ought to deal with their Muslim pupils. These concerns included facilities for prayer, proper Muslim dress and diet, and respect for Muslim perspectives in the school curriculum, particularly in RE, drama, music and sex education. The reaction of the city council was to set up a joint working party of experts rather than politicians. Three years later, the result was a set of official education authority guidelines issued to all schools advising them on how to meet the religious and cultural needs of pupils. It was remarkable that the discussions had not included the demand for Muslim voluntary aided schools. This appears partly to have been because there was not a consensus within the Muslim Liaison Committee that this was required. But it was also because many among the Muslim leadership were concerned to try to obtain as much cooperation as possible from the city within the school system and therefore to the benefit of as many as possible of the Muslim pupils, where a separate system would only have benefited a minority. Another factor was that Birmingham had retained about six secondary girls' schools, mainly in response to the demand of Muslim and other minorities, so that that particular pressure was less than elsewhere. The city council was also well aware that if it did not meet Muslim demands to some extent, it would be encouraging more extreme demands for voluntary aided schools.

Although the Education Reform Act and the political and educational debate around it had an agenda far wider than the issue of this discussion, some parts of it were strongly influenced by the increasing polarisation on ethnic and religious issues outlined above. While the Act left the old provisions regarding voluntary aided schools alone, the provisions for religious education and school worship became a major debating point while the bill was being considered in the House of Lords. The government had intended to leave the existing provisions untouched, but a group of lords wanted to reintroduce the Christian nature of traditional religious education. The pressure was such that the government had to give in and, after consultations led by the Bishop of London, new clauses on RE and school worship were accepted. These now require a mainly or broadly Christian content in both fields, with some space admitted for other world faiths. Schools which have a community for which such a pattern is not appropriate can apply for exemption to a local Standing Advisory Committee on Religious Education, set up to reflect the educational and religious interests of the local community.

The Education Reform Act also further strengthened the role of parents and the local community in running schools, even to the extent of handing over control of large parts of the individual school budget to the board of governors. As a result, by the end of the 1980s, a number of schools around the country had boards of governors with a substantial proportion of Muslim members, sometimes chaired by a Muslim parent. The additional facility granted to schools to opt out of local authority control and instead receive funding directly from central government has given many schools a road towards local control and autonomy which previously could only have been achieved by obtaining voluntary aided status. So it was soon suggested that the Islamiah School might apply for such 'grant-maintained' status when this became possible for private schools from April 1994.

In the event, it was to be another four years before such an application was successful. By the end of 1996, Islamiah had again applied for public funding, on this occasion as a grant-maintained school. The application went forward with the support of the local education authority, the official education inspectorate and the civil servants of the Department of Education. But the Secretary of State, in whose hands the final decision rested, turned down the application, as he turned down several others which came in with equally strong support, making it clear in the process that he was opposed to Muslim schools. When the new Labour government came to power in May 1997, it brought with it a policy which had already admitted the legitimacy of Muslim schools for several years. In January 1998, the first two Muslim schools were granted official status, namely the Islamiah in Brent and the Al-Furqan in Birmingham. More recently, a further nine schools have also been granted public status. There remain some 167 Islamic independent schools operating privately, some of which are in the process of seeking public approval. Some 2,000 Islamic educational institutes and mosques provide Islamic confessional training to approximately 250,000 Muslim children. Education is often free, but parents are encouraged to donate money if they can afford it, and teachers are often volunteers or possibly paid imams. It is an impressive ongoing educational feat.

CHAPTER 5

The Netherlands and Belgium

THE NETHERLANDS

Immigration

Immigration involving Muslims started in the Netherlands after 1945. The first small groups arrived as Indonesia became independent in 1949. Among the mainly Christian Moluccan soldiers of the Netherlands East Indies Army were about 1,000 Muslims. By the early 1980s, this group was estimated to number about 1,500. As the Moluccans had not been expected to stay for long when they arrived, they ended up in temporary camp accommodation and were only slowly moved to more permanent housing after some years.

A more substantial number of Muslims came from the Dutch colony of Suriname (Dutch Guyana): some of them were part of the Lahore Ahmadiyya movement. From the mid-1960s, labour migration from that colony started to increase, reaching 5,500 people entering in 1970. Talk of more restrictive immigration laws led to a doubling of the rate of immigration by 1974. An explosive rise to 36,000 entries in 1975 could be attributed to the coming of independence, after which Surinamese not living in the Netherlands would lose Dutch citizenship. After independence, immigration continued under a bilateral agreement, mainly for family reunification, until the agreement expired in 1980. The majority of the Surinamese were Christian, but an important number were of Indian origin and continue to call themselves Hindustanis. By the early 1980s, it was estimated that about 30,000 of the Surinamese living in the Netherlands were Muslim and a further 90,000 were Hindu.

Apart from these special cases, there was little immigration until the 1960s. For a long time, the country considered itself overpopulated, but by this time the available internal labour pool was exhausted, and industry started looking for workers from around the Mediterranean. After first making bilateral recruitment agreements with Italy, Spain and Portugal, the turn came to Turkey in 1964. Agreements followed with Morocco in 1969 and with Tunisia and Yugoslavia in 1970. By this time, there were 92,000 foreign workers in the country, the largest single group being the Turks. Despite a short recession in 1967, immigration continued to increase sharply until it was stopped in 1974. However, as elsewhere, a policy of permitting family reunion ensured that the numbers would continue to rise, and that the gender distribution would change dramatically. Statistics from 1971 indicate that there were nearly 43,000 Muslim men from Turkey and North Africa in the country, but fewer than 5,000 women. By 1977, the ratio between men and women had become 4:3. In 1982, there were 148,000 Turks and 93,000 Moroccans in the country, and by 1989 these figures had increased to 176,500 and 139,200 respectively.

Dutch statistics include reference to religion, and in 1989 the Central Bureau of Statistics gave a figure of 405,000 Muslims of foreign origin. Estimates suggest that there may be as many as 3,000 Dutch converts to Islam.

During the 1980s and especially the 1990s, there was a marked rise in the number of people seeking asylum which also brought in new groups, particularly Iranians, Iraqis, Somalis and Afghans. The official statistics of 1999 indicated that the total population of Muslim origin had now risen to 700,000, of which the largest groups were Turks (285,000), Moroccans (247,000), Surinamese (36,000), Iraqis (28,000), Somalis (26,000), Iranians (17,000), Pakistanis (15,000) and Afghans (15,000). 'Statistics Netherlands' estimated a total of 825,000 Muslims in 2007. Turks and Moroccans were still the largest groups by far and both categorised themselves as Sunni (89 per cent). Shi'as are mainly of Iranian descent. Alevis comprise 7 per cent of the Turkish group. By 2010, the number had grown substantially and a new estimate put the number of Muslims at 907,000.

The economic recession of 1973–4 brought calls for restrictions on foreign workers' rights, with the aim of encouraging their departure. Proposals for a payment to leave were rejected, but rules were introduced making work permits more closely dependent on employers, and residence permits dependent on adequate housing. The effect of these restrictions was minimal, and by 1981 the government had changed towards a policy of integration, as it realised that the majority of the immigrants were likely to be permanent settlers. In 1986, foreigners were given the right to vote and to be elected to local councils. Acquisition of Dutch citizenship has been extensive; it can be acquired after five years of residence if all papers are in order. Almost all Muslims hold Dutch passports. Many have dual citizenship even if the general rule is that earlier citizenship has to be renounced: for example, Turkish citizenship cannot be abandoned and refugees are not required to. Muslims make up slightly more than a quarter of all Dutch citizens born outside of the Netherlands, or who have at least one parent born abroad.

Legal structure and associations

The Dutch constitution grants freedom of religion within the law for all religions, Christian or otherwise. In a constitutional amendment of 1983, the state adopted the principle of strict separation between church and state: the principle of laicism, not dissimilar to French principles. Dutch government policy continues to be to abolish gradually the remaining privileges of the traditional churches. At the same time, the churches play an important institutional role in Dutch public life. This is a role which is generally recognised in the concept of *verzuiling*, 'pillarisation'. Four traditional pillars are identified: Roman Catholic, Reformed and Re-reformed (both Protestant of Calvinist origin), and secular/humanist. This structure has dominated the educational system and the printed and broadcast media, but over recent decades it has been weakening. It is no longer possible, as it was in the past, to identify particular political parties or trade unions with particular church adherence, and clearly the state has withdrawn from involvement with the institutional church, certainly to the extent that it no longer provides subsidies for church-building.

In some quarters, it was suggested that the new immigrant communities should be inserted into Dutch society as new pillars. For a time, this was expressed, for example, in the government's providing financial support for the acquisition or building of property for mosque purposes. This support was available only to the communities from countries with which the Netherlands had a labour supply treaty: Morocco, Turkey and Tunisia. The argument for this was that Islam, as also Hinduism, was a newcomer which lacked the advantages of the historical Christian communities. However, as part of the increasing policy of laicism, this policy was discontinued at the end of 1983. This decision was taken in spite of a report by a government commission established to look into religious facilities for ethnic minorities. The commission had reviewed the whole field and had concluded that the policy of government subsidy should be continued. The commission's report, published in 1982, was rejected by a liberal and socialist coalition which was reluctant to reverse the increased laicist nature of the Dutch state. It is notable that in the absence of such government funding, not insignificant amounts have been contributed by private persons and institutions, as well as local churches, towards local mosques and prayer-houses.

On the political front, however, measures for integration proceeded, significantly with the granting of local voting rights to foreigners in 1986. After low initial voting levels, not helped by official discouragement on the part of the Moroccan government, participation has increased. But voting patterns have been different, with a much higher proportion of Turks voting for ethnic parties than has been the case among Moroccans and the Surinamese.

The 1982 government report included a description of the situation in the four main centres of Muslim settlement, namely Amsterdam, Rotterdam, The Hague and Utrecht. It identified forty-nine mosques and prayer-houses, thirty-three of which were spread evenly between Amsterdam and Rotterdam. Each city had one mosque at that time, using the definition of either a purpose-built structure or a building previously used as a church, as is the case with a former Lutheran church in Utrecht. By 1989, the number of mosques and prayer-houses in the country was estimated to be about 300, a dozen of which had been purpose-built, spread over about 100 cities and towns. A dozen years later, construction activity had burgeoned with thirty purpose-built mosques. In 2014, there were more than 450 mosques, approximately 100 purpose-built. Most mosques were run by a Turkish (245) or a Moroccan (150) organisation. The Netherlands is one of the most important centres in Europe for the Lahore Ahmadiyya movement, which has five mosques.

This growth has been closely associated with the activities of ever more organisations, mostly identified with specific ethnic groups. Muslim organisational life can be divided into the establishment phase, running up until the 2004 murder of artist Theo van Gogh, and after, the cooperation phase. Among the ethnic groups, the Turks are probably the best organised. The Turkish Islamic Cultural Federation (TICF) was founded in 1979; by 2014, it coordinated 140 mosques. It works closely together with the Turkish Department of Religious Affairs (*Diyanet*), which provides the TICF with the imams that it employs in its member mosques. While the Federation seeks to train its imams in Dutch language and culture, to the extent of supporting a few of them to attend Dutch university courses, its aim of establishing a corps of functionaries who can help the community to deal with Dutch society is frustrated by the Turkish government policy of seconding imams only for limited periods of three or four years.

The Foundation Islamic Centre in the Netherlands is smaller and has its main office in Utrecht. In 2014, it coordinated thirty-eight mosques. This is the Dutch branch of the *Süleymançi* movement, whose European centre is in Cologne, Germany. It refuses to cooperate with the *Diyanet* and has to get by with unofficial imams. Of equal size is the *Milli Görüş*. The Alevis have about thirty local associations. The Nurcus, with six mosques, have their main following among Kurds rather than Turks.

The Moroccan community is less well organised than the Turkish. The major organisations are both identified with the Moroccan monarchy. The *Amicales des ouvriers et commerçants*, started in France in 1973, came to the Netherlands in 1975. The Union of Moroccan Muslim Organisations in the Netherlands (UMMON) was founded in 1978 and claims to have about 150 members (in 2014), but it has a very low public profile. A number of Moroccan mosques exist independently of these two large organisations, preferring to keep their distance from the monarchy. This tendency of 'free' mosques is supported by the left-wing Committee of Moroccan Workers in the Netherlands (KMAN). A major mosque in Utrecht has found regular support in Libya, and smaller groups of Darqawi and Alawi Sufis exist. The *Tabligh* movement branching out from France is particularly active in Moroccan mosques, as are groups originating in the Muslim Brotherhood.

Despite the assumed monarchical connections, mosques associated with UMMON, just like other Moroccan mosques, have to find and employ their own imams, as they are not supplied by Morocco on the Turkish pattern. This has created problems for the employment of imams under Dutch labour legislation, which exempts priests and similar religious functionaries from employment regulations. A High Court decision in 1986 determined that imams had the status of priests, with the result that, if dismissed, they could not receive unemployment benefit. The small mosque communities are, of course, not as well established as the churches, so dismissed imams have been left destitute.

The Muslims among the Surinamese find their inspiration in South Asian Islam. Related to the Deobandi-based World Islamic Mission is the Society for the Welfare of Muslims in the Netherlands, centred in the Taibah Mosque in Amsterdam. About ten mosques are linked to this organisation. In Amsterdam and The Hague, Indian and Pakistani Muslims have come together in mosque projects, while in Rotterdam the Pakistanis have their own mosque. The Barelwi trend is represented among the Surinamese by the *Jama'at Ahle Soennat Nederland*. Since 1982, they have held large, well-attended celebrations in The Hague to mark the birthday of the Prophet.

The smallest Muslim community, originally only about 1,000, but also the oldest, is that of the Moluccans, a Muslim minority within a mainly Christian ethnic minority. In 1951, they opened their first mosque in a demobilisation camp in the north of the country. They were later resettled near Rotterdam and in North Brabant, and two mosques were constructed. As part of an agreement with the Moluccan community, representing a recognition of the Moluccans' support for the Dutch during the Indonesian struggle for independence, these two mosques were, exceptionally, built with government subsidy.

Until 2004, attempts to create national umbrella organisations have foundered on internal differences here as elsewhere. The Muslim Organisations in the Netherlands Foundation brought together the TICF and UMMON with very little practical effect. The *Islamitische Omroepstichting* was established in 1980 to implement the right to produce religious broadcasting. With specified amounts of weekly time on radio and television, the Foundation was to represent both Turkish and Moroccan interests. However, for the first few years, the better-organised Turkish side dominated the organisation, and only in the late 1980s was a more even-handed arrangement achieved. In 1975, mainly at the initiative of Dutch converts to Islam, the Federation of Muslim Organisations in the Netherlands was formed. Its success in representing the whole Muslim community was limited, and after a few years it was dissolved. Many of the individuals involved then proceeded to found the Muslim Information Centre (MIC) with its office in The Hague, from where for a time it produced a regular magazine called *Qiblah*. The MIC particularly sought to explain Muslim concerns to the Dutch political and social structures, and worked on the principle that the Muslim community is an integral and permanent part of Dutch society.

In the late 1980s, a new government commission was set up to consider the relationship between the government and the religious communities. It was chaired by Professor Hirsch Ballin, who later became minister of justice. In its report, this committee recommended that centres for the pastoral care of Muslims and Hindus be set up in the armed forces and in prisons and other penitentiary institutions. The recommendations did not meet with much favour in the political establishment.

However, by 2004, media attention around the murder of Theo van Gogh, some imams' derogatory comments on homosexuals, and recurrent criticism of Muslims and Islam by some public voices, accentuated the need for a Muslim national representation able to collaborate both with Dutch authorities and with each other. The most successful, if not the only, organisation that came out of the process is the Muslim Contact Agency (CMO, *Contact Moslims en Overheid*) organising most Muslim groups, excluding the Ahmadis. CMO is now a regular collaboration partner of the Dutch Minister of Integration and Immigration. The organisation is often consulted by media and civil society to explain Muslim views and wishes. CMO is frequently criticised for not standing up for Muslim values enough by less integration-oriented Muslims.

Christian–Muslim relations

Within the Dutch churches, there has traditionally been a strong missionary and evangelical tradition, but one which at the same time has been extremely concerned about social justice. In many local churches, especially in the cities, the latter tradition has often held the upper hand, and the Netherlands therefore has one of the best records of local churches helping Muslim groups to establish themselves with meeting places for worship and obtaining planning permission for mosques. Some quarters within the churches were also quick to see the possibilities of the new Muslim community acquiring a place within Dutch society as another 'pillar'. This readiness may, of course, be interpreted as a process of seeking allies in a struggle to preserve the principle of *verzuiling* at a time when it was having to retreat.

In the mid-1970s, the Reformed Church in the Netherlands gave a watching brief on Islam in the country to one of its officers in the mission section. At the end of the decade, a separate office was created, whose incumbent has been very active since in the press, in meetings in local churches and in relations with Muslim representatives. At about the same time, the Roman Catholic church gave an Islam brief to its migration office, the *Cura Migratorum*. There was close cooperation between the two offices from an early stage, in particular in the production of a magazine appearing every two months entitled *Begrip*. In the early 1980s, a third member was added to this work in the form of an officer appointed by the other Calvinist church, the Netherlands Reformed Church.

This officer, a woman, has since concentrated on women's and youth work to complement the work of the other two.

The last decade has seen an increase in interfaith dialogue. At least three out of four mosques are regularly involved in dialogue projects or meetings, and in several cities there are interfaith councils on which Muslim organisations are active. As elsewhere, as public, anti-Islamic opinionated pundits increase their activity, so do interreligious dialogue supporters.

Education

The Dutch school system is divided into two sectors, both funded by the state. On the one hand are the public or state schools, sometimes called neutral schools. On the other are the confessional schools, Roman Catholic or Protestant. This is an organisation which is a remnant of the *verzuiling* mentioned earlier.

Islamic matters can appear in a variety of ways on the school timetable, in subjects such as history, geography and intercultural projects. Since August 1985, a new subject, 'spiritual currents', has been added to the curriculum of the 'foundation school', which combines nursery and primary. This is supposed to be an objective introduction to the world religions and other currents of belief and philosophy, such as humanism, and includes introductions to Islam, Hinduism, Buddhism and so on.

Children from ethnic minorities receive 2.5 hours per week of teaching in mother tongue and culture of origin within school hours and a further 2.5 hours outside. The content of these classes is determined in outline and is not planned to be a time for religious instruction. The detailed content is very dependent on the individual Turkish or Moroccan teacher, who often includes an element of Islamic instruction within this period. This is particularly true of the Moroccan teachers; Turkish teachers are more likely to put across a secularised view in the Kemalist tradition.

In the confessional schools, religious education is determined by the school administration and is taught by members of the teaching staff with support from church-based religious education experts. As a result, different schools have adopted different policies in relation to Muslim children. Some have taken the view that the confessional school serves only the confession, so any Muslim children who seek admission are expected to follow the Christian programmes of the school. At the other extreme are schools which have dropped all reference to Christianity as a basis of the school and welcome all religions equally. A third model is the schools which retain Christianity as their base but make space for and encourage respect for other religions. In this case, separate Islamic instruction may be offered in cooperation with a local imam.

The neutral schools do not offer religious instruction outside the content of the subject 'spiritual currents'. However, the law states that if at least twelve parents demand it, the school must provide religious instruction in the religion concerned, and this law is valid for Muslims as for Christians and other religions. The various churches provide teachers in these circumstances through an ecumenical body set up for that purpose. In the absence of a similar Muslim organisation, the local imam is likely to be called in by the school. In practice, it has only been possible for a few local authorities to respond positively to such demands. The difficulty has been to find Muslim teachers who have the educational qualifications and sufficient command of Dutch to be able to provide religious instruction in a form satisfactory to the Dutch education system. Clearly, also, some authorities have set conditions not only of teacher qualification but also of the nature of the Muslim organisation supporting such teachers, which are known to be very difficult to meet.

In 1988, a change in government policy meant that it became possible for Muslim schools to be opened on the same pattern and under the same conditions as the traditional Christian schools. By 2000, thirty-two such Muslim schools had been opened. In 2014, there were forty-one. Several of these have come together in an Organisation of Islamic Schools Boards. This alliance has drawn up guidelines for regulations in participating schools and also concerns itself with monitoring the approaches to the teaching of Islam and the treatment of Muslim children in the general school system. A further experiment which has been taking place in one school since 1989 is the so-called 'cooperation school' which is jointly run by Christians and Muslims. This has had a limited effect in most of the timetable, except that in religious education there are both joint lessons and separate confessional instruction.

Operating on limited resources, an Islamic University was started in Rotterdam in 1998, supported primarily by private businessmen. The university was still not acknowledged by the national university system in 2015, but it has survived. In fact, it has been joined by yet another private, unrecognised initiative in Rotterdam: the European Islamic University. Following lengthy discussions of the pros and cons, two academic centres for imam training were established in 2005, one in Leiden, the other in Amsterdam. However, the Leiden courses were discontinued in 2011 because of a lack of students.

Outside of school, most mosques provide regular instruction in the Qur'an and Islam. Mosques belonging to the TICF usually offer three to four hours per week, while the *Süleymançi* mosques sometimes offer as much as three hours per day. Sources differ as to the rate of attendance in such mosque schools. A survey done in 1983–4 by a Moroccan scholar obtained a figure of about 4,500 children registered as attending regularly in mosques served by imams appointed by the *Diyanet*. Attendance at the remaining Turkish mosques was estimated at about 2,500. The total of 7,000 at that time represented a little over 20 per cent of Turkish children of compulsory school age. By the end of the 1980s, estimates of attendance at mosque schools had risen to between 60 per cent and 80 per cent.

BELGIUM

Immigration

Belgium has traditionally been a country of labour immigration, recruiting in particular from central Europe for the coal mines and the iron and steel industries. After the Second World War, more workers were recruited through bilateral arrangements with Italy and Spain, a system which continued in effect until 1963. In that year, bilateral agreements were ended, and immigration was left to individual initiative.

Shortly before this, Belgian consulates in Morocco had started to invite Moroccans to go to Belgium to work. Later, Turks also started to arrive, in particular as the export of labour became an important part of Turkish economic policy. In August 1974, the Belgian government imposed strict conditions on the entry of further foreign labour but remained one of the most liberal countries in Europe as regards the immigration of spouses and children. Until 1977, the state even offered to cover half the moving costs of families going to Belgium. A foreigner who had a job was then entitled to bring in spouse and children under the age of eighteen, a figure which was reduced from twenty-one in 1984.

The effect of these developments is evident in population statistics. In 1955, there were only about 4,000 North Africans in the country. The census of 1970 counted 39,000 Moroccans and 21,000 Turks. In the part-census of 1977, these figures had risen to 81,000 and 60,000 respectively. For the next few years, immigration of families continued to raise these totals, Moroccans to 105,000 in 1981 and Turks to 64,000. The growth was now slowing down, but it did continue to grow at not insignificant rates to reach 123,000 Moroccans and 72,000 Turks by 1985, when there were also 11,000 Algerians and 7,000 Tunisians. But by this time the growth was primarily due to births, since the annual net rates of immigration had fallen to just a few thousand.

There are no statistics on religion, but observers estimated that the total number of Muslims in 1989 was in the region of 250,000. During the 1990s, the emphasis shifted to the arrival of refugees, averaging 12,000 arrivals annually of all origins in the mid-1990s, until the Kosovo crisis at the end of the decade pushed the figure up to 36,000 arrivals in 1999. By the end of the decade, estimates of 370,000 Muslims were common. In 2015, the Muslim population is thought to number between 410,000 and 450,000. The majority of Muslims (80 per cent) have either Turkish or Moroccan background. Legislative changes between 1990 and 2002 opened up access to Belgian citizenship to the extent that what once was unusual is now common: an estimate of two-thirds of the Muslim population hold Belgian citizenship in 2015.

The distribution of Muslims across Belgium reflects the nature of the immigration. The greatest concentration is in Brussels, a city whose population is 25 per cent foreign, large numbers of whom reflect, of course, the fact that Brussels is the headquarters of both the EU and NATO. Approximately 17 per cent of the population in the region of Brussels is Muslim. A significant proportion of the remainder are in the industrial areas of the French-speaking south. Large numbers of Turks have also settled in Flanders, especially in Antwerp, Ghent and Limburg.

Legal structure and organisations

Like France, Belgium has inherited a Napoleonic legal system, but it has gone its separate way in the relationship between religion and state. On both sides of the language divide between Flanders (Dutch-speaking) and Wallonia (French-speaking), the country is overwhelmingly Roman Catholic. While there was an anti-clerical movement during the nineteenth century, it did not result in the split between church and state which France adopted in 1905. In the Napoleonic style, the Belgian state continued to give recognition to the Roman Catholic church, the Reformed church and the Jews. The Anglican church was added to this list because of the very close connection at one time between the royal families of Belgium and the United Kingdom. Recognition means that the religious institution has control over the teachers and curriculum administered by the state for the children of adherents in school. It also means that the clergy are paid by the state. Lack of recognition does not limit the freedom of other communities to practise their religion, to have their places of worship or to organise their own religious instruction outside school.

The first mosques were founded in Brussels by Moroccans in the early 1970s. Turkish mosques came with the later immigration. By 1982, a study identified sixty-six mosques in Brussels and the French-speaking part of Belgium. Five years later, the total for the whole country was estimated at 130, and by the year 2000 this figure had gone up to 312, including six purpose-built. The latest estimation was made in 2004 and counted 333 mosques.

Most of the Moroccan mosques are independent of organisations, although the Moroccan *Amicales* do have some influence. The most important single influence appears to be the cultural mission of the Moroccan embassy which brings in teachers of religion, Arabic and Moroccan culture seconded either to Moroccan associations or through the Islamic Cultural Centre for official religious instruction.

On the Turkish side, the Directorate of Religious Affairs (*Diyanet*) is active enough to have influence over at least two-third of Turkish mosques. In an ambivalent relationship with the Islamic Cultural Centre (see below), the *Diyanet*, working through the attaché for religious affairs in Brussels, appoints imams and teachers to Turkish mosques and school classes in such a way that they are recognised by the state. It has also acquired control of a number of associations and their properties, in such a way that the *Diyanet*, on behalf of the Turkish government, retains a certain degree of influence over the Turkish Muslim émigré community and stands to profit from the sale of redundant property should an association close down.

Of growing significance has been the *Jama'at-al-Tabligh*, whose presence stretches back two decades. The movement chose from the beginning to register its centres as associations under Belgian law, even though it was not legally necessary to do so and though the law of the time required that three-fifths of the founders should be Belgian citizens. This non-Muslim element has gradually been moved aside, and the law has since amended this requirement. In the ten years between 1975 and 1985, twelve mosque associations were founded by the *Tabligh*. In 1985, the movement took the initiative to establish a Federation of Mosques and Islamic Cultural Associations as an umbrella body which was an attractive alternative to the domination sought by the Islamic Cultural Centre in Brussels. By one account, the pressure that the *Tabligh* were able to exert through this federation led to the dismissal of the founder-director of the Centre.

This was, in fact, not the first attempt to create a rival to the Centre. In 1977, a group of Belgians, Turks and Moroccans had established the Association of Islamic Culture and Religion. The purpose of the group was to create a Muslim institutional life not only independent of the Centre but also independent of the influence of the Turkish and Moroccan governments. The Association has had only limited success, although it has succeeded in ensuring the appointment of a few teachers of religious education. In so doing, it appears to have challenged the Centre to be more visible and consistent in its own procedures.

The main point of interest in the Belgian context is, however, the role of the Islamic Cultural Centre itself and its relation to the Belgian state. The Centre was founded in 1969, and the government gave it the Oriental Pavilion of the Parc du Cinquentennaire in a ceremony in which the minister of justice symbolically handed over the keys to King Faisal of Saudi Arabia. After internal reconstruction, it housed a library, offices, information service and a mosque. The board of trustees is chaired by the ambassador of Saudi Arabia, and a significant proportion of its funding comes through the Muslim World League. For some years, it functioned as the headquarters of the European Council of Mosques, which was established by the League to support the foundation of mosques and related services for the Muslim communities in Europe.

The Belgian state guarantees freedom of religion to all residents, but the constitution also provides that ministers of religion shall receive a salary from the state. To regularise this, a law of 1870 provided a framework for the financial organisation and the provision of religious education at state expense for four recognised religious communities: Roman Catholic, Protestant, Anglican and Jewish.

Soon after the Islamic Cultural Centre was opened in 1969, voices began to be raised in Parliament in support of also recognising Islam, with the justification that the Muslim community was larger than both the Anglican and the Jewish. There had also been a recent history of interest in Islam and the Arab world, as more and more international organisations established offices in Brussels. Arguments in support noted not only the numbers of Muslims, at that time about 100,000, but also the expectation that a significant proportion of them would settle permanently. Recognition of Islam, it was felt, would contribute positively to this process of settlement. Additionally, the interventions of some politicians suggest that foreign policy considerations in relation to the Arab world at the time of the 1973–4 oil embargo were not irrelevant.

The first attempt to legislate was a bill in the Senate in 1971, which failed due to lack of time. The following year, it was revived and referred to the Commission of Justice for investigation. The Commission found that recognition was not simply a matter of extending the provisions of the 1870 law to cover Islam. It proposed specifically that the public financial subsidies, and therefore the Muslim communal organisation, should be based on provinces rather than the much smaller communes, or local councils. The financial responsibility was to be divided between the state, which would take care of the salaries of imams and up to 30 per cent of the construction costs of buildings, and the provinces, which would carry the housing of imams and any further construction and maintenance costs of mosques.

The law was finally passed on 19 July 1974. It made provision for the recognition of Islam and established that the organisation was to be based on the provinces in the same way that the other communities were based on communes. The implementation of the law and recognition of the bodies and regulations related to the new law depended on further detailed work culminating in royal decrees and further legislation.

In 1978, a royal decree established the territorial organisation of the Muslim community and the way in which its temporal affairs should be governed. It determined qualifications for membership and elections, leaving open the possibility for different forms of election where particular Muslim minority groups might feel their interests threatened by a majority. The Islamic Cultural Centre was to be responsible for overseeing the first establishment of these committees. Three years later, a new law laid down the salaries which the state would pay to imams. To determine this, a parallel was drawn to the pastors of the Protestant church, both in terms of the salary levels and in terms of the rankings of imams as between 'first-rank imams' and ordinary imams; the 'Imam Director of the Islamic Cultural Centre' was in a rank of his own.

For several years, the legislation and its associated decrees remained inoperative, apart from in the educational field, which will be reviewed later in this chapter. The main obstacle was the delay in establishing the committees which were to oversee the affairs of the community. This delay was due partly to the usual difficulties in achieving sufficient cooperation among various Muslim groups, and partly by the reluctance of the Ministry of Justice to recommend recognition of any committee which was not felt to comply with the requirement of the 1974 law that it be representative of the whole community. By 1983, it appears that papers were ready for the recognition of an Islamic structure for the province of Brabant, but the royal decree granting recognition was never issued.

By the mid-1980s, the Belgian authorities were increasingly ambivalent with regard to the implications of the 1974 recognition. Public opinion had changed in reaction to events in the Islamic world, especially in Iran and Lebanon. This change was brought home in the context of the demonstrations in Brussels on 20 April 1986 against the US bombing raid on Libya. The demonstration turned into a strong public statement of Islamic identity, much to the surprise of the organisers themselves. The press and broadcast media emphasised the demonstration as an expression of Islam in its 'fanatical', 'fundamentalist' and '*intégriste*' garb.

By the late 1980s, the understanding of the role of the Islamic Cultural Centre as a coordinator of the Muslim community had broken down, probably irretrievably. The situation had not been helped by the unsettling ways in which the Centre leadership had been changing. The first director, Muhammad Alouini, a Tunisian, was replaced in 1985 because of widespread dissatisfaction with alleged high-handedness on the one hand, and lack of effectiveness on the other. He was replaced by Abdallah al-Ahdal, a Saudi of moderate tendency. He soon came under attack for not being sufficiently orthodox. His murder in March 1989, at a time when he was seeking to calm tempers over the Rushdie affair (see Chapter 10), only served to convince Belgian public opinion that Islam was violent and dangerous.

The government began to seek to create a new representative body to take over the Centre's role, in the shape of a Higher Council of Muslims in Belgium, which was to include representatives of the Muslim World League, Muslim ambassadors and representatives of the immigrated Muslim communities. Still no provincial Muslim organisation had been recognised and therefore no Muslim officials, other than teachers, had been receiving government salaries. Finally, in 1998, an Executive of Muslims in Belgium (*l'Executif des Musulmans de Belgique* – EMB) was formed to carry the institutional recognition granted a quarter of a century before. It consists of seventeen members elected by a wide ballot to reflect the ethnic make-up of the community as a whole. The EMB is organised into five departments reflecting the responsibilities flowing from the 1974 recognition. One of these has as its first task to review the whole field of provision of Islamic instruction for children in the schools. Others will deal with issues like 'chaplaincy' in prison and the army, regulation of halal slaughter, production of programmes for broadcasting, and financial control.

Internal squabbles, including filed lawsuits, have disrupted the work of the executive body and the election thereof. The last elected executive body only had a mandate until the end of 2009. However, a temporary board upholds the everyday work with the help of the Belgian authorities.

The high rate of acquisition of Belgian citizenship has been reflected in Muslim success in elections. In 1988, the first Muslims were elected onto local councils in Flanders, and more entered the Brussels regional council in 1994. The 2000 election placed Brussels well ahead of most local authorities in Europe when major ethnic minority voting placed ninety-one Muslims, including thirty-three women, onto the council of 650 members.

Education

Already at the beginning of the 1980s, the presence of Muslim children in school was marked, especially in the Brussels region with its 8 per cent Muslim population. In 1982, it was estimated that there were 35,000 Moroccan children in school and nearly 22,000 Turks altogether, nearly two-thirds of them in the Brussels region, where they were concentrated in just four localities. This figure represented an increase of about 50 per cent over the previous five years. In Brussels, nearly forty schools had a Muslim population of over half, and nine of them had over 80 per cent Muslim children.

As in several other European countries, the Belgian education system is divided into two sectors, the public and the private. On the public side, schools are run by the state, by the provinces or by the local authorities. The private sector consists overwhelmingly of the 'free' schools, which are confessional, mostly Catholic. Muslim children generally attend the public schools, partly out of preference and partly because Catholic children have priority of access to the Catholic free schools. Even so, about 10,000 Muslim children were attending Catholic schools in the early 1980s, and by 1984 over twenty Catholic nursery and primary schools had more than 50 per cent Muslim pupils.

The reaction of the schools to this Muslim presence has been mixed. In the public sector, the main development has been the expansion of Islamic religious instruction. In the Catholic free schools, the individual schools have developed a variety of practices. Some schools have allowed Muslim children to withdraw from Catholic religious instruction, while others have not. In Antwerp, in a few Catholic schools with almost totally Muslim pupils, Catholic religious instruction is no longer given. Some schools have made local arrangements with imams or other Muslim leaders to take Muslim religious instruction either in school hours or outside school hours in school buildings. A few schools have linked with the system of Islamic religious instruction organised by the Islamic Centre in Brussels. Most regret the lack of central guidance on the part of the Catholic church.

In fact, the church has only limited resources to guide it in dealing with Islam. In Brussels, there is a *Centre al-Kalima*, which has been concerned mostly with social work among immigrants of Muslim origin. Its director has often been a White Father with experience in the Arab world, and he has been able to give some advice. But the church does not have a secretariat or special office, as is the case in many other countries in western Europe.

It should be noted that, as against a very mixed and often negative experience in the education system, the experiments in intercultural education which were started in the 1970s in Limburg stand out. Here, the local policy was one of positive integration encouraging the preservation and development of immigrant culture. The policy was assisted by the fact that the city had a generations-long history of integrating immigrant communities into the mining industry. The role of the schools in relation to children and their parents has been regarded as crucial in this policy, but they have not had to bear the burden of the policy on their own. Advocates of Limburg's policy point out that, as the economic recession took hold during the late 1980s, the region has not experienced the kind of racist nationalism which has characterised, for example, Antwerp.

The main feature of the Belgian education system in this connection is the system established on the basis of the 1974 recognition. In the public sector, religious instruction is organised according to the so-called education pact between the church and the strong laicist tendencies. This pact was formulated in a law of 29 May 1959, amended in July 1973. Two hours per week can be devoted to religious instruction at the demand of parents. This instruction is to be given by teachers approved by the state as well as by the organs of the religious community concerned.

The 1974 recognition of Islam had the immediate implication that Muslim children should have rights similar to Catholic, Protestant and Jewish children. This could not, however, be fully implemented until the necessary amendments of the law of 1959 could be made. In the meantime, a circular from the Ministry of Education encouraged schools to start offering Islamic religious instruction. The necessary amendment came in a law of February 1978. As a result, the Islamic Cultural Centre of Brussels is the official Muslim organ for the approval of the curriculum of Islamic instruction and the approval and appointment of the teachers to be paid by the state.

The effect of these changes was swift. In 1978, the Islamic Cultural Centre had sixty-eight teachers on its books, a number which had risen to 193 by 1982. Over the same five-year period, the number of schools served rose from 140 to 445, three-quarters of which were primary schools, the rest secondary. By 1982, over 20,000 students were taking part in Islamic religious instruction, about 40 per cent of the possible total. By 1988, 510 teachers were serving over 36,000 pupils. About one-third of the teachers were Turks, the rest Moroccan. In 2009, the number of teachers had risen to 700, but in addition some 850 public schools had made their own arrangements to provide Islamic religious instruction to some 30,000 pupils, generally thought to be half the actual amount of Muslim pupils.

This rapid growth, especially in the first years, was not only a reflection of the great demand but was also a result of the positive attitude taken by the Ministry of Education to the implementation of the new system. During the mid- and late 1980s, the expansion slowed down partly because the limits of demand had been approached but also because the system had become more regulated. Technically, the teachers are employees of the state and therefore ought to be Belgian citizens, a requirement which the Ministry tended to ignore. This situation was regulated in 1986 with a requirement that teachers should have been resident in Belgium for at least five years to be eligible for exemption from the citizenship rule. Since then, the Ministry has become markedly reluctant to grant approval to new teachers.

Quite apart from the religious instruction within the state and free school systems, most mosques have their own supplementary system of Islamic instruction, often using the resources of the same teachers who are recognised by the government. Given its responsibility for approving teachers, the Islamic Cultural Centre of Brussels had organised courses for teachers of Islam and had plans to establish some form of permanent teacher-training institution, though these never materialised. There have also been plans drawn up in various quarters for Muslim free schools parallel with the Catholic system, but such plans began to meet administrative resistance on the part of the government in the late 1980s. As part of the turning of public opinion against Islam in the late 1980s, two suburbs of Brussels decided in 1987 to withdraw the facility for Islamic religious instruction, a decision which they have stood by despite extensive criticism.

One of the first acts of the new imam of the Islamic Cultural Centre in 1989 was to open an Islamic primary school in the Centre. At first met by widespread protests concerning the legality of such a move, the imam's careful defence succeeded in satisfying the authorities that the teaching being offered met the legal requirements. The school was therefore permitted to continue. It was clear that the basic reason for opening the school was the continuing lack of Islamic religious instruction in the two Brussels suburbs. Elsewhere, the existence of such teaching has meant that there has hardly been any of the pressure for separate Islamic schools which has grown in some other countries. All in all, there are only three Islamic schools in Belgium; the latest opened in 2013 and is run by Moroccan Muslims. The Gülen movement has opened six schools in Belgium reported to be quite successful. The schools are not Islamic as such, but attract pupils who are Turkish and Muslim.

In recent years, a few university programmes have tried to attract Belgian students with the ambition to become imams. For example, a master's programme at the University of Antwerp has been developed in collaboration with the EMB. At the University of Louvain-la-Neuve the *Centre interdisciplinaire d'études de l'Islam dans le monde contemporain* organises an education directed both to Muslims and non-Muslims with the aim, among others, of satisfying the needs of an imam. Outside the university structure, Muslim organisations offer training programmes.

CHAPTER 6

The Nordic countries

DENMARK

Denmark joined the Europe-wide search for migrant labour in the late 1960s with an initially almost unrestricted labour immigration policy. Estimates in 1968 suggested that there were then about 2,000 Muslims in Denmark, but many of them will have belonged to the Ahmadi community, which had already built a mosque in 1967 in a Copenhagen suburb. This new immigration meant that by 1970 over 8,000 Turks, 2,000 Pakistanis and nearly 9,000 North Africans had entered the country. In the following few years, immigration restrictions were gradually imposed. Early in 1973, these restrictions were lifted, only to be followed towards the end of the year by a full stop to labour immigration, while permitting the continued entry of dependants as part of a policy of family reunion.

By the early 1980s, family reunion and some continuing labour immigration had brought the total for Turks and Pakistanis to nearly 16,000 and 6,600 respectively. By this time, there was also a growing Moroccan community of 2,000 to 3,000. The following decade saw one of the most radical changes in immigration patterns of any European country during this period. While the Turkish community continued to grow, reaching 30,000 by 1991, the Pakistani community stagnated – although it should be noted that many Pakistanis have moved to Denmark as UK citizens and do not therefore appear as Pakistanis in the official statistics. The change came as a result of unrest in the Middle East. The official data for 1981 recorded a total of 463 nationals of Lebanon, Iran and Iraq combined. Ten years later, the government recorded 2,800 Iraqis, 9,000 Iranians and 3,200 Lebanese residents, a combined total of 15,000! Of course, not all of these were of Muslim background, especially among the Lebanese and, to a lesser extent, among the Iraqis, but the majority were. By the end of 1990, therefore, the total number of Muslims estimated for Denmark was between 55,000 and 60,000, and the second-largest national group had arrived within the decade. In this development, one also finds the reason for Denmark adopting one of the harshest immigration and refugee policies of all the countries of western Europe. While this slowed down immigration, it did not stop it – the war in ex-Yugoslavia produced a new wave of refugees – until a new right-of-centre government with a strong anti-immigration policy came to power in November 2001. It quickly tightened up already very tight entry policies with almost immediate effect. By this time the total number of Muslims had risen to about 150,000.

During the following ten years, Muslims became the object of public and political debates with regards to two issues: immigration and immigrants; and security and threat. The terrorist attacks in Europe and the US, the threats in connection with the so-called cartoon crises (see chapter 10), Danish military engagement in Afghanistan, and the successful intervention by Danish Security Police (PET) in Islamically motivated terror plans in Denmark, taken together, created a tense atmosphere. Politics changed again in 2011 when a new centre-left government removed some of the most restrictive regulations on migration, and public debate moved on.

In 2014, the number of Muslims was estimated at 250,800 based on statistics on nationality. The largest group regarding national background was the Turkish (22.2 per cent), then Iraqis, Lebanese (including many Palestinians from refugee camps), Pakistanis and Somalis, all being approximately half to a third of the size of the Turkish group. According to a study from 2008, Sunni Muslims comprise the majority (67 per cent), while Shi'ites make up 14 per cent. The remaining 19 per cent were Ahmadis, Alevis or heterodox Sufis.

In 1991, the right to vote in local elections was extended to foreigners who satisfied the residence requirements, and soon there were members of local councils of Muslim background representing a variety of parties. Most tended to prioritise their ethnic interests or represent the general interests of immigrants, rather than Muslim concerns. A few Muslim political activists sought to work with the Christian People's Party on issues of shared ethical and religious principles. At the same time, a growing number of Muslims who had acquired Danish nationality became active in the national political parties and, for the first time, two politicians with a Muslim background were elected to parliament in the 2001 general election.

Muslim organisation in Denmark has over time been weak at the national level. While there locally are a number of mosques (115 in 2006), and a number of Muslim associations, the formation of national councils has been slow. It took until 2006, when thirteen local associations founded the Council of Muslims (*Muslimernes Fællesråd*). At least three other competing umbrella organisations exist. Another type of national organisation is Young Muslims in Denmark (*Muslimske Unge i Danmark*), formed in 1995. Its main purpose is to inform about Islam and arrange social activities and lectures for members who share a Danish background, regardless of the ethnicity of their families.

Milli Görüş and *Jama'at-al-Tabligh* have been present in Denmark for many years, but the largest Islamic organisation in Denmark is the Danish Turkish Islamic Foundation (*Dansk Tyrkisk Islamisk Stiftelse*) which is organised through the Turkish *Diyanet*. *Minhaj al-Qur'an* has substantial following, even among youth, while *Hizb al-Tahrir* has probably made more noise in Denmark than it has anywhere else in western Europe, with the exception of Britain, even though it is estimated to have only 50–500 active members.

Denmark has incorporated freedom of religion in its constitution since it first became a democratic monarchy in 1849. However, the religion of the state and the monarch was declared to be Evangelical Lutheran, and the Lutheran established church remains a department of state to this day. This means that church affairs are governed by a central government ministry, rather than a church synod, and that clergy are government employees. Registration of births, deaths and marriages falls under this Ministry of Church Affairs, and normally the local Lutheran pastor is also the official registrar. The very small Christian communities outside the Lutheran church have the legal status of 'recognised faith community': the main ones are Roman Catholic, Methodist, Baptist and the Jews. It has been argued from the side of the government that this status is now defunct, and that it is therefore irrelevant for new communities like the Muslims. While it is true that the freedom to exercise one's religion within the bounds set by the law is not affected by 'recognition', there are certain disabilities inherent in not having such recognition, since in many places the state church pastor was the only civil registrar. In recent years, however, officials of other religions, including Muslims, have been accorded similar status.

Given the nature of the established church, it cannot enter into relations with Muslim organisations except as a government department. It is left to voluntary associations to represent the various approaches of the church. There were, of course, agencies involved in socially oriented work, but only the missionary societies were aware of the religious dimension of immigrant Muslim communities. Naturally, some of them saw this as an opportunity for proselytising. However, the largest society, the Danish Missionary Society, which had many generations of work in the Arab world and India behind it, as well as more recent serious efforts at expanding its work among the 'folk-Christians' in Denmark itself, saw it as quite reasonable to start specific work on Muslims in Denmark. In 1979, the Society appointed a full-time officer, with a social work background, with the sole purpose of making contacts with Muslims. He was to try to understand their priorities and to interpret them to the church and society at large; his job was not to seek converts. This work has continued, and during the 1980s a meeting centre was established in one of the inner-city areas of Copenhagen. Shortly afterwards, a second was established in another part of the city, specifically for women to meet.

In the early 1980s, a combination of events in the Muslim world and the growing presence of Muslims in Denmark led the state research councils to start a seven-year research project on Islam in the modern world, of which a major part was devoted to Islam in Denmark. In the process of this project, it was established early that the work had to be done together with Muslims. As a result, the researchers were very closely involved with the various Muslim organisations, and Muslim representatives took an active part in the series of seminars which the project organised. Relative to the size of the country and of the Muslim population, this project was probably the most heavily funded and concentrated undertaken in any part of western Europe during the twentieth century.

The experiences of Muslim groups with Danish authorities have been mixed. In some areas, local government has been ready to make the necessary arrangements, through planning and other practices, to support the opening of mosques or to make appropriate burial space available. In other areas, the experience has been less positive, especially where fire and hygiene regulations have been used to hinder the establishment of Muslim free schools of the kind discussed below.

On the other hand, the Danish authorities had made arrangements for the provision of halal meat at a very early stage. Denmark's traditional concern for its agricultural exports led it to become one of the pioneers among European suppliers of agricultural produce and expertise to the Arab world. During the 1970s, the Muslim World League representative in Copenhagen was accepted as the authority guaranteeing the halal nature of Danish meat exports, especially of poultry. By the end of the decade, the bulk of poultry exports went to the Muslim world, with the result that the poultry available in most Danish supermarkets today is halal and includes Arabic text to that effect on the packaging! Denmark has thus also become the main supplier of meat to the Muslim communities in neighbouring countries, where restrictions remain tight.

The process of immigration had an effect on schools only with some delay, and it was not until the second half of the 1970s that major growth in numbers of pupils from Muslim backgrounds began to take place. Records for 1975 indicated that there were 467 Turkish children and no Moroccan children in the age group 6–14. Five years later, the figures were respectively 3,138 and 326. In the same period, the number of Pakistanis increased from 48 to 1,275. By 1985, there were 559 Moroccans, nearly 2,000 Pakistanis and over 4,000 Turks, giving a total, when smaller Arab and other Middle Eastern groups are included, of almost 7,000 Muslim pupils. The majority of these pupils, both then and since, have been concentrated in and around Copenhagen. However, it should be remembered that the more even spread of Turkish residents across provincial towns compared to other nationalities is reflected also in their distribution in schools.

The city of Copenhagen was the first education authority to be faced with substantial numbers of children from Muslim backgrounds. The first priority was language teaching, and the pattern of initial intensive Danish teaching before incorporation in mainstream classes, which was pioneered in Copenhagen, became the model for the rest of the country. In 1972, following recommendations from the Council of Europe, work was begun to offer children teaching of their mother tongue as well.

During and since the 1980s, as Muslim pupil numbers have continued to rise, there has also been a major movement out of the city of Copenhagen to the new public housing estates in the western and southern suburbs. At the same time, developments in syllabus and curriculum took place, which widened the geographical and cultural references. The teaching of Christianity in schools, required by law, became religious education with space for teaching about Islam and other religions as well as the continuing teaching of Christianity; in this field in particular, teachers and educationists looked to British models.

The Danish school system dates back to the introduction of compulsory primary education in 1814. During the romantic and nationalist movements in the middle of the century, there was a highly successful endeavour to create 'free' schools funded by the state but set up by parents and answerable to them. This parental right to organise the education of their own children was enshrined in the constitution of 1849. Ever since, it has been accepted that if a group of parents come together to start a school on a particular ideological, religious, educational or other basis, they have the right to do so and to have an amount of state subsidy which represents the saving to the state of not having to provide for their education itself: the subsidy can cover two-thirds of such a school's budget. Over the decades, a variety of such schools have been founded: Christian of various denominations and tendencies, Jewish, ecological, socialist, and so on.

This system has provided Muslims with probably the most favourable circumstances of any European country for the establishment of Muslim schools. The first was started in Copenhagen in 1978. A study in 1987 identified six. Four of these schools were Arab-led and two Pakistani; the main intention behind the latter has been the preservation of Urdu as mother tongue. One of the Arab-led schools, the Islamic School, is explicitly, and not only from its title, established on an Islamic basis and has had some success in attracting the support of families from a variety of ethnic backgrounds. Two of the Arab-led schools were started by groups of Palestinians and have exclusively Arab pupils. The fourth Arab-led school serves mostly Turkish pupils. In 1986, these six schools had a total of 451 pupils, two-thirds of whom were Arab. The number of schools had reached seventeen in 2000 and twenty-two in 2012, catering for the education of almost 4,000 pupils. The majority of pupils with a Muslim family background go to public schools as do most pupils.

Despite the public subsidies, such schools still need to find their own funds, especially to enable them to acquire buildings. This has sometimes placed them in a situation where they have been unable to pay teachers' salaries, and they have had to appeal for further financial support from parents and sympathisers. Local authorities have occasionally used their powers to delay opening such schools by being strict on safety and health regulations. The very ease of establishing a free school has been identified by some Muslim observers as a disadvantage. One school, with mainly Iraqi support, was established in 1980 but had to close a few years later. In another instance, a conflict among the support group of one of the more successful schools led to a split and the establishment of a new one. Both such developments have not helped the children's educational experience. Still, most schools have succeeded with the task of giving their students a good education and according to the Ministry of Education, 41 per cent of pupils from Muslim free schools progressed into upper secondary school, compared with the national average of 26 per cent.

SWEDEN

Sweden as a country has probably undergone a greater transformation in its character as a result of immigration than any other European country since 1945. In 2013, 19.5 per cent of the population were either immigrants or descendants of immigrants. However, half of the immigration has come from other Scandinavian countries, mainly Finland, and much of the rest from other European countries. The main early influx of workers from Muslim countries came after the mid-1960s from Turkey, together with some Yugoslavs. Since 1967, work permits have had to be obtained before entry. This allowed the Swedish authorities to regulate more closely the process of entry at a time during the 1970s when industrial labour needs were to all intents and purposes being filled by immigrants from Finland.

As elsewhere in the 1970s, the nature of Muslim immigration changed towards family reunion, but there was also a significant move towards the entry of refugees on a large scale. Sweden had, until the early 1980s, possibly the most liberal refugee policy in Europe. Not only was it easier to enter Sweden as a refugee, but the processing of applications was generally faster than elsewhere, and the virtual absence of unemployment until the very end of the decade ensured that the authorities could interpret applications liberally, knowing that work could be found. As a result, more Turkish citizens entered, as did Iranians in large numbers after the revolution, as well as Lebanese and Palestinians. Many of these were, of course, not Muslims. While many of the Turkish citizens were in fact Kurds, many others were Syrian Orthodox Christians from the villages and towns of eastern Anatolia. Equally, many Lebanese, and some Iranians and Palestinians, were Christian. This makes it particularly difficult to estimate total numbers of Muslims in Sweden. According to Muslim sources at the end of 1978, there were 37,000 at that time, while another source estimated 22,000. The large refugee influx since then, plus continuing family reunion, has continued to raise the figure. According to estimates, based on immigrants from Muslim countries and their children (taking into account Christians and others arriving from these countries), the Muslims in Sweden amounted to 100,000 (1988), 200,000 (1996), 300,000 (1999), 400,000 (2005), and 500,000 (2015).

Permanent settlement permits can be issued after only one year of legal residence, and the acquisition of Swedish citizenship requires only five years of residence. Especially among the refugees there is, therefore, a high take-up of Swedish citizenship. Statistics from 1988 thus showed that almost one-third of the Lebanese and half the Pakistanis and Syrians had already become Swedish citizens, and that the rate was rising for both Turks and Iranians. As Sweden has allowed dual citizenship since 2000, adding Swedish citizenship without renouncing former citizenship has become an attractive opportunity for many, but no official figures regarding Muslims exists.

One estimate suggests that as many as 50 per cent of the Muslims in Sweden live in the Stockholm region. Apart from southern Sweden, where the Bosnians have concentrated, Turkish distribution is even across the major cities, especially in Stockholm, Gothenburg and Malmö. Muslim immigrants are overwhelmingly employed in industry, primarily the metal-based ones. But a large proportion are also employed in unskilled jobs in the service sector (restaurants and hotels) and in public institutions, such as cleaners in hospitals and schools, especially in the Stockholm region, or are self-employed running minor businesses. Through the period of recession during the 1980s, Sweden was only minimally affected, but even so, unemployment rates among immigrants tended to be double those of native Swedes. Youth unemployment among foreigners was particularly high until a special employment programme came into effect in 1984. Even so, gaining a foothold on the labour market for an immigrant takes, on average, seven years and immigrants born outside Europe tend to have a hard time finding employment. Somalis are among the least successful with an employment rate of only 20 per cent as of 2009, while Bosnians had a success rate on a par with native Swedes. However, the generation growing up in Sweden, getting a Swedish education, is generally doing well on the labour market.

In the mid-1960s, a major reform of immigration and settlement policy took place. This involved a substantial investment in teaching Swedish to the immigrants, both adults and children. An Immigration Board was established, and after a lengthy commission investigation, the state adopted a multicultural policy in 1975. This policy had three objectives, namely full equality between immigrants and Swedes, freedom of cultural choice for immigrants, and cooperation and solidarity between the Swedish majority and the ethnic minorities.

The new policy has been put into action in a number of ways. Government funds have been made available to immigrant associations, and both press and broadcasting in minority languages have been supported. In 1976, foreigners with three years' residence were for the first time allowed to vote and to stand for office in local elections. From the 1980s, legislation against discrimination and hate crimes was developed, especially during the first decade of the twenty-first century. Anti-discrimination and anti-racist work has increased both through governmental initiatives and economic support to civil society organisations, which includes initiatives against discrimination and hate crimes directed towards Muslims.

These developments have also affected Muslim communities. The establishment of associations, including religious ones, is relatively easy in Swedish law, so by 1990 there were forty-five registered congregations claiming 70,000 members; in 2014 it was estimated that there were at least 150 congregations, a highly uncertain figure. A more precise one pointing to a similar number of congregations is that, in 2006, 166 persons had the role of imam, most of them (108) unpaid. Although most of these congregations have some form of mosque, few are purpose-built: five Sunni mosques, one Shi'ite, and one Ahmadi. A couple of mosques are renovated churches but most are housed in basements or apartments. The experience of constructing such a mosque in Malmö, the first Sunni mosque in Scandinavia, illustrates some of the difficulties which are experienced, not only in Sweden. In Malmö, the Muslim community was given a plot of land for a nominal rent. They were able to raise sufficient money, much of it from abroad, to start construction. The building was finished but with major bills outstanding, as promised gifts had failed to materialise. At one time, the city authorities reclaimed control of the mosque until the finances were finally sorted out and the Muslim community could take over the building in 1984.

In 1995, permission was given to build a mosque in central Stockholm after overcoming years of opposition. Objections from Swedish quarters included the view that it would be stylistically and culturally inappropriate. Ironically, the building that finally was renovated to house the mosque was a former electric power station in central Stockholm, a listed building designed by Ferdinand Boberg in 1903, inspired by Moroccan Islamic architecture! More substantially, there were objections that in Stockholm Muslims on the whole do not live in the city centre or the inner-city districts. Public housing policy has meant that many immigrants have been allocated modern apartments in blocks in expanding suburbs and outlying towns, such as Södertälje, some 30 km west of Stockholm. In such housing estates, the policy of providing for cultural pluralism has meant that facilities for places of worship have been included in local plans. Most mosques, as a result, are small, but mostly adequate, community buildings with little public prestige or visibility attached. Some of the major employers of Muslim immigrants, such as the SAAB aeroplane and car factory in Trollhättan, have provided prayer rooms within the factory. In 1985, the Shi'ite Muslims of Trollhättan built the first Shi'ite mosque in the Nordic countries. They were Indian-Ugandan refugees expelled from Uganda in 1972 by military dictator Idi Amin.

Among the Turkish Muslims, the formation of organisations is much on the pattern of Turks elsewhere in Europe. The *Süleymançi* movement has been active, although not with the strength seen in Germany, partly because of the difficulty of ensuring control over local developments from distant Cologne. The Swedish government has consistently refused in all spheres to coordinate its policy on immigrants and ethnic minorities with the governments of the countries of origin, insisting that it deals only with the communities and their representatives in Sweden. As a result, the Turkish *Diyanet* does not have any official representation, although some individual mosque leaderships do maintain good relations with the relevant attaché at the Turkish embassy.

For many years, Sweden had a unique relationship between the state and the religious communities. The Lutheran Church of Sweden had been a state church since the Reformation, funded by a church tax, but was self-governing through its General Assembly. The right to belong to other Christian denominations was introduced in 1873, but not until 1951 did the law guarantee full freedom of religion, including the right not to belong to any religion. In 2000, the church and state were finally completely separated.

From the 1950s, the view developed that Swedish society, and therefore the state, should welcome differences of religion and life-view within fundamental agreed limits. As an expression of this, the state should be impartial towards the various religious communities. A policy was therefore established that the state provides financial assistance to religious congregations outside the state church, through denominational federations, to parallel the church-state cooperation in, for example, the church tax. Once a religious federation has established a structure with membership lists and processes for appointing leaders and religious officials satisfactory to the legal requirements, the federation is entitled to support from public funds once it has reached a certain size. This support is distributed through the Commission for State Grants to Religious Communities (SST, *Nämnden för statligt stöd till trossamfund*), once created (in 1971) to financially support mainly the Protestant free churches that had historically been oppressed by the state. In 1975, Muslims, together with the Orthodox Christians, became eligible for support. Local Muslim communities have had comparatively good financial circumstances as a result. The first national Muslim federation was established in 1974. Due to internal differences, new umbrella organisations have occasionally been set up. In 2015, six such exist, five Sunni and one Shi'ite. All work together in a cooperation council responsible to SST. The federations have been instrumental for the government when trying to communicate with the Muslim population of Sweden. As a result of the church–state separation, a new administrative category called registered religious community (*registrerat trossamfund*) was created. Some Muslim organisations have been accepted as such and now have the right to collect membership fees through the general taxation system.

Such recognised congregations are responsible for arranging marriages and burials in forms acceptable to the community. In both cases, this means negotiating with the authorities. Marriages also have to be acceptable to the Swedish civil authorities to be valid in Swedish law, while burial facilities are negotiated with the local authority.

The ritual slaughter of animals for food is not permitted in Sweden without prior stunning. For a long time, the Muslim organisations were the main route through which halal food, especially meat, was obtained. However, most Muslims have come to accept the practice of stunning, which is also supported by several Muslim authorities globally through fatwas (legal opinions). Today there is Swedish halal food produced, especially chicken. Due to the globalisation of the food market, imported halal food is obtainable from regular food stores in major cities.

Since 1962, religious education has been non-confessional, and the church has had no privileged rights to influence the syllabus. Through successive curriculum reforms in 1969, 1994 and 2011 religious education became a teaching of history, values and life-stances, which includes extensive reference to the views of the main religions, including Islam, in these matters. Between 1962 and 1996, parents had the right to withdraw their children from religious education lessons but very few did. In 1997, this right was taken away, the argument being that religious education is non-confessional and information about other religions is important for all citizens. It is expected by the system that the Muslim community is responsible for its own religious instruction of children, just as are the other religious communities.

Since the mid-1970s, major reforms have been introduced into the Swedish school system to cater for children of foreign background, and Sweden has become a model, in the eyes of many educationists, for the integration of foreign children into the main schools system. On the one hand, the government has recruited widely among ethnic minorities to find teachers, or people who could quickly be trained, to take care of children from their own background. Soon after these reforms started, it was recorded that fifty different languages were being catered for. The basic pattern has then been for foreign children to start their school life in classes for the newly arrived. Special intensive Swedish classes are available so that they can be integrated into the main education system as quickly as possible. Foreign and ethnic minority children continue to have the right to supplementary hours in mother tongue and culture, and there is no doubt that some Islamic instruction is incorporated by the teachers in this guise. At times, when large groups of children with the same foreign language background have arrived in a particular city, a solution has been to organise teaching in, for example, Arabic and then as pupils grow older introduce more and more Swedish.

Compared to Denmark, the development of publicly subsidised Muslim 'free' schools was late. Because of a change in legislation in 1992, the first Muslim free school was able to open in 1993 in Malmö. In 2009 there were nine Islamic schools and six additional Arabic schools stressing Islam. The free schools are financed by the state, but in return the schools have to follow the nationally imposed curriculum and may only add to it, not remove anything. The vast majority of Muslim pupils attend public schools, as do most pupils in Sweden.

NORWAY

Industrial labour migration into Norway was late compared to other European countries, and during the first few years remained comparatively slow. During these years, Pakistanis were the only prominent group, but due to refugee migration Norway has a more diverse Muslim population in 2015.

Official statistics in 1980, a few years after economic immigration had been restricted, gave 2,384 Turks, 1,286 Moroccans and 6,828 Pakistanis as being resident in the country. By the beginning of 1990, these three groups had more than doubled, and to them had been added substantial number of Iranians (5,381) and a few from other countries of origin. Together with other smaller communities, a total of 36,000 could be suggested for 1990. By 2000, the total had risen to about 70,000, and in 2013, approximately 220,000, of which 39,000 were of Pakistani origin, 33,800 Somalis, 30,600 Iraqis, 21,300 Iranians, 20,500 Turks, 17,900 Bosnians, 15,200 Kosovo-Albanians, 15,600 Afghanis and 11,400 Moroccans, as well as a smaller number of Lebanese and Palestinians. How many of these self-identify as Muslim is not known, but 55 per cent of the estimated number of Muslims are members of a Muslim organisation (120,882). The Muslim community is by far the largest non-Christian group in Norway.

The largest proportion of these people lives in and around Oslo, with much smaller numbers in the major coastal cities between Oslo and Bergen. Most of the Muslims resident in Oslo are of Pakistani origin – the smaller number of Turks are more evenly spread between Oslo and other cities. The Pakistanis appear to be the group which has moved furthest in the process of settlement, as indicated in the relatively large proportion of established families – thus, the 1990 figure of 40 per cent of Pakistanis being children under the age of fifteen is quite close to similar estimates for Britain with its long and well-established Pakistani communities. As years go by, the average age of the Muslim population increases, but is still younger than the national average.

Norway allows naturalisation but is restrictive regarding dual citizenship. To be able to apply – if one is a non-EU citizen – one needs to have lived in Norway for seven years with all papers in order. As more and more Muslims feel they have settled in Norway, they increasingly become Norwegian citizens.

Norway has traditionally been a very self-consciously Lutheran country, like its fellow Scandinavians Denmark and Sweden. Its constitution guarantees freedom of religion, although the extent to which this freedom was to be practised was questioned in some quarters during the 1970s, when plans were produced to build a central mosque in Oslo. According to a recurrent attitude survey, 40 per cent expressed scepticism towards Muslims and the building of mosques in 2012; this was however 11 percentage points less than two years earlier. For the last two decades, the populist nationalistic Progress Party (*Fremskrittspartiet*) has warned of Islam, sometimes using Sweden as a warning example of how far the Islamisation will go if nothing is done. The Progress Party was forced to rethink its rhetoric because of the terror attack of 22 July 2012 when a lone radicalised nationalist murdered sixty-five young leftists at a summer camp and bombed a governmental building in downtown Oslo. The reasons given in a manifesto posted on the Internet by the perpetrator were that the political acceptance of multiculturalism, especially Islam, was destroying Norway and the West. His act was aimed at the establishment which allowed it and at the coming generation of politicians of the same mind-set.

Official statistics include data on the membership of religious associations outside the state church. In 1980, for the first time, these statistics identified Muslims (1,006). Over subsequent years, the number grew much faster than the total 'ethnic' Muslim population as described above. By 1985, it was over 8,200, by 1990 almost 20,000, and in 1998 over 40,000. What this astounding increase reflects is clearly the growth of organised Islam during the period: in just three years, from 1988–90, the number of Muslim 'congregations' registered in the same statistics almost doubled to thirty-two. In 1998, there were thirty-five Muslim associations in the region of greater Oslo alone. It should be noted that the Norwegian authorities rely on organisations' self-description for classification, so this figure includes the Ahmadiyya group. The largest of these organisations by far is clearly the Oslo-based *Jama'at Ahl-e-Sunna*, founded in 1976. Its membership is Punjabi and its leadership is closely integrated into the Sufi network of the Chisti order. The group took the initiative to construct the, thus far, largest mosque in Norway in 2006. Apart from it, there are six other purpose-built mosques. In 1993, a joint Islamic Council of Norway (*Islamsk Råd Norge*) was established, which in 2014 represented about forty Muslim organisations with some 60,000 members, roughly half of the organised Muslims in the country. The council has enjoyed financial support from the government since 2007.

Until 1997, the school curriculum included a choice between Christian religious instruction according to the Lutheran tradition, teaching of moral and life stances, and complete exemption. In that year, a new syllabus was introduced combining moral and life stances and teaching about the main world religions, of which Christianity, not just in its Lutheran form, was to occupy just over half of the teaching and world religions one-quarter. The curriculum soon came under attack, both from the Humanist Society (*Humanistena*) and from religious leaders from faiths other than the Norwegian State Church. In 2008, after a ruling from the European Court of Human Rights, the government revised the curriculum creating more space for other religious traditions than Lutheran Christianity and for secular worldviews. While Norway has a 'free' school option similar to Denmark's, access to its benefits is more tightly controlled. A single application to set up a publicly funded Muslim school was turned down in 1995 and, as of 2015, there are no Islamic free schools. However, there are a few Muslim kindergartens.

FINLAND

The oldest component of the small Muslim population of Finland are the Tatars who came as traders during the nineteenth century, when the country was part of Tsarist Russia. In 1925, eight years after independence, they established the Islamic Congregation of Finland in response to the state giving Islam official recognition. Today a fully integrated and comparatively well-off community concentrated in Helsinki, the Tatars have two congregations in Finland with 610 members (in 2012). The immigration which started at the beginning of the 1990s was a new phenomenon. From various countries, but with a high proportion of Arabs, these immigrants were supplemented by an influx of Somalis during the civil strife in Somalia in the 1990s. As of 2014, the total Muslim community in the country stands at 60,000–65,000, roughly 1 per cent of the total population. The vast majority are Sunnis, with about 10 per cent Shi'ites.

While Islam has existed as a recognised religion since 1925, such recognition does not bring with it particular privileges. Only the Lutheran and the Orthodox churches have a church tax collected by the state.

The Tatars were the first to have their own centre including rooms for prayer and community activities. They built the first purpose-built mosque in the Nordic countries. The wooden mosque of Järvenpää was inaugurated in 1942 and in 1960 a small mosque was built in Helsinki. In 2015, there are almost sixty places converted to mosque use. Founded in 2006, the Islamic Council of Finland (SINE, *Suomen Islamilainen Neuvosto*) coordinates twenty-five Islamic associations. SINE is funded by the Finnish state. Its main activities, apart from providing education and information, are as a collaboration partner of the state in matters of burial, cemeteries, Shari'a and religious education in public schools.

By Finnish law, the Religious Freedom Act of 2003, religious instruction must be given in the religion of the children if at least three pupils demand it within a municipality. In 2001, the University of Helsinki, the Helsinki Education Authority and the Ministry of Education established a training course for teachers of Islam and a working party of Muslims and educationists has now put together a series of textbooks. Religious education in Finland has to be non-confessional with no religious practice permitted, yet pupils are separated into different religious groups. A coming curriculum change in 2015 will strengthen the demand that every pupil should learn about the religions of others. The Tatar community had its own primary school between 1948 and 1969. Efforts by the other communities to obtain permission for a Muslim school have so far foundered on the absence of funding and suitable organisation.

CHAPTER 7

Southern Europe

SWITZERLAND

As in many other European countries, it was the Ahmadiyya movement which first brought a Muslim presence to Switzerland. Based in Zürich since the end of the nineteenth century, it built up its work on a Europe-wide scale, though with only minimal impact in Switzerland itself. It was only when a mosque was constructed in Zürich in 1963 that the Swiss public paid attention, with fears being expressed that the intention was to make Switzerland Muslim. Reactions were more muted when another mosque was built in Geneva, funded by Muslim governments, especially that of Saudi Arabia, intended to serve the Muslim community attached to the various international organisations based there.

Both of these ventures remained generally isolated from Swiss society. The period of labour migration which led to the creation of a larger Muslim community came significantly later than elsewhere. Only in the late 1960s did Switzerland begin to experience a major immigration of workers from Muslim countries, primarily from Turkey and southern Yugoslavia into the northern, German-speaking areas, and from North Africa mainly into the French-speaking areas. In the late 1970s, Switzerland allowed family reunification, paving the way for a second wave of immigration. With this growth in the Muslim community has come a greatly increased activity of organisations and mosques, which have made themselves noticed in native Swiss society to a degree that was not the case with the older centres in Zürich and Geneva.

Starting in 1850, Switzerland has a long tradition of carrying out national censuses every ten year. Since 2000, this has been done annually through estimations using local government registries. The census of 1980 recorded 56,625 Muslims living in Switzerland. In between censuses, one has to rely on regular publication of numbers of foreign residents. If 95 per cent of Turks are Muslim, then there were 54,000 Turkish Muslims in the country at the end of 1988. Possibly around 20,000 Yugoslav Muslims, representing 20 per cent of all Yugoslavs, 12,000 North Africans and about 5,000 Swiss citizens should also be added. Swiss labour law makes room for large numbers of seasonal workers, who particularly tend to come from ex-Yugoslavia. One intelligent estimate of the total number of Muslims in the country at the end of 1988 suggests about 100,000, since there were also smaller numbers from the East Mediterranean

Arab countries, from Iran, the Indian subcontinent and Indonesia, as well as a notable number of Muslims with French and German nationality. By the time of the 1990 census, the number of Muslims had risen to over 152,000. The census of 2000 included a question regarding religious belief for the first time: 310,807 persons were recorded as Muslim residents, a doubling since the last census. Due to changed statistical methods, the quality of data has somewhat declined. For 2010, statistics estimated a total of 295,798 Muslims, a lower figure than for 2000! Researchers tend to estimate the figure to be 400,000 instead, and 450,000 for 2013.

A major part of the growth can be attributed to immigrants and asylum seekers from former Yugoslavia and other hot spots, to the extent that they today make up over half of the total Muslim population of the country. The second largest group is people originating from Turkey. Naturalisation is possible in Switzerland, the general rule being a requirement to having spent twelve years in the country. In 2014, about 35 per cent of Muslims had Swiss citizenship, mostly due to naturalisation rather than conversion. As elsewhere, the Muslim communities are concentrated in the major cities: Zürich, Bern, Basel, Lausanne and Geneva. The ethnic national distribution is uneven around the country with Turks and people from former Yugoslavia showing a preference for the German-speaking parts of the country. The French-speaking cantons have attracted a higher proportion of North Africans, who tend to include a relatively high number of professional and better-off families.

It follows from the national origins indicated that most of the Muslims are of a Hanafi background, but that there are also a significant number of Malikis. The other Sunni *madhahib* (law schools) are represented in smaller numbers, as are *Ithna 'ashari* (Twelver) Shi'ites and Alevis. Most political-religious movements of the countries of origin are to be found, with the more 'fundamentalist' movements having developed a good deal of support among workers in the larger urban areas. While many organisations concentrate on advice and cultural work, there appears to be little explicit contact between activities in Switzerland and the political events of the country of origin.

There are still only four purpose-built mosques, one in Winterthur run by Albanians, opened in 2005, one in Wangen run by Turks, opened in 2009, and the two mentioned above. Since the formal adoption during the 1970s by the major international Islamic organisations and governments of the view that the Ahmadis are not Muslims, the Ahmadi mosque is used exclusively by followers of that movement. Funded primarily by the Saudi government, the large mosque in the Petit-Saconnex district particularly serves the international community attached to the major UN-related and other organisations based in Geneva. The vast majority of the approximately 240 smaller mosques and prayer rooms are to be found in apartments or converted houses and usually owe their existence to private initiatives. In a national referendum of 29 November 2009, unprecedented in Europe, the building of minarets was prohibited. However, the building of minarets has been discussed in several places in Europe and in, for example, two Austrian states, complicated planning regulations have in effect banned minarets.

In recent years, there has been a very lively organisational activity, with many new associations being formed for a variety of purposes. Most are wanting to found and build Islamic centres, and others seek to support the cultural traditions in the form of leisure and free-time activities.

Swiss law has made very few concessions to the presence of Muslims. Slaughter of animals for food according to Islamic rite remains forbidden without prior anaesthetisation, and if this is not accepted halal meat has to be imported from outside the country. Only recently has a movement begun which, supported in some Swiss quarters, is calling for halal food to be made available in public institutions, especially in hospitals and prisons, and for employers to take account of the religious requirements of their Muslim employees. However, some cantons and local governments have agreed arrangements for Muslim burial plots in their local cemeteries and days off school for the main festivals.

Many, mostly German-speaking, Swiss cantons have legislation by which certain religious communities can achieve a status of public recognition. In such cases, the main Christian churches are usually recognised. In some cantons, demands have been made for recognition also of Islam. Such recognition would bring with it the right to give Islamic instruction during school hours instead of, as at present, in free time. As of 2014, only two Alevi organisations have been officially recognised by the canton of Basel-Stadt. In other cantons, such as Geneva and Neuchâtel, there is a complete separation of religion and state on the French model.

There are no Muslim schools in Switzerland; all Muslim children follow whatever form of public education system is laid down in each individual canton. So-called integration courses are offered to Turkish and Yugoslav children with the purpose of teaching mother tongue and culture, but, as both the states in question are secular in ideology, there is seldom a religious element in these courses. On the other hand, the Department of Religious Affairs (*Diyanet*) of Turkey, through its religious attaché in Zürich, has been seeking support for a programme of religious instruction on the authorised Turkish model to be introduced for Turkish children in Swiss schools. Since 2002, some Islamic religious education has been given to Muslim pupils in public schools in four municipalities, approved only locally. The optional classes are in German and do not distinguish between different Islamic groups.

In the meantime, Muslims continue to rely on Qur'an schools independent of official control and frequented out of school hours. Many parents prefer these courses to the official integration courses with their secular bias. Especially in the Turkish case, one consequence is the contradictory messages which children will receive, with the official Kemalist view of Turkey in the integration course being contrasted with the traditional Islamic view given in the Qur'an school. The bulk of the teaching in the latter consists of learning the Qur'an in Arabic, which also attracts children from non-Turkish Muslim families. The nature of these schools differs widely due to the lack of any strong central organisations in Switzerland, and there are parents' groups trying to organise Qur'anic teaching in Turkish and with a more 'modern' approach. The fact that all this activity takes place in languages foreign to the Swiss means that there is a good deal of freedom and flexibility, which the efforts of the Turkish authorities have only to a certain extent succeeded in limiting.

Outside the economic and narrow political sphere, there is little contact between the Muslim communities and the wider Swiss society. In a few places, it has been possible to form meetings of Christians and Muslims, with particular success in Geneva. But at local level, contact tends to take place when there are problems, a fact which strengthens the reservations of local officials or Christian clergy, who probably already have congregations which are hesitant about anything Muslim. The Swiss Catholic bishops' conference has given its support to a working group set up to study the issues arising out of the Muslim presence in Switzerland and to offer concrete suggestions to solve particular problems of a pastoral nature.

Two such recurring issues are conversion and mixed marriage. In fact these are related, because despite the existence of a number of both Muslim and Christian groups with conversion as their purpose, the vast majority of conversions result from mixed marriages. In 1984, official statistics showed a total of 3,500 nationals of Muslim countries married to Swiss women, a figure which may have doubled in the following five years and which is bound to increase yet further as young Muslims who have grown up in Switzerland reach marriageable age. What is not known is how many of those who marry convert sooner or later to the religion of their spouse, although an estimate made in 1982 suggested that about 500 French-speaking Swiss had become Muslim.

AUSTRIA

Islam in Austria has become dominated by Turks, since labour immigration started during the 1960s, reaching its peak during the following decade. The census in 1981 showed a total of 77,000 resident Muslims. Of these, 53,000 were Turks, 11,000 Yugoslavs and 5,000 of various other nationalities. A further 7,000 had Austrian nationality, some through naturalisation and the rest from old Muslim families settled during the Habsburg period, predominantly from Bosnia. By 1987, the total was estimated to have passed 100,000, and a decade later the figure had risen to 300,000, of which the largest groups by current nationality were about 140,000 Turks and 35,000 Bosnians. Estimates suggest that there were around 500,000 Muslims in Austria in 2009.

There has been a comparatively high rate of acquisition of Austrian citizenship, especially among the almost 90,000 Bosnians who were given asylum in the years after 1992. About half of the Muslim population were Austrian citizens in 2009. About half of this Muslim population is concentrated in the area of Vienna, followed by the industrial provinces of Vorarlberg and Lower Austria in the west.

As elsewhere, the vast majority are employed in manufacturing and service industries, although there are a significant number of diplomats and businessmen in and around Vienna in connection with the various United Nations, OPEC and other international agencies headquartered in the city.

Austria inherited from the empire a system of legal recognition for religious communities. In the mid-1960s, the first attempt was made to persuade the Austrian state that laws of 1874 and 1912 recognising Islam were still in force and could be reactivated to cover the new situation. In 1964, the goal of gaining recognition was written into the by-laws of the *Moslemischer Sozialdienst* (Muslim Social Service). From 1968, a series of negotiations with the Ministry for Education and Art started, firstly to seek clarification as to whether the old laws were still valid or whether a new legal basis had to be found. Formal applications were submitted in 1971. When it became clear that the government had decided to take the view that the existing laws were satisfactory as a legal foundation, a new application was submitted in April 1979 by the Islamic Religious Community of Austria (IGGiÖ, *Islamische Glaubensgemeinschaft in Österrich*). Recognition was granted two weeks later, at the beginning of May.

The main advantages to flow from recognition were access to Islamic religious instruction within the school system, regulated access to the public broadcast media, and certain tax advantages. But recognition also required a formal structure for the Islamic community in the country. According to the decree of 1979, there was to be a national council, a smaller executive and a chief mufti. Local congregations were to be organised in a similar manner. Elections held in 1980 to constitute the community were marred by rivalries among various ethnic and political-religious groups, leading to fights at the scene of the election. No elections were held for a number of years after that, and in May 1987 five major Muslim associations requested the Austrian authorities to ensure that a more representative council be elected. This led to a new organisation of the Muslim community, based on local government regions. Each local community had its own elected executive body and elected the sixteen or more members of the national Shura Council. This was the highest official organ of the community and appointed the local imams. The Council in turn selected from among their own the ten members of the Council of Elders, at least five of whom had to be religious scholars. The chair of the Elders was the formal representative of Islam to the outside world and president of the community. The Council of Elders provided religious guidance and advice and also selected the chief mufti. Muslims of other denominations protested against the monopoly given to the Sunni dominated IGGiÖ, and in December 2010 a court decision ruled that it was violating religious freedom not to open up for other Muslim groups to apply to be recognised. Since then two Alevi organisations and one Shi'ite have been registered as religious denominational communities.

By 1987, there were about thirty registered Muslim associations in Austria, mostly Turkish with a few Arab and Persian ones. The oldest still-active association is the *Moslemischer Sozialdienst*, or Muslim Social Service (MSS), founded in 1962 by Austrian Muslims of Bosnian origin. Having achieved recognition in 1979, it continued for a time to act as executive committee for the national council elected in 1980.

By 2014, the situation has totally changed. IGGiÖ is still an important organisation but several others have risen to prominence; some cooperate, some do not. There are hundreds of Muslim associations. Most Turkish associations, although formally falling under the umbrella of the national council, act independently and sometimes have a tense relationship with both it and the MSS. The two main groupings represented among the Turks are the *Süleymançis*, with the title of 'Union of Austrian Islamic Cultural Centres', coordinating thirty-four associations and forty-three prayer rooms, and the *Milli Görüş*, running the Austrian Islamic Federation with forty-four associations and some sixty mosques. A large number of mosques are controlled by the *Diyanet*, which organise sixty-five associations and their prayer rooms. The Gülen movement is also present, even if a formal organisation is not set up. There is also a Bosnian federation, and an Albanian one, two Alevi and one Shi'ite. Ahmadiyya, *Hizb al-Tahrir* and different Salafis are also active, even if on a minor scale.

After lengthy consideration and argument, a new *Islamgesetz* (law on Islam) was passed by parliament in early 2015. It was controversial in that it forbids foreign funding of Islamic organisations and seeks to control which versions of Qur'an translations may be used. Legal challenges are expected.

Recognition has had its main effect in making Islamic education available as part of the state school curriculum. From the school year 1982/83, the state funded Islamic religious education during school hours. In 2013, according to IGGiÖ, there were 430 teachers in Islamic education catering for about 57,000 pupils in 2,000 schools. In 1987, the number of pupils had been about 15,000. Teachers are paid by the state but must have the approval of the national Muslim council, which is also responsible for providing the curriculum and approving textbooks and examinations. Since 1998, IGGiÖ has run the Private Academy for Islamic Education providing training for teachers. In 2006, a Master's degree in Islamic Religious Pedagogy was launched at the University of Vienna. Since 2013, the main Alevi organisation has had the right to organise its own religious education. Presently, there are six private Islamic schools, all of them in Vienna. Two of them are run by the Islamic Centre in Vienna serving the diplomatic and business communities. One of these operates in Arabic and is funded by Saudi Arabia. The other works in German and the teachers are provided by the Austrian state.

ITALY

For the last century or more, Italy has been a country of emigration. Its people have migrated to North America, across the Mediterranean, and more recently to South America and Australasia. Both during the great depression in the early 1930s and then again after 1945, Italians emigrated to the industrial north of Europe. In France and Germany, Italians were among the main sources of labour migration during the 1950s and early 1960s.

However, by the end of the 1970s there were the beginnings of an awareness that Italy was also becoming a country of immigration. On the one hand, this was a continuation of the phenomenon of North Europeans and North Americans making a degree of permanent home for themselves, as well as due to the fact that Rome joined the ranks of cities such as Geneva and Vienna, becoming the home of international agencies such as the UN Food and Agricultural Organisation. Of itself, this attracted a disproportionate number of diplomats and businessmen of Muslim origin. Additionally, the presence of the Vatican invited international Muslim organisations to look to Rome as one, if not the only, seat of Christian leadership.

On the other hand, one saw the beginnings of an economic immigration across the Mediterranean. The difficulty in taking the account on from this point is the lack of any even slightly reliable statistics, official or otherwise. In 1977, a survey was conducted at the behest of the Interministerial Committee on Migrations, which suggested a total of 300,000 to 400,000 foreign workers originating from North Africa, Eritrea and Somalia, Greece, Yugoslavia, Spain, Portugal and the then EC countries. Of these, North Africans were estimated to total between 70,000 and 100,000.

The underlying problem here has been the lack of any effective control and administrative apparatus. Thus, in 1981, official data for Moroccans with registered residence indicated fewer than 2,000, while the trade unions claimed that the true figure was closer to 30,000. The SOPEMI (*Système d'observation permanente des migrations*) report of the Organisation for Economic Cooperation and Development (OECD) for the same year estimated a total of 1 million foreigners in Italy, while another report for the following year gave a range of between 300,000 and 700,000!

In the mid-1980s, studies indicated that a large proportion of the immigrants from North Africa and other developing areas of the world were working in the southern half of the country without official status. They appear to have been employed in domestic service, shipbuilding and fisheries, but an increasing proportion was also finding work as unskilled labour in manufacturing industry further north.

By this time, the issue of immigration had arrived at the point where the Italian parliament felt it necessary to start investigating the situation, with a view to updating the legal situation regarding immigration and foreigners' status from the antiquated laws of the early Mussolini years of the 1920s. This period of review came to a head during 1989 and 1990, by which time pressure had grown from other member countries of the European Community for Italy to bring its immigration laws into some degree of harmonisation with the rest of the Community.

At this time, the first serious attempts to estimate the Muslim population of the country were made. While Muslim institutions were quoting totals of between 0.5 and 1 million, more disinterested observers were preferring figures in the range of 200,000 to 300,000. The main reason for this discrepancy may very well have been a high rate of 'irregular', and therefore unrecorded, immigrants, as a more serious statistical study published in 1991 indicated. This study was based primarily on the 1991 statistics on resident foreign nationals published by the Ministry of the Interior, on the strength of which, data on religious origin were extrapolated. This suggested a total of almost 300,000 legal residents of Muslim national background, mostly of various Arab origins and a substantial group of 24,000 Senegalese. The inevitably unreliable data for irregular residents would suggest that, for example, the true figure for Albanian Muslims is closer to 20,000, rather than the official figure of 1,500! By the year 2000, extrapolations from official statistics on foreign nationals, and estimates of unrecorded immigration, were producing a total of possibly 700,000 people of Muslim background. Over the decade, all groups had grown markedly; notably, the number of Moroccans had doubled and that of Pakistanis trebled. But the greatest impact had been caused by the series of wars in the territory of former Yugoslavia. The total of Albanians by nationality had risen to 142,000, not counting tens of thousands more from Bosnia, Serbia, and especially Kosovo, Montenegro and Macedonia, many of whom do not appear in official figures. In 2010, according to ISTAT (the national bureau for statistics), the two largest national groups from Muslim countries residing in Italy were Albanians (482,627) and Moroccans (452,424).

Estimates from 2014 put the population of Muslims between 1.5 and 2.2 million. The major reason for the increase is the political crises in different countries in both Sub-Saharan Africa and North Africa. Most Muslims are not Italian citizens since naturalisation is difficult, although possible. The number of irregular migrants has been very large over the years. In 2008 it was estimated that 651,000 irregular migrants were present in Italy. How many of these were

Muslim is impossible to know. Through regularisation processes the estimated number of irregulars had been halved by 2013.

Taking the data for recorded foreign residents as a guide, the concentrations of Muslim population are to be found particularly in Rome and Milan, followed by Turin, Palermo and Naples. The province of Emilia Romagna also has a large Muslim population, but spread more evenly among its urban centres, especially Bologna and Modena. Outside Palermo, several Sicilian towns have smaller but notable Muslim populations.

Islam had made itself noticed before it became a national issue, but only in connection with particular local developments. In Catania in Sicily, a mosque was built in 1980 to serve a mainly North African community (though it is no longer in use). Eight years after that, another purpose-built mosque was opened in Milan. But more attention was attracted over the years by the fate of the mosque in Rome. The plan for a vast, prestigious building in Rome can be traced back to the early 1970s, when it had the support of the then Shah of Iran. The plan gained the official support of the Italian government when it was endorsed by the prime minister during an official visit to Saudi Arabia – much to the annoyance of some Roman Catholic leaders, who felt that some reciprocal gesture by the Saudi government could have been requested. Construction was, however, delayed for several years as opposition groups used all the avenues offered by planning regulations to obstruct the project. It was finally inaugurated in 1994, in the presence of representatives of a number of Muslim governments and organisations, the Italian government and the Vatican. The mosque can house more than 12,000 people and is one of the largest in Europe. Apart from these early mosques, eight additional mosques have been built in Palermo (1990), Brescia (1990s), a second one in Catania (2012), Ravenna (2013), Colle Val d'Elsa (2013), Albenga (2013), Turin (2013) and Agrigent (2015).

The public attention attracted by the politics around the Rome mosque tended to obscure the growth in the number of small local mosques and prayer rooms. In Italy, as elsewhere, this would appear to have been closely related to the settlement of Muslim families. In 1980, reliable sources indicate that there were only seven locations exclusively dedicated to regular worship and community activity. This number grew by over twenty in the following decade and again doubled by the end of 1992. If one adds to this the number of locations which are regularly used for worship, mostly some form of community hall, the total number of mosques in Italy reached close to 200 by the end of the 1990s, and is estimated to be more than 750 in 2014. By far the largest proportion of these is Moroccan, a community in which the proportion of people who retain some degree of adherence to Islamic practices is much higher than among the much more secularised Albanians.

At the end of 1980, the public debate on the new immigration regime had brought into focus the extent to which official policies and bureaucratic procedures were unprepared. Suddenly, local authorities, social services, schools, the legal system and the other institutions of local and national government found themselves at a loss in dealing with the petty practical challenges which had long since been faced in many other parts of Europe. At the same time, the country also found itself suddenly having to deal with a new vocal right-wing nationalist movement of the kind which countries such as France had become accustomed to some years earlier. The tension was exacerbated by the pressures from the north towards integration and harmonisation into the European Community following the Maastricht treaty of 1992, a pressure which had been drawing Italy's attention away from its historical and more obvious interests in the Mediterranean cultural and economic zone.

Apart from the Rome mosque and its associated Islamic Cultural Centre of Italy, there are few organisations which have achieved national prominence. The Union of Islamic Communities and Organisations in Italy (UCOII, *Unione delle Comunità e delle Organizzazioni Islamiche in Italia*), established in 1990, claims to represent most mosques. In 1998, and then again in 2000, initiatives were taken to establish a *Consiglio Islamico d'Italia* to act as a common representative organisation. It mainly brought together the members of the UCOII and the Rome mosque, but membership has been rejected by the two main organisations representing mainly Italian converts but with significant profiles in public awareness, namely the Islamic Religious Community (COREIS) and the Association of Italian Muslims (AMI).

The weakness of the *Consiglio* and the quite public disagreements among the main Muslim groups have contributed to the inability to achieve official recognition. Apart from the Roman Catholic church, for which there is a concordat with the Vatican, the Italian state has over the decades concluded 'ententes' (*intesa*) with a number of the smaller religious communities, primarily various Protestant groups and the Jews. In 2000, new agreements were made with Buddhists and Jehovah's Witnesses, but a new right-of-centre government, led by Silvio Berlusconi, and a centre-right parliamentary majority meant that neither of these agreements was ratified by parliament, and that official interest in reaching an agreement with the Muslim communities effectively disappeared.

Even though the Muslims of Italy have not managed to gain legal recognition, they are free to organise religious education at schools when there is a significant number of pupils of the denomination in question, as are all religious groups. However, organisers will bear the costs. No Muslim group has used this possibility this far and no Islamic private school has opened. Instead, Muslim pupils can chose between participating in Catholic religious education or take part in alternative classes for non-religious pupils and pupils of other faiths. Both classes are optional. According to statistics, about 11 per cent opt out of the Catholic religious education, but the background of these pupils is not known.

SPAIN

The Muslim presence in Spain is characterised by three elements. On the one hand is the cultural heritage of the Islamic period, particularly marked in architectural treasures, which ended in 1492 with the conquest of the last Muslim kingdom, that of Granada. As Islam has again become a feature of the social scene in Spain during the last few decades, some Muslim groups have appeared which claim to be the heirs of that period. At the same time, as part of the country's reorientation following the return to democracy after the death of Franco in 1975, increasing attention has been given to the Islamic heritage, especially of Andalucia.

Numerically much more significant, however, has been labour migration. Much of this was temporary, transient and unregistered, as it started to grow during the 1960s. Many Moroccans found temporary work in the tourist industry of the Mediterranean coast while they were looking to moving on to France. Thirdly, there has been the more long-term process of labour immigration into the country's most industrialised region, Catalonia. It was here that many men from the former Spanish protectorate of the northern sector of Morocco went to find work during the 1960s and 1970s.

As France and other European countries further north closed their borders to labour immigration in 1973 and 1974, many Moroccans found themselves stuck in Spain, while others found themselves being forced back south out of France. This quickly led to a population of some 100,000 Moroccans in Barcelona for a time during the late 1970s. But in Spain, as elsewhere, this development also led to a new process of family reunion and settlement, and therefore of permanence. The last major wave of immigration came during the late 1980s and early 1990s, as people sought to enter before Spain joined the stricter immigration regime being adopted by the European Community. The first step in this move was the introduction in May 1991 of stricter visa requirements, which was followed at the beginning of 1993 by the coming into effect of the Single Market and then Spain's adherence to the so called Schengen accord on internal and external passport controls.

It remains difficult to estimate the number of Spanish residents of Muslim background because of the high proportion of unregistered people. An estimate from 1986 suggested a total of some 175,000, of which 110,000 were Moroccans, 20,000 from Sub-Saharan Africa, 30,000 from the Middle East, and 15,000 from South and South-east Asia. A 1990 estimate indicated a total of 250,000 Muslims, at a time when official government records showed fewer than 10,000 Moroccans legally resident! By 2013 estimates were suggesting a total of between 1,300,000 and 1,700,000, of which migrants of Moroccan origin were the largest group. Approximately a third of the Muslim population are believed to be Spanish citizens.

Family reunion has led to a very speedy development of Muslim organisa-tions. The first mosque to be built in modern times was in Marbella, opened in 1981, followed in 1983 by the Abu Bakr Mosque in Madrid and, in 1992, the Saudi-financed Islamic Cultural Centre in Madrid. Since then major mosques have opened in Valencia (1992), Fuengirola (1994), two in Granada (2001, 2003), and Malaga (2007). The two towns that Spain still holds in North Africa, Ceuta and Melilla, harbour four additional major mosques. There were an estimated 1,279 smaller mosques and prayer-houses in 2013.

In November 1992, Spain joined the small number of western European countries to grant a form of recognition to Islam. This was part of the post-Franco policy of moving towards a system of neutrality towards religion. The accord was reached between the Spanish government and the Islamic Commission of Spain (*Comisión Islámica de España*), an alliance of the two main federations of Muslim associations, and was similar to the accords reached with other religious communities previously, including the Roman Catholic church. Since 1992, the number of Islamic associations which have joined the Commission and thus gained access to the privileges accorded by the recogni-tion has grown. The accord permitted Islamic religious instruction in both public and private schools, the right to set up Islamic schools and the recogni-tion of religious rights of Muslims in the armed forces, hospitals and prisons, as well as recognising Muslim marriage ceremonies within the limits of the general civil law, certain tax exemptions, and the right to religious holidays, including time off work from an hour before sunset during Ramadan. Provision for halal food, including the slaughter of animals, was also granted. The accord also encouraged local authorities to make provision for Muslim burial, a process which has been slow. A problem has been that the two original federations have not permitted other federations to become part of the Islamic Commission. By creating a competing organisation, Muslim federations managed to pressure the government to amend the agreement from 1992 allowing for new federations to enter the collaboration. As of October 2012, 35 Islamic federations were registered as part of the Islamic Commission.

One of the most successful Muslim organisations in Spain has been the *Jama'at al Tabligh*, with its members coming from either North Africa or its British base. *Tablighi* activities started in the mid-1980s in Catalonia but by the turn of the century had spread all over Spain. Most *Tablighi* communities are part of the Union of Islamic Communities of Spain, one of the two original federations recognised by the Islamic Commission and thus recognised by the state and covered by the 1992 agreement. The *Tablighis* concentrated their work on developing personal piety and on social work. However, *Tablighi* organisa-tions came under suspicion in connection with the train bombings in Madrid, 11 March 2004, and the subsequent supervision of extremists, because arrested alleged terrorists claimed to have been in contact with them.

Two private Muslim schools offer the official Spanish curriculum and are recognised by the Ministry of Education. One serves primarily the diplomatic community in Madrid; the other is attached to the Islamic Cultural Centre in Madrid. Following the 1992 recognition, the Islamic Commission in 1996 made an agreement with the government intended to provide religious instruction for Muslim children in state schools. Its implementation was first hampered by financial problems and the absence of agreement on the content of the syllabus among the member associations of the Commission. By an agreement of 1996, this teaching was initially to be financed by a direct government grant to the Commission, which would then take responsibility, but subsequent legislation has transferred the financial responsibility directly to the Ministry of Education. Finally, in the school year 2003–4, specific Islamic education was offered at a number of schools. This activity has grown immensely, and in 2014, forty-six teachers were engaged in giving Islamic religious education. However, as 243,437 Muslim pupils were registered in the Spanish educational system, to offer Islamic RE to all would, by estimation, require at least 400 teachers! Islamic organisations developed teaching materials and launched a textbook for primary education (*Descubrir el Islam*, Discover Islam) in 2006 and teaching materials for secondary education in 2009.

PORTUGAL

The first major immigration of Muslims took place in the mid-1970s in connection with the process of decolonisation. The largest single source was people of Indian origin from Mozambique, probably two-thirds of the total Muslim population today, with a further 20 per cent being black Africans originating in Guinea-Bissau. By 1990, the population had reached some 15,000. Smaller numbers have arrived at various times from other countries in Africa, or have been 'illegal' settlers in other parts of Europe seeking to take advantage of occasional government amnesties permitting regularisation of residence during the 1990s. By the year 2014, the total Muslim population was estimated at between 48,000 and 55,000, some 8,000 of whom are Isma'ilis. Given that Portugal's colonies in Africa were legally regarded as part of metropolitan Portugal, a significant majority of these people hold Portuguese citizenship, and those who do not, need six years of legal residence to acquire it.

Over half of the Muslim community lives around Lisbon, concentrated in immigrant areas which it shares with Hindus who are also of colonial Asian descent, and with others of African origin. The Isma'ilis live mostly in Lisbon, with smaller numbers in Porto. Only in the Muslim communities of black African origin is poverty and unemployment a major problem. In 2010, some thirty places of worship had been established, and by 2014 six full mosques with minarets had been built. The first of the latter was opened in 1982 in the

Laranjeiro district of Lisbon, and the second was opened the following year in Odivelas, also in Lisbon. The large central mosque in Lisbon opened in 1985. Apart from these, the towns of Coimbra, Oporto and Funchal (on Madeira Island) have their own mosques.

In 1996, the government invited broad consultation with a view to revising the law on religious freedom, which dated back to the period of the Salazar dictatorship. Most of the responses to this invitation came from various Protestant groups, but Muslim associations also took an active part in the debate, putting forward their own particular concerns. The debate provided the motivation for Muslim and Jewish groups together to form an alliance of non-Christian religions. Before 2001, there was no formal recognition of Islam in Portugal, but Muslim associations were expected to register officially under the law of association. But since the passing of the Religious Freedom Act of 22 June 2001 religious denominations with a presence in Portugal for at least thirty years may gain rights on a par with the Catholic church. The main Islamic organisation, The Islamic Community of Lisbon (*Comunidade Islâmica de Lisboa*), was recognised a couple of years ago as a Registered Religious Community. Government officials have cultivated positive relations with the major Muslim associations, and the government has tended to be represented at the opening of mosques. However, at the same time, it seems clear that public awareness of the Muslim past and present is minimal, and thus there is nothing like the attention given to the Islamic heritage which can be seen across the border in Spanish Andalucia. The new religious freedom act stipulates that if a minimum of ten pupils need religious instruction in their own faith this should be organised. In 2014, there were no schools with enough Muslim pupils in the same age group to offer such training.

CHAPTER 8

Family, law and culture

Social and economic considerations

The process of immigration has been the main factor in determining the basic working and living conditions of the majority of Muslims, certainly of the immigrant generation itself. They came with little European language ability, to find employment in the less skilled parts of industry. Their educational qualifications were low, and those which they had were only recognised sparingly. Housing conditions were poor. The effect of racial discrimination has been to perpetuate these conditions and, to a great extent, to pass them on to the children.

This is not the place to present a general survey of the social and economic conditions of non-European immigrant and ethnic minority communities in Europe, a field in which a substantial literature has accumulated. Much of this literature relates of course to Muslims, since in mainland Europe most such communities are Muslim in origin. This circumstance makes it particularly difficult to make any judgement as to how far their social and economic circumstances are affected by the fact of these communities' Muslim identity. While there is no doubt that the conditions affect very strongly Muslims' reaction and adaptation, it seems absurd in such circumstances to attribute to Islam, as a religion, any alleged social or economic shortcomings attributed to Muslims in Europe.

In Britain, however, the circumstances of the immigration have brought not only Muslim communities but also Hindu and Sikh communities from generally similar areas, namely particular regions of the north of the Indian subcontinent. Here, one has a situation where it is possible at least to attempt a comparison, and so we can refer again to the circumstances outlined in the opening paragraph above.

A number of surveys have shown the extent of these circumstances, in particular four major surveys on racial disadvantage, conducted in 1966, 1974, 1982 and 1994. However, there are significant differences in these areas, as the third survey showed with reference to English-language ability. In 1982, three-quarters of Bangladeshi women and a slightly smaller proportion of Pakistani women spoke little or no English, while the same was the case with half of Bangladeshi men but less than a quarter of Pakistani men. These differences are symptomatic partly of the later arrival of Bangladeshis and partly of the extent to which women conducted their lives within the community. In contrast, English fluency among people from India and East Africa was much more widespread – less than a quarter of East African Asian women spoke little or no English. This lack of English fluency appears to have had surprisingly little influence on people's ability to find work, with less than 10 per cent of Asians reporting having had difficulties in finding employment because of language problems. The 1996 survey showed that these populations were now overwhelmingly fluent in English, especially among those who had grown up in the UK or had lived there for more than twenty-five years. The one notable exception was that the figures for women of Pakistani or Bangladeshi origin were consistently below the average.

Three-quarters of Asian men and almost 90 per cent of Asian women had no qualifications when they came to Britain. The men entered unskilled or semiskilled industrial work, especially in textile and metal manufacturing. Here they worked in shifts, often under foremen of the same origins, and it was the foremen who had sufficient English to be able to mediate between their workers and the management. By the early 1980s, some diversification had taken place, with people moving out of manufacturing industry into service industries, but men of Pakistani origin were still concentrated in manufacturing – over two-thirds in 1982, a figure which had fallen to not much more than one-third by 1994. Another sign of such diversification is the growing number of self-employed, particularly in retailing and catering, which in 1994 accounted for two-thirds of men of Bangladeshi origin. Here, it is notable that self-employment is higher among Bangladeshis and African Asians than among Pakistanis, probably, in the case of the former two groups, because they tended to arrive during the periods of high unemployment during the 1970s and 1980s and, in the case of the latter group, because of the higher proportion of traders and professionals.

This experience of unemployment struck the ethnic minorities particularly hard, especially Pakistanis and Bangladeshis, with almost one-fifth of the men out of work in the early 1980s according to one survey, and almost one-third according to another. Unemployment rates among people of Pakistani and Bangladeshi origin have tended to remain stubbornly around twice the national average, with female rates significantly higher. The combination of low-paid work and unemployment has meant that household income among Muslims has averaged substantially below the national average. This is emphasised further by the reluctance of Muslim women to enter the labour market. Only 18 per cent of Muslim women had work in 1982, and most of them were in the age group 20–34. Twelve years later, the figure was only marginally greater. In fact, 80 per cent of the economic inactivity of Muslims in Britain can be explained by the low level of female participation in wage labour.

This comparatively low household income is only partly compensated for by the fact that Asian households tend to be larger than average. Most of the extra members of the household are children – the average Asian household in 1982 had two children – but there also is an average of almost three adults as against the general average of two per household, and this extra adult often contributes to the household income. In 2001, the average Muslim household size was 3.8, while the national average was 2.4.

The first phase of immigration was characterised by single men lodging together in houses owned by earlier immigrants, often from the same village or region. As wives and children joined, it became necessary to find more private accommodation. At the time, local councils were major landlords of rented property, but the system of waiting-lists worked against recent immigrants. Among people from the Indian subcontinent, there was also a preference for owning property, a preference which could be satisfied when the extended family's resources were mobilised collectively. In any event, this support was necessary partly because as Muslims they were reluctant to enter into loan arrangements in the traditional British mortgage market, and partly because the mortgage lenders tended to restrict mortgages to ethnic minorities to certain inner-city districts. As a result, by the early 1980s over three-quarters of Pakistani families lived in property which they owned. Bangladeshis, on the other hand, again because they have tended to arrive later and therefore after council house-allocation policies became more flexible, are much more likely to live in rented public housing – less than a third owned their own homes in the early 1980s, although by the mid-1990s this proportion was close to half. The same figure is given in the early twenty-first century.

During the late 1980s and the 1990s, central government policy of privatising much of public housing, combined with local authority policies of urban renewal meant that the rate of private ownership, especially among Bangladeshis, grew significantly. At the same time, the quality of such housing had improved so much that between 1982 and 1994, houses inhabited by people of Pakistani and Bangladeshi origin without central heating had declined from two-thirds to less than one-third. However, in the early twenty-first century, Muslim households experienced homes to be overcrowded to a higher degree (32 per cent) than for example Christian households (6 per cent), a clear indication of having low income.

Throughout, there is an underlying tone of racial discrimination. Early experience of racial discrimination and abuse by ethnic minorities in Britain was felt particularly by Afro-Caribbeans, and they clearly retain a much more sceptical attitude towards the fairness of British institutions than do Asians. This even extended to expectations of employers and police in dealing with minorities, at least in the survey conducted in 1982. On the other hand, this Asian belief in the fairness of British institutions is identified with the older, immigrant generation. Young people are rather more disillusioned, and the growing history of racial attacks, particularly against Bangladeshis in East London in the 1980s and then the 'crises' of the 1990s, contributed to a growing disillusionment, certainly about police attitudes, into the twenty-first century.

Much of this will be recognised by observers of Muslim communities elsewhere in Europe, while other aspects will be different. It is also evident that the factors causing disadvantage, emanating from within the Muslim communities, can be attributed to the particular peasant background of the immigrant generation rather than to Islam. Certainly in Britain, all the more recent evidence shows clearly that the proportion of children of Pakistani background outperforming the national average is growing, when a decade earlier they had underperformed and were a common cause for concern among educationists. However, this has been matched by a much larger proportion of all children underperforming the national average.

Behind this improvement lies the centrality of family cohesion felt within the Islamic tradition generally, as well as its particular strength in the Indian subcontinent. It is at this level of the family that Muslim communities in western Europe may be most profoundly affected by the process of migration and settlement. It has legal implications, in terms of the legal norms and contexts of the countries both of origin and of settlement, and it has its implications for the changes taking place as the generation born or brought up in Europe reaches maturity and establishes the families of the next generation.

Family

Attitudes to the nature of the family and the internal relationships among family members are central to personal and cultural identification. Migration changes both the family structure and its context, and thus challenges the perceptions and traditional ideologies of family. In the case of European and Islamic norms, the law is a particularly critical forum in which to test the issues. This is so, not only because of the distinct, separate histories of European and Islamic norms and their enshrinement in specific legal systems, but also because the varying relationships between cultural norm and family law reflect the complexities of the transition through which the Muslim family has passed over the last two centuries.

We can identify probably four areas of analysis which need to be taken into account when looking at Muslim family structures and processes in this context. First, there is the fact of migration and partial family reunion itself. Second, the physical environment plays a role. Third, there are the variations of culture among the regions of origin and, fourth, the stereotypes and mutual perceptions which can so significantly determine the nature of the first personal or collective encounter between Muslim and European.

In the context of the growth of Muslim communities outlined in previous chapters, Muslim family structures and processes have been particularly affected. There is not merely the fact that families have been reunited, although in modified forms, in the years after 1962 in Britain and 1973–4 in mainland Europe. That fact has itself had further consequences in a large variety of ways. The men, who had previously been on their own, now had direct responsibilities for wives and children. This entailed involvement in practical matters relating to health, housing and schooling. The whole family therefore became much more extensively related to public officialdom. This put Muslim families into situations which were usually difficult, often embarrassing and occasionally traumatic. Women had to go through antenatal care and give birth in the impersonal surroundings of city hospitals, without the accustomed support and presence of female relatives. Occasionally, a young son might be the only available interpreter. The bureaucracy involved in entry and residence formalities, in dealing with the welfare services and housing authorities, and in arranging schooling for the children were all daunting and often frightening.

Many of these new experiences were not specifically or uniquely linked to the move from the country of origin to Europe. They were as much the experiences of moving from village to city, and they would have been experienced in similar ways had the move been from the Punjab to Karachi, rather than to Birmingham. There were particular European elements in the process all the same – apart from the difficulties associated with preserving family links over the much greater distances. These European difficulties arose specifically from differences of language and culture. Officialdom did not understand the immigrants, and it took a long time before anything like adequate moves were made towards providing competent interpretation from Urdu, Turkish, Arabic, and so on. Such language barriers were only exacerbated by the monolingual bias of European national cultures and the common expectation that 'they should learn our language'. The language barriers also served to underline the cultural misunderstandings, of which there were many – even when there was direct communication. This was most obviously the case with expectations relating to women. Women joining their husbands were more likely to be illiterate and to have no experience of urban society, let alone European society. On the other hand, European officials and care staff did not understand or felt a need to respect traditional gender relations or role patterns in the parts of the Muslim world from which the immigrants came. Nurses, social workers and teachers tended to expect women, as they expected all individuals, to speak for themselves, without referring constantly to male relatives for advice or spokesmanship. There was also a failure to appreciate the authority structures within families as regards the relationship between parents and children, an area where the educational professionals in particular felt frustrated.

In the same way that these experiences during the 1960s, 1970s and 1980s served to encourage a 'them and us' analysis within European thinking and policy discussion, so they did also among the Muslim immigrant communities.

In the latter case, one of the resources to which they were increasingly inclined to turn was the Islamic element of their heritage. This trend provided the detailed content of a tendency which a number of observers have noted. In a study of Bengali Muslims in Bradford, Stephen Barton noted that the religious identity of the individual tended to remain linked with the family. In other words, the locus of the family provided the focus of religious belonging. When the family moved, so too did the locus of the individual member's religious life. Practically, this meant that while the family remained in the country of origin, the individual migrant, usually male, could reasonably clearly distinguish between the secular sphere of the life of employment and society, which was in Europe, and the life of belief and piety, which was mostly at home. When the family came to join him, that distinction became more difficult to make. His Islam was no longer something 'over there' or purely private. It now became an active factor in his everyday family and working life. It is no coincidence, therefore, that the process of family reunion sparked the first major expansion in the numbers of mosques. This aspect will be dealt with in the next chapter, but there were implications of other kinds which have more directly affected the character of Muslim families in Europe. Here, there are questions arising out of the relationship between extended and nuclear families, as well as gender roles and generation expectations.

The physical environment in which Muslims settled had a significant effect on the way in which family life and structures evolved. Most obvious were the constraints of climate and of traditional domestic architecture in the urban areas of Muslim concentration. The climate in northern Europe forced domestic family activities indoors into accommodation designed for small nuclear families. Even if the climate were more favourable, the vertical columns of apartment blocks in many European cities, no less than the strings of terraced housing more characteristic of Britain, would make social intercourse difficult. The physical environment and the climate in Europe prevent nuclear households from forming a functioning extended family life of the kind which was common even where the norm was a nuclear household, as it often was, for example, in Turkey.

The other characteristic of the physical environment which has appeared over time has been the gradual concentration of Muslim immigrants into certain specific urban districts. While this flowed naturally from the common pattern of chain migration, the persistence of residential concentration has caused both politicians and scholars concern. In the late 1960s, some scholars suggested that the receiving society imposed restraints which forced immigrants into particular areas. There was certainly a widespread practice by estate agents and local housing authorities which served to exclude immigrants from specific districts. But other scholars suggested that just as significant a factor was the desire of the immigrant communities to live close together. Today, urban geographers have tended to confirm that migration patterns and ethnic identities have influenced the growth of residential concentrations in ways which allow for an interplay between the choices of the immigrants within the constraints imposed by the context of settlement. Economic historians have stressed that ethnically homogenous areas may in fact have a positive effect on economic integration. According to some analysts, reflecting more recently on the urban street clashes of English northern towns in the early summer of 2001, local policies of encouraging cultural and religious particularism under a banner of 'multiculturalism' have reinforced such residential segregation.

Of course, official housing policies have not been without influence. Difficulty of access to local council housing waiting-lists in Britain was a major reason why South Asians, including Muslims, had to resort to purchasing private terraced housing. The public housing policies of Sweden around the Stockholm and Gothenburg conurbations have greatly influenced the location of ethnic minority communities, as has the public housing policy in for example France and Denmark. A study of residential patterns in the Netherlands suggests that public housing policies tend to have a socially and geographically immobilising effect when they are restrictive. Thus the policy of Utrecht did not stop immigration, but forced it into poor housing which was difficult to move out of. On the other hand, a more liberal policy in Amsterdam – on the principle of 'bring your family, then we'll sort out housing' – seemed to allow for more mobility. But it has also given scope for cultural backgrounds to play a more active role, and in consequence the Surinamese have tended to move on faster than the Turks, while Moroccans have been least mobile.

The element of cultural particularities brought by particular groups and families cannot be ignored. This has sometimes been a sensitive question. On the one hand, European political and social analysts often emphasised the common experience of immigration and discrimination in a socialist analysis which in Britain brought all ethnic minorities under the umbrella term 'black'. This was severely criticised by academics with a background from South Asia preferring 'Asian' instead of 'black'. During the 1990s and the early twenty-first century, 'Muslim' has become the dominant category used (and misused). On the other hand, many Muslims have emphasised the unity of the *ummah* and talked of Islam as the culture, ignoring the sometimes substantial differences, even contradictions, in the heritage, way of life and attitudes of different Muslim ethnic and cultural groups.

We have already referred briefly to the tendency of different groups to concentrate in different cities and in different parts of cities. The variations behind such choices of residence are also an important factor, especially in the immigrant generation, in how family life is organised. Official statistics, as well as many social surveys, have concentrated on national origins as factors of variation and, occasionally, on educational or social background. But within countries there can be substantial regional variations which may be quite deep-rooted. One can mention the contrasts among Kashmiri, Punjabi and Pathan in Pakistan, or those between Berber and Arab in Algeria. During the 1980s, it became increasingly clear that the distinctions between Kurdish and Turkish citizens of Turkey had implications beyond merely the social, implications which were further complicated by the overlapping tensions between Sunni and Alevi. In addition, the distinctions between urban and educated as against the majority of peasant origin were more or less open and persistent, especially among the Turks because of the historical tensions between Kemalist secularists and traditional Muslims.

A fourth element which has to be kept in mind is the initial perceptions with which the immigrants and the hosts met each other. On the one hand was a European perception of superiority regarding people from Africa and Asia, reinforced by the recent experience of empire, sometimes mixed with resentment at empire lost, to which were added conceptions about Islam which could often be traced back to the Middle Ages. On the other hand were the perceptions of Europe of the immigrants themselves. This was more complex, depending very much on where they came from and the circumstances of the migration. For many, there were no great expectations of open hospitality or help towards settling – which was not usually the original purpose, in any case. But there were mixed experiences of decent or not-so-decent treatment at the hands of employers and officials. Some employers in Germany were quite quick to make, for example, worship facilities available to their new Turkish workers, while others hardly provided decent accommodation. Groups which had come as refugees during the early years often came with quite high expectations which were rudely disappointed. This particularly applied to those Algerians, the Harkis, who had thrown their lot in with the French during the war of independence.

Muslim families and the law

Before proceeding to a more specific discussion of the family and the law in the European situation, it is necessary to consider the general context both in the countries of origin and in the European countries of settlement.

Muslims bring with them to Europe a complex of perceptions about the norms of family life, the roots of which can be identified in four categories. First, there is the Shari‘a with its extensive rules and principles on family law and personal status based on the Qur’anic injunctions – it should be remembered that it is in these areas that the Qur’an has the most extensive and detailed set of rules. Developed over centuries of scholarship and legal practice, the Shari‘a has traditionally operated according to four Sunni schools (*madhahib*) and three major Shi‘ite ones. In all the schools, there has been some scope for accommodation to local custom, in particular with its recognition of *‘urf* in the Maliki tradition of North Africa and *'adat* in the Shafi'i school of South-East Asia. The Shari'a was also able to be adapted to local custom through the practice of the Islamic judges, *qadis*, who at the local level often preferred to take note of local social and political relations in their application of the legal rules. However, it seems clear that the fullest effect of Shari'a law tended to be felt in the urban areas.

In the countryside, the Shari'a in its formal shape was always more open to compromise with local custom (the second category) to the extent, often, that it was the local village or tribal customary law which held sway with only limited obeisance to the principles of Shari'a. This has meant that, in specific areas, family custom has occasionally been in harmony with Shari'a and more often at variance with it. This has tended to be the case especially in marriage customs and the ceremonials and duties associated with marriage. In many areas of the Muslim world, aspects of customary law which are in direct contradiction to the Shari'a have prevailed, especially in women's rights to inheritance. Depending on the point of view of the orthodox Islamic perspective, there are also areas which can be considered either a variation or a contradiction of the Shari'a; hence the widespread practice of arranged and sometimes enforced marriage, or the practice in parts of Pakistan of a form of adoption.

The last two elements in the equation are the categories of legislation and administrative procedures. Although the latter were a factor before the incursion of European powers in the eighteenth and nineteenth centuries, the weight of their influence reflects their essential European origins. Technically, in Islamic terms, there was no legislation before the colonial period, although in practice there were extensive regulations on the application of law, especially in the Ottoman empire. But on the whole, this affected areas of the Shari'a other than family, particularly commercial, tax and land rent law. Very soon after British influence began to extend through the Indian subcontinent, the beginnings were made on legislation to also affect Muslim family law. This expanded after Britain took over direct rule in 1858, but it remained piecemeal. It was not the British practice to codify areas of the law, and the changes which were introduced tended more to be the results of British-controlled courts establishing new precedents. The Ottomans were the first to codify law in the form of the Mecelle promulgated in 1869. In 1917, they legislated for the first time to effect changes in traditional Shari'a family law. Under the influence of colonial rule, and then as part of modernisation processes initiated by states independent after the Second World War, almost every Muslim country in the Arab world and Iran has codified family law in such a way as to include reform. In other countries, legislation has been passed affecting specific parts of the law, usually to improve the situation of women in marriage and divorce and, in the Sunni world, the situation of orphaned grandchildren in inheritance.

In some ways, the spread of administration has been more pervasive than legislation. Some of this has come about simply because of the requirement of registration of births, marriages and divorces. This requirement of itself extended the control of the law, whether in its traditional Shari'a form or otherwise, to areas which had previously been able to ignore it. In some countries, a marriage could only be registered if it conformed to – or could be made to appear to conform to – the official requirements. A birth or a divorce could only be registered if the marriage had been registered properly. Similarly, the status of a woman's subsequent marriage depended on the administrative procedures of her previous divorce being satisfied. Establishment of inheritance rights depended on all these registrations being completed, and in recent decades the right to enter a European country in order to join family has been crucially dependent on having papers in order. In addition, countries such as Egypt and Pakistan have enforced reforms in their marriage and divorce laws through attaching conditions to registration rather than legislating directly on the point at issue.

As a consequence, the perceptions of what is legitimate or illegitimate in family relations among Muslims settled in Europe are related very much to what particular combination of these four areas of norms – Shari'a, custom, modern legislation and current administrative practice – they bring with them, as well as to the specific content of each of the four. So one notes claims by men of Pakistani origin before British divorce courts for the return of all the gifts they have given to their wives during the marriage, or the conflict when a family wishes to bring into the country an adopted child, usually a nephew, from the Punjab. Earlier one saw quite a high frequency of officially unrecognised Turkish marriages or divorces because of a persistent ignoring of registration requirements in Turkish villages only relying on a combined customary and Islamic practice. Due to better administrative practices and negative consequences when migrating inside or outside of the country, to a large extent this has been replaced with a practice of both registering marriage officially and marrying according to local custom (in 2007, 82 per cent were such marriages in the towns and villages of the Kurdish region).

The European context into which migrants of such backgrounds have moved is one which on the surface is monolithic. But beneath this surface lies a historical reality which before the modern period tended towards the plural. The development of the law in western Europe during the medieval period was characterised by a very slow bringing-together of legal and customary traditions traceable to the varieties of Germanic and Celtic heritages, overlaid by Roman traditions interpreted to differing degrees through Christian ecclesiastical perspectives. From the seventeenth century, humanistic and secularistic philosophies reinterpreted or opposed such complex traditions. From the eighteenth century, culminating during the nineteenth century, a process of unification and codification took place. In conjunction with a progressively more centralised judiciary, legal profession and legislative process, this ended in the pattern of one legal system and one law being applied to the territory controlled by a nation state. It should be noted that, for the purposes of family law, the state-territory can differ from the state-territory controlled by the political state, as in the case of Britain, where the family law of Scotland differs from that of England and Wales.

There remains, however, a recognition that personal legal status cannot be rigidly dependent on one's geographical location at any given moment. It would be disastrous for family stability if crossing a border entailed an automatic change in the mutual rights and obligations of the various members of a family unit. In medieval Europe, stability was maintained by the fact that the church was the arbiter of most family matters, and as the church was one, migration across political boundaries had little effect. With the development of national legal systems, it was the family law of the state to which one belonged which was the arbiter. It became an accepted principle of International Private Law that one's family law of origin moved with one across boundaries. In this way, courts in a given country would find that they had to apply foreign law within their own jurisdictions. However, the choice of foreign law is made by different criteria in mainland Europe and in Britain. In most mainland European countries, it is the nationality of the parties concerned which determines the choice of law, while in Britain it is the domicile, one's 'permanent home', which is the determining factor. Throughout, the formalities of the country have to be observed; it is in the substance of rights and duties that the foreign law gains entry into a domestic system. Thus, Algerians marrying in France have to observe the French rules for formalising the marriage, but the marriage which is created is an Algerian one, and the French courts will in principle enforce the rights and duties laid down by Algerian law. Equally, the French courts will, in principle, have to recognise the marriage of two Algerians or, for that matter, two French partners properly formalised in Algeria; in the first case, the substance of the marriage is governed by Algerian law, while in the second it is governed by French law.

There comes a point when European courts will refuse to implement the foreign law fully. This is when it runs up against what are conceived of as basic principles of morality and public order. This particularly affects divorce, where the general European expectation is that the dissolution of a marriage must go through a judicial procedure. Consequently, most European countries find it difficult to recognise a traditional unrestrained Islamic *talaq*, the declaration by a man divorcing his wife. However, in most Muslim countries, legal reforms have made a judicial hearing incumbent on both parties for a divorce to take effect, although there remains some doubt as to whether the family arbitration council procedure of Pakistan is a judicial or an administrative procedure. European countries also find it impossible to recognise the marriage of minors, which was made legal again in Iran after the Islamic revolution, and no law regulates a minimum age of marriage in for example Yemen and Saudi Arabia, but local custom requires that puberty has been reached before a marriage is consummated. Generally, the average age of entering into marriage has increased in most Muslim countries in recent decades.

For most Muslims, this complex analysis tends to remain irrelevant until they come into contact with some aspect of public administration which will refer to family or personal status law. This need not happen only in direct relation to family courts, as in a case of divorce. The legal personal status of an individual determines access to social welfare payments, status in taxation, entry into the country for settlement or visits, and so on. In each instance, an applicant will have to show that a marriage exists or has ceased to exist, or that children belong to the parents as claimed. The first hurdle is likely to be to persuade a bureaucrat to accept foreign papers; the obstacles raised here can range from a matter of translation to allegations that the papers are forged. Ultimately, a case will go to court, at which point the court will resort to the rules of International Private Law. But most Muslims in western Europe of the immigrant generation come from rural backgrounds, which have only partly adapted to the urban-based legal systems of the past or the present. So, resort by a French court to the rules of Algerian law imposes on the parties concerned the tensions between the countryside and the town in Algeria. The fact that this is taking place in a French court only serves further to confuse. The German–Turkish situation is likely to have been the most extreme because of the gulf between the official position in Turkish law, where the family law code is based on the Swiss law of the 1920s, and the rural custom which remained strong until recently and in many areas ignored the law and the registration procedures. As a result, German courts often found themselves imposing a Turkish family law which was as alien to the Turkish parties to a case as German family law would have been.

The law in certain countries

The particular areas of family law which cause problems tend to be in recognition of polygamous marriages, the status of enforced marriages, divorce and the custody of children. There are variations in the particular details of how individual European countries deal with these issues, but in general terms the issues are similar across mainland western Europe. Where there are significant differences, they tend to be related more to the country of origin than to that of settlement. So the problems arising when dealing with Moroccan marriages and divorces are similar in Belgium and France, while those related to Turks are similar in Belgium and Germany. In the following, therefore, we shall look briefly at the issues in Belgium and Britain as examples.

Belgium will recognise polygamous marriages validly entered into in countries which permit polygamy, while not permitting such marriages to take place in Belgium itself. This, incidentally, does not create too much of a problem with social security payments, because these are usually paid to employees; that is, usually the husband rather than the wife. A more common problem than polygamy is marriages forced on young Moroccan women to prevent them marrying a man of their own choice, especially if he is Belgian and a non-Muslim. Since a woman, according to Moroccan custom, cannot enter a marriage without the consent and presence of her guardian, usually the father, she has no other option than to accept such a marriage or to escape from home and break all her ties with her family. Another issue has been pro forma marriages with the purpose of legalising the situation of one party (entry visa, work permit, naturalisation, and so on). Some Belgian courts have annulled such marriages against the objection of some legal experts that it represents an intrusion into the private life of an individual, in that it questions individual motivations.

In the case of divorce, if one party is Belgian, Belgian law applies; if both are foreign, foreign law applies. Before the most recent reform of Moroccan family law in 2004, there were complications, particularly when a Moroccan man returned home to Morocco, registered a valid *talaq* against his wife in Belgium, and remarried. Belgian courts could in this situation effectively intervene only where they had physical jurisdiction, usually in questions of custody and maintenance. Since Moroccan law today requires a judicial process with both parties involved and present, this situation does not arise in the case of Moroccans any more. The laws are similar in, for example, Algeria, Tunisia and Turkey.

In matters of custody of children, Belgian law takes precedent for children resident in Belgium, with the interests of the child being of primary concern. The courts tend to give custody to the mother if the father is a Turk or a North African, although the father feels entitled, and often is, according to the law of nationality. Consequent cases of removal of children from Belgian jurisdiction by the aggrieved party are not common, but do cause great suffering and attract media attention. In the event of death, if both parents are foreign, Belgian courts grant custody according to the foreign law.

It is worth noting that Belgian courts have increasingly started to take cultural expectations into account when reaching decisions in individual cases. What seems to be happening here, and is possibly happening in other mainland countries, is that the judiciary is looking behind the watershed of Napoleonic codification and reviving a pre-Napoleonic 'common law' tradition. Such cultural considerations have been fiercely criticised by nationalist and populist press and politicians and in social media.

In general terms, the law of France is similar to that of Belgium. However, it should be noted that after a number of disputed custody cases in France relating to children of Algerian fathers, the respective governments reached an accord in 1988 establishing procedures for dealing with such instances. It should also be noted that the Harkis, the *musulmans français*, as they are French citizens in accordance with the Evian agreement, are subject to French personal law.

The Federal Republic of Germany appears, at the legal level, to have little problem in dealing with the family law of resident foreigners of Muslim background. Apart from the Turks, the largest number of Muslims is from the former Yugoslavia, and in both cases the family law of the country of origin is of a European type, in the Turkish case adapted from a 1920s Swiss code.

As more and more people of Turkish origin take up German citizenship under the reforms of the late 1990s, the potential for legal conflict should decline – although this is likely to focus attention much more closely on claims founded explicitly on religious grounds.

The International Private Law rules of England tend in practice to be rather more complicated because of the criterion of 'domicile' rather than nationality. While the legal definition of domicile is comparatively straightforward, it is case law which determines the elements needed to establish that a domicile in England has been acquired; in other words, it is not purely a matter of acquiring permanent residence. However, as most Muslims are now settled in Britain, have acquired UK citizenship and have children born and growing up in the country, the courts tend to assume that an English domicile has been acquired. As a result, English, or Scottish, law is usually applied. But there do remain instances where a foreign law has to be called in to help solve a case. As the community retains very close connections with the parts of the extended family still living abroad, the frequency of marriage or divorce cases across the frontiers has only diminished to a limited extent. Traditionally, English law refused to recognise any marriage or consequences flowing from any marriage conducted in a polygamous system, regardless of whether the particular marriage in question was polygamous or not. A combination of court cases and legislation has now effectively banished that view into legal history. At the same time, however, new definitions have been introduced which do not always function well together: permanent residence and intended matrimonial home have been added to domicile as criteria for determining which law should apply in a particular instance, and they sometimes overlap, with consequent uncertainty as to which criterion should take precedence. Lawyers often find this difficult to sort out, so one wonders how ordinary members of the community cope!

This situation may be part of the reason why Britain is the only European country in which the demand has with some persistence been made for the introduction of some form of Islamic family law into the domestic legal structure for Muslims. The first recorded demand for this came from the Union of Muslim Organisations in 1975 in a petition to Parliament. It would be wrong to suggest that the demand has widespread support, but it has had sufficient support for it to be raised at regular intervals since. Parallel to discussions about recognition, Muslim legal experts have drawn up marriage contracts and wills taking both British and Islamic law into account. It is difficult to estimate the popularity of these, but the phenomenon is spreading in different European countries.

It is not surprising that until the late 1980s inheritance hardly figured on the list of legal issues arising out of the Muslim presence in Europe. The age distribution of the community was so concentrated in the younger and child-bearing ages that the death rate in relation to the community size was minute. In addition, outside Britain, Muslims in Europe have owned only very little immoveable property, their land and houses being in the country of origin. All European laws are agreed that moveable properties, such as bank accounts, are distributed by the personal law of the deceased; only immoveable property is subject to the law of the country in which it is situated. In Britain, where the community is older and the number of deaths has therefore started to rise, many Muslims own property in an economy where home-ownership is common. But with children staying in the country with the full status of citizenship, passing on immoveable property to them in accordance with English law shows little tension in relation to expectations of custom. With the passing of time, it seems inevitable that in most of western Europe, as the number of deaths starts rising with an ageing community, there will be problems of conflicts of law and expectations over the disposal of immoveable property. There will be complications arising out of dual nationality, which during the last two decades increasingly have become allowed in several European countries, for example in Belgium, Denmark, France and Sweden. In some countries, like Germany, dual citizenship is accepted but with restrictions. Polygamous marriages may not be numerous, but the legal problems which they can give rise to are. There are instances where a *talaq* may be recognised in one country but not in another, with implications for inheritance disputes between spouses.

In many European countries, though hardly at all in Britain, the issue of mixed marriages has become a subject of special interest. One must, however, be clear what a mixed marriage is in this context. On the one hand, we are talking of a marriage between someone who is Muslim, at least in ethnic and cultural background, and someone who is usually of some European national-ity, and who may be a lapsed Christian, agnostic, atheist or just areligious. Anecdotal evidence suggests that one is most often talking of a liaison between a nominal Muslim and an areligious European. Such marriages place enormous stresses on the families and the parties themselves. The parties bring into the marriage often very different expectations. If the couple have been married in a European country and then later move to the country of the non-European partner, the change in circumstances adds further pressures. The result is a very high failure-rate of such marriages, with all the consequent possibilities of dispute over property and custody of children; in fact, the vast majority of inter-national custody and property disputes arise out of mixed marriages.

Of course, so far as the law is concerned, it is not religion but the law attached to the parties which determine whether the marriage is mixed. This fits well with the rules of International Private Law which refer to national legislation, not to religious adherence. So, if a particular national law, like the Lebanese, refers to a religious law, this is coincidental to the European court, which will regard itself as implementing Lebanese law, not some form of Muslim or Christian law.

The few countries which collect statistics in this area do so by nationality, so while we may guess at the numbers of mixed-faith marriages, we can only say something certain about the number of mixed-nationality marriages. Thus, French data from 1981 recorded a total of 26,000 children of mixed marriages. For the year 1983, West Germany recorded over 2,000 marriages between Turkish and German citizens, of which nearly 400 were between a Turkish woman and a German man; more than 1,700 further marriages with other 'Muslim' nationalities were recorded in the same year. While the rates have gone up since then, the change has not been of major significance. Statistics show that the vast majority (more than 95 per cent) of Muslims with a Bangladeshi or Pakistani background, both men and women, living in Britain and Norway married someone with the same national background. Anthropological research suggests that marriage patterns differ for migrants with an Arab Muslim background; in particular, men of this background marry, to a higher degree, outside their respective national, religious or ethnic group.

There is evidence that access to a European court system may of itself be contributing to changes in attitudes and perceptions. Faced with situations which are felt to be difficult, either party has the option to accept them and cope, or to reject them and seek a remedy. In traditional society, the second option was usually to be found in internal family negotiation and pressure, so a resolution might be found by identifying and using the interests and powers within the family. There was little scope for appeal to a principle – even an Islamic principle – other than as one part of a larger complex of factors. Access to a court in a European country appears to add a further option, namely to go outside the traditional system. Unpublished research has analysed the divorces before the Birmingham divorce court in 1983–4. By using names as a guide, it was possible to identify almost 200 cases involving Muslims over the two years, eighty-four in the first year and 112 in the second year. It should first be noted that this amounted to less than 2.5 per cent of the total number of divorce cases in a population which at that time made up less than 10 per cent of the city, and which was very highly concentrated in the 'divorcing' age range. So the Muslim divorce-rate was very low. By 1984, two-thirds of the divorce petitions had been initiated by wives, and half of these on a claim of cruelty by their husbands. For both years, well over half of the husbands' petitions for divorce were on the basis of desertion or separation, again an indicator that a wife had taken an initiative to resolve an unsatisfactory situation. According to later research (2007), divorce patterns are similar to the wider population's, with the addition of stating the reason 'leaving a forced marriage'.

Cultural changes

It is inevitably in the field of family life that the meetings of cultures resulting from immigration and settlement are concentrated, and law is, of course, not the only external factor which imposes constraints or opens up possibilities. Cultural change arises also from other pressures. We have already pointed to the new circumstances brought about by the very process of migration. Such circumstances have consequences on family relations which defy generalisation.

In some situations in the country of origin, where the extended network of nuclear households is broken up by migration, women left behind to administer the absent men's remittances have gained an experience of autonomy and responsibility which cannot be undone when they themselves join the migration, but which can create tension through its challenge to the traditional male role. In other situations, the ideological power of purdah (i.e. the public female seclusion) is such that it can become a central element in the defence of identity and thus lead to an isolation of individual women in the immigrant community.

Moving into low-paid jobs in Europe, working unsocial hours, and consistent exposure to much higher rates of unemployment: none of these factors have of themselves led necessarily to Muslim families trying to augment their total income by sending wives and young people into the employment market. The Muslim communities of Indian subcontinental origin in Britain have consistently shown a lower level of household income than those of Sikh and Hindu families. This is evidently attributable to a great reluctance to allow adult women into the wider job market, a reluctance which is explicable in terms of the strict Islamic purdah of an Indian subcontinental tradition. The kinds of income which women can earn in such circumstances are of the lowest-paid kind, such as manual tasks like sewing on a home-work, piece-rate basis where there is no protection of the collective kind offered by trade unions or government inspection. The lack of interesting job prospects also influence the life expectancies and choices of women.

However, this is clearly not a phenomenon associated with Muslims generally. While the description would be recognisable for large sections of the North African communities in various parts of western Europe, it does not apply to Turkish Muslims. Women of the immigrant generation from Turkey have a much higher level of industrial employment than Muslims of other origins, regardless of which country one looks at. Similarly, it is clear that Muslim communities of South Asian origin show a very different pattern if one looks at people of merchant and professional backgrounds. In Britain, this would be the case particularly with those who have come from Kenya or Uganda. It is evident that being Muslim does not necessarily entail similar choices of lifestyle or gender role by groups which differ in economic, social and cultural background and experience.

Changes in family relations are not restricted to those between male and female, especially as children arrive, go through school, mature and marry. Parents of the immigrant generation are often accustomed through their own backgrounds to their role being both authoritative and authoritarian. In a traditional context, changes certainly took place, but gradually, so that new situations had a major area of connection with what went before. The change arising out of immigration has usually been sudden and profound. Any similarities are likely to be coincidental and minimal. As children grow up, parents find that their own experience becomes irrelevant. As they try to guide their children in matters of behaviour, choice of companions and careers and, most significantly, marriage, parents often find themselves being authoritarian because they can no longer be authoritative.

In this process, an appeal to an Islamic model often becomes a major, and sometimes a central, element in the developing relationship. But by the very nature of that appeal, a factor is introduced into the relationship between parents and children over which neither party has control and through which external parties are offered entry. As discussed earlier in this chapter, the customs of large segments of the cultures from which Muslims in Europe originate are to be found in rural-based oral traditions which combine a variety of elements, only one of which is the 'high' Islamic tradition of urban scholarship. The villagers migrating to the European cities brought with them this complex baggage in a form which was perceived as an integrated whole. If part was to be defended as Islamic in the face of children's growing challenge to parental authority, then the whole had to be defended on that same basis. This is at least one reason why Muslim movements of the more 'popular' kind (Barelwis, Sufi *tariqas*, and so on) retain a strong following in Europe.

But the parents are challenged in this from two quarters. Their children are likely to have an educational background which their parents do not share. On the one hand, the children are proceeding en masse beyond the basic primary education of at least some of their parents. On the other hand, the children are receiving an education which encourages questioning. The situation in which the children are growing up is one where the parents' inherited answers to specific problems can only work by isolating themselves in an inward-looking cultural enclave. Large numbers of young Muslims – the proportion differs from community to community – are seeking to develop responses to their own felt needs and perceptions of the future, responses which can work in the European context, responses which allow them to be European without breaking with Islam.

To take one example, the practice of Punjabi parents arranging marriages for their children, a mixture of Islamic practice and a particular local customary process, is adapting to new circumstances. More and more, the children are taking the initiative to make the first introduction, the parents are brought in through a process of negotiation, and the final arrangement is thus the product of a family consensus. Increasingly, the gender roles are also changing within such a marriage, especially if the couple is reasonably well-educated. There is a sharing of domestic and childcare responsibilities, coupled with an expectation that both parties may have careers to follow. Often, these choices are explained as being legitimately Islamic, even as being more correct, in Islamic terms, than the practices of their parents.

In fact, there is growing evidence that young people are meeting formally and informally in small groups on a regular basis to discuss the source texts. Qur'an and Hadith are explored as fresh texts, without the intervention of centuries of Islamic scholarship. In consequence, the texts are interpreted in the light of current needs and with methods which are based on the intellectual tools acquired through education in European schools. These hermeneutical methods are hardly systematic, but in the process of the exercise there is a growing awareness of the need for a more systematic mode of analysis.

The first need which arises is a desire to have access to the original texts. For Muslims who are not Arabic speakers, this has obviously meant learning the Arabic of the Qur'an. During the late 1980s, there was a great expansion in Arabic courses within the Muslim communities in Britain, and many young people have since chosen to make Arabic the subject of their first university degree. More than half the annual intake of undergraduates choosing to study Arabic at British universities today are British Muslims, a group which was completely absent four decades ago. The question of language as a tool for religious study is more ambiguous among Turks. During the 1980s, again, it seems clear that Arabic regained a position previously lost at the height of the Kemalist reforms. But Turkish retains a position which clearly goes beyond the definition of 'mother tongue' and transgresses into the field of a religious language. On the face of things, North African and other native Arabic speakers should have a more direct and simple access to the pristine sources of Qur'an and Hadith. However, they are faced with the much more subtle challenge of distinguishing between modern and Qur'anic Arabic.

While the children are thus implicitly, and sometimes explicitly, challenging the validity of their parents' Islamic defence, the parents are also being challenged from another direction, namely by the Muslim organisations and their leaderships. This is especially the case with those movements and organisations which fall within the general family of *Salafi*, puritan and Shari'a-based, such as sympathisers with the so-called Wahhabis, Muslim Brethren, *Hizb al-Tahrir* and the followers of Mawdudi. From these quarters, there is a distinct and clear criticism of the various forms of accommodation which have been made over the centuries between 'high' Islam and local social and religious customs. This has meant not only a rejection, in varying degrees, of the traditions of the Sufi orders, but also a comprehensive attack against popular forms of religious expression which do not find sanction in the Shari'a. The activities and teachings of such movements often imply very strongly a serious critique of what most 'ordinary' Muslims – certainly those of the immigrant generation – have regarded as their way of life and devotion.

A final factor contributing to the weakening of traditional Muslim cultures in European cities is the fact that, in that situation, the cultures themselves are being mixed. The differing cultural entities, which tend to define themselves as Muslim, lived distinctly from each other until migration started. The migration into cities brought them into touch with each other and imposed a necessity of interaction which had previously been minimal. When the migration was into a European city, the self-definition as Muslim immediately drew attention to the differences: why should this marriage or burial custom or that conception of a patriarchal family be more correctly Muslim than another practised by a neighbour?

The holistic nature of the traditional village culture, bringing together a variety of historical components into an integrated whole, at first sight seems to coincide with the ideological statement of Islam as a 'complete and whole way of life'. But the two are, in fact, in conflict, as the latter tends to seek to purify the former. The circumstances of migration, the situation into which Muslims have settled in European cities, and the adaptations which are being made, especially as the young grow up to be the first European Muslim generation, all impose the need to analyse. The old way has to be analysed into discrete parts so that Islam can be identified. The emphasis of the identification of Islam can be on the Qur'an and Qur'anic principles or it can be on aspects of the Shari'a tradition. In either case, one proceeds to 'reassemble' these Islamic components, together with the components arising out of the migration and settlement experience, into a new complex whole which functions more successfully in European urban, industrial life. As a universal religion with a long historical experience of successfully integrating into new cultures, it would be extremely surprising if Islam were not to follow exactly this kind of path also in Europe.

Among young Muslim intellectuals, such developments proceeded apace in the 1990s. On the one hand, movements such as *Jama'at-al-Tabligh*, *Minhaj al-Qur'an* and the Muslim Brotherhood, all initially introduced into Europe from bases in the countries of origin, have taken on distinctly European forms. On the other, individual scholars, most notably Tareq Ramadan, have embarked on a search for an independent and rational investigation of what it means to be a Muslim in contemporary Europe. These debates find expression not only in externalities such as dress and organisational structures, but also in the increasing attention being paid to theological and legal substance. In this debate, classical Islamic concepts drawn from medieval debates among scholars of jurisprudence are being revived, most centrally North African ideas out of the Maliki *madhhab*, around the principles and fundamental purposes (*maqasid*) of the

Shari'a as divine intent, and how these can be interpreted flexibly into situations particular to time and place. Of importance also is the development of Islamic advice about the minority situation (*fiqh al-aqaliyya*) offered by organisations, individual scholars, and states, easily accessible on webpages. One such organisation, growing in importance, is the European Council For Fatwa Research headed by Qatar-based scholar Yusuf al-Qaradawi.

CHAPTER 9

Muslim organisations

In any consideration of the development of Muslim organisational activity in western Europe, three main processes of establishment can be identified: groups which arose out of the community and its own perceptions of its needs; groups set up as extensions of organisations and movements in the country of origin; and groups set up by governments or government-related agencies.

During the first phase of Muslim immigration, the migrants were mostly men on their own coming for a limited period. The fact that they were men on their own meant that requirements of religious practice were minimal – it was usually sufficient to be able to pray. This minimal religious practice was further marginalised by the expectation of imminent return home. The situation changed fundamentally when the migration of Muslim workers became an immigration of Muslim families. Firstly, the sense of temporariness began to weaken, to be replaced by a sense of permanence. Secondly, the presence of wives and children critically widened the scope for interaction with the surrounding society, especially in education, health and social welfare, as indicated in Chapter 8. As a result, large areas of traditional culture came under question, creating a need for the construction of institutions which could either help defend tradition or lower the level of tension.

It is necessary first to attempt to present an overall perspective on the processes involved in establishing Muslim organisations in Europe and an identification of the factors, both in origins and in the European environment, which have affected the nature of organisations. Certainly in Britain, and probably elsewhere in Europe, these elements have been a major force in determining the balance between and the character of the institutional integration of Muslim communities.

The context of origins

The study of Muslim communities in Europe has suffered from a lack of awareness of the complex of structure and culture from which the communities come. It is certainly fair to complain that, on the whole, British race relations and ethnic minority studies have, with the partial exception of some social anthropologists, shown either ignorance or lack of interest in the contexts out of which the immigrated communities have come, which is somewhat surprising in view of the oft-repeated assertion of the weight of imported 'cultural baggage'. However, the situation has vastly improved in the last decade. The setting up of the Cardiff-based Centre for the Study of Islam in the UK is an important step towards establishing sound scholarship.

In any consideration of the growth and role of Muslim organisations in Europe, it would seem to be absolutely essential to consider the situation in the countries from which the relevant communities have come. This is not a simple matter, since all of these countries, by the era of major emigration, no longer contained the more or less stable and integrated cultural complex which had developed through the Islamic phase of their history. Even in the Anatolian part of the Ottoman empire (roughly equivalent to modern Turkey), arguably the most recently Islamicised major region of emigration to Europe, a cultural *modus vivendi* had been reached between Islamic, Arabic, Persian, Turkish and long-standing folk cultures which justifies the application of the epithets 'stable' and 'integrated'. The disruption in stability had been caused to a great extent by the expansion of European influence, which imported a new set of criteria and constraints, initially of an economic and military nature, but which quite quickly became cultural and intellectual, even civilisational.

Consequently, the Muslim organisational tendencies, which have formed the roots of those we see about us in Europe today, are the product not only of traditional Islamic processes but also – and very significantly – of the organised Muslim reaction to the expansion of European influence during the last few centuries. This is most clearly the case in the Indian subcontinent, where various reform movements appeared to defend and reassert Islamic ideals in the context of expanding European power. The earliest of these appeared in the eighteenth century, as the Mogul empire was weakened after the death of Aurangzeb. A second phase, which has led directly to many of the organisations of the present, arose in the context of direct British rule after 1858. More recently, much of the Muslim organisational activity of Turkey has arisen out of the dramatic change of circumstances associated with Kemal Atatürk's policies during the 1920s.

Such contexts have contributed to influencing the nature of organisations as well as their language and agendas. The impact of political and economic change has meant that many of the organisations in question have selected for emphasis those aspects of Islam which are perceived most to differentiate it from foreign influence. Usually, such aspects have tended to be based in the Islamic law, the Shari'a, and the training of cadres well qualified in Shari'a has been high on the agenda. In some movements, this has been extended to a programme of re-Islamicising the state. The availability of new organisational structures has often been used to great effect, as in the case of the Muslim Brotherhood in Egypt and, perhaps even more remarkably, by the *Jama'at-i-Islami* in Pakistan.

In some ways, such 'modern' organisations, almost always of Sunni back-ground, resemble the traditionally more hierarchic and structured forms of Shi'ite sects. On the other hand, the looser forms of the Sunni tradition also continue to be found. These are so loose that they deserve the term movement rather than organisation. They tend to be held together by some form of loyalty to or identification with the personality and ideas of a founder, and to that extent there is a similarity even with the Sunni law schools, the *madhahib*, where there is a continuity of teaching rather than of structure.

The traditional Sufi orders cannot be ignored. Traditionally, they have exhibited a wide range of organisational forms, some so loose that they can hardly be considered orders in any meaningful sense, others tightly structured and controlled with a hierarchical leadership. These orders have shown a remarkable ability to survive, even as their social base, especially in towns and cities, has disintegrated with economic and social change. A variant on this are the village- and tribal-based spiritual orders, where authority is vested in 'holy men', such as those described by Gellner as 'saints of the Atlas' or the *pirs* of the North Indian countryside.

Whatever the social base or nature of such organisations and movements, they have in common a foundation in some form of Islamic legitimacy. Gellner identifies three types of such legitimacy, namely the Qur'an, including its exten-sion with reference to the Tradition (Sunna), the consensus of the community (*ijma'*) and the line of succession. Different organisations and movements derive their legitimacy from one or more of these sources in varying proportions. Gellner's assertion that the Qur'an sits in ultimate judgement is, arguably, over-stated, as it is possible that it may become the property of a particular tendency and that in this manner the interpreter gains control of the text, at least so far as his adherents are concerned. In such a case, the consensus would seem to have an equal role to play. Within certain Shi'ite sects, and according to some of Ayatollah Khomeini's statements, the line of succession, that is, through the imams, has an authority surpassing that of the Book. With this proviso, it is pos-sible to identify the functioning of these three types of legitimacy continuing in the movements of the modern Muslim world, as well as in the movements and organisations to be found in Europe.

The establishment of organisations

The immediate and critical change brought about by the reconstruction of forms of community life among Muslims in western Europe was that organisa-tion became necessary. However much movements and organisations in the Muslim countries of origin may have been thriving, there was not an intrinsic necessity for specifically religious organisations with particular goals in order for ordinary Muslims to be able to lead their daily religious lives. The mosque was available as a community facility and did not have to be linked to a particular organisation, although many were. In fact, during the twentieth century in many countries the government has taken over responsibility for this service through its Ministry of Religious Affairs or of *awqaf* (religious endowments) – much like the government in Denmark is responsible for the church there. The Islamic religious education of children tended to be something naturally available, whether in formal classes in school or mosque or to be imbibed through the general Islamic content of the culture – all of this without individual families having to make any particular effort to make the facility available.

The one exception to this picture has been Turkey where, in a sense, this migration from effortless Islamic practice to a situation where conscious efforts had to be made to create facilities had already taken place as the result of Kemalist reforms. In consequence, movements such as the *Süleymançi* or the Gülen, with their respective vast educational activities, are in some sense much more 'European' movements than most of those originating outside the Turkish experience.

The context into which Muslim families settled in Europe was one where nothing could be taken for granted in terms of access to Islamic facilities. In fact, there are indications that many Muslims perceived the non-Muslim environment as being actively inimical to things Islamic: a study of the Pakistani community in Oxford suggests that many wives saw themselves as joining their husbands to 'save' them from being estranged from their culture and religion. The provision of facilities for prayer, teaching Islam to children, access to halal food and proper burial – these and many other matters which had been taken for granted at home now had to be consciously sought out.

The needs were met by the formation of Muslim organisations primarily through two routes. Certainly during the earlier phases, the most common process was local community initiative, often the work of a few individuals only who identified a particular requirement which they then proceeded to meet. The kinds of organisations being created thus were not necessarily explicitly Muslim; most were probably ethnic-, regional- or village-based. The Muslim organisations were especially related to mosque projects and, in parallel, to the establishment of some form of Islamic instruction for children. However, from a comparatively early stage, organisations and movements from the countries of origin began to set up agencies or branches in Europe. With time, they have come to dominate the scene, as the smaller local groups have found it useful to have access to the power, resources and prestige of these larger movements.

Beyond such general remarks, the detailed process of organisation has to be considered in relation to the constraints imposed by the European context, and those constraints vary significantly according to the circumstances of individual countries. The most influential element has been the particular legal system governing association, with funding sources being a further factor. In most of Europe, the public authorities offer financial advantages to organisations with educational, cultural and, sometimes, religious aims. But to take advantage of this, the association has to have a form which the public authorities will recognise. This usually means registering under a law of associations and meeting the criteria laid down by the law. Thus, Muslim organisations have had to adopt committee structures, the concepts of membership and officers, regular subscriptions, annual general meetings, voting, and so on.

Such forms of organisation have traditionally been alien to Islam, at least in its Sunni variant, with its absence of church and hierarchy. It is perhaps no coincidence that the few organisations which already had aspects of such structures in their countries of origin were among the earliest to find success in transferring their activities to Europe. As obvious examples, one could point to the *Jama'at-i-Islami* from Pakistan and the *Süleymançis* from Turkey.

The variations in the European legal context have resulted in significant differences in the extent and nature of organisation. In Britain, the criteria in law for setting up an organisation are minimal. No registration is required, although there are tax advantages in satisfying the requirements of the Charity Commissioners, as there can be legal advantages in registering as a company. A consequence of such lack of definition has been a proliferation of organisations, many with ambitious titles and consisting of a private address, a letterhead, and little else. French and Belgian requirements that organisations needed to have a minimum number of French or Belgian citizens in their leadership have been an important obstacle in the way of such proliferation. When France in 1981 abolished the special requirements for associations of foreigners, the consequence was a major growth in the number of associations, although still not on the British scale.

Continuing development

Once established, the elements influencing the further development of such organisations become more complex. Funding becomes a major consideration, as does the continuing earning of legitimacy. Related to these aspects are developments both in the countries of origin and in the country of settlement, and sometimes the development in other Muslim environments around the world.

Settlement in Europe has not entailed the severing of relations with the country of origin. Primarily, of course, family relations have been preserved and with them links to the locality of origin. Local developments thus retain a direct effect on the immediate interests of the migrated communities.

Wider developments – political, economic and social – in the countries of origin, however, also continue to have a major effect on the Muslims in Europe through a variety of channels. For individuals and groups with political ambitions, the émigré community represents an arena for operations free of the constraints at home. This was very evident during the 1970s in West Germany, when various Turkish political groupings, banned in Turkey, could raise resources and support. France had experienced something similar during the Algerian war of independence and arrested thousands of Algerians in France to deprive the revolution of support. More recently, the Pakistani community in Britain has been used by both Benazir Bhutto and her opponents in this manner. A similar process has taken place among the Kurds in Sweden and Germany. The recruitment of supporters and fighters to different wars presented as jihad has become an increasing phenomenon, recently reaching culmination in relation to the campaigns of so-called Islamic State since it proclaimed a caliphate in 2014.

Such political developments also affect the European environment in which Muslims have to operate, usually in a constraining manner. Perceptions of Islam and Muslims in the wider European society have been determined much more by international political events than by the settled Muslim communities themselves. The Iranian revolution, the Lebanese civil war, the activities of the Palestinian resistance as well as the many conflicts in the Middle East between 2010 and 2015, which are likely to continue for some time, have all tended to strengthen the inherited anti-Muslim bias of centuries, a sentiment which has often easily been reinforced by racism and racist movements. The effect of such hostile public opinion has consistently been to limit the space in which Muslim organisations can constructively manoeœuvre, and some have adopted the only other alternative, namely aggressive self-assertion.

Developments of European origin impose their own influence on Muslim organisations, either directly or indirectly, by changing the context in which they operate. Thus, immigration policy affects organisations both indirectly, through context, and directly. On the one hand, they are forced to move immigration policy higher up their agendas and find difficulties in recruiting staff, while on the other hand immigration policy has tended to encourage a more strongly racist or xenophobic atmosphere. Policy statements made by prominent politicians seeking votes usually ignore the negative impact on the minorities whose votes are not deemed worth seeking. Major policy changes, as with Britain's educational reforms since 1988, can have a significant impact on Muslim organisations which were not intended, even if they were considered. Events such as the affair of *The Satanic Verses* have had quite dramatic effects on the whole scene of organised Islam in Britain.

There is little doubt that questions of funding are interlinked with all these various factors. Very few organisations, other than the smallest and least ambitious, are not dependent on funding sources outside their own membership or circles of sympathisers. There are a few organisations which, as branches of government to some degree, are funded by a government to perform the functions determined by that government. The best example of this is the West German branch of the *Diyanet*, DITIB. In most cases, however, organisations have to form and to formulate themselves in such a way as to attract the necessary funding.

Much has been speculated about the extent of funding by wealthy Arab states, but very little research has been done into either the actual extent or the possible concomitant influence. In Britain, it was noticeable that the number of annual mosque registrations grew suddenly between three- and four-fold from 1974. There is little doubt that this was associated with the rise in oil prices, but there is equally little way of knowing how much of that growth was based on Arab money, how much on hopes of Arab money, and how much simply on growing self-confidence.

In very few of the cases where mosques and organisations are known to have received substantial gifts from the oil economies is it possible to show a direct correlation between funding source and subsequent policy. The fact that DITIB in Germany, through the Turkish *Diyanet*, or the Islamic Foundation in Britain have theological lines and adopt policies which are in harmony with those of Saudi Arabia, even if not in total coincidence, is evidence of an initial mutual sympathy and common interest rather than of a Saudi-dominated relationship. Iraqi funding for a mosque in Birmingham did not make that mosque a mouthpiece for Saddam Hussein, nor did the Muslim College in West London or the main mosque in Malmö (Sweden) take orders from Qadhdhafi's Libya.

There is little doubt that some imaginative presentation work is done in relation to funding sources, as well as some judicious selection. Organisations with explicitly Sufi, or *pir*-related, or other 'unorthodox' tendencies simply do not bother to approach official Saudi sources. The fact is that most funders, private or governmental, are simply insufficiently aware of the specific circumstances of their applicants and are seldom in a position to assess the use to which their gifts are put. There is, of course, a degree of interrelationship as regards general theological and political tendency, but the mediating and interpreting role played by the personalities directly involved ensures that that interrelationship is usually open and flexible. A growing trend is that financiers demand a seat on the board if they fully finance a mosque or a cultural institute.

While the degree of influence of Muslim funding sources remains wide open to question, the influence of European funding sources is much more direct, both on agendas and on organisational structure. European funding of Muslim activities has come either from governmental agencies or from trusts.

As indicated previously, to get access to such sources, organisations have had to adopt structures which are recognisable by the potential funder, structures which are often a break with traditional forms. Sometimes this remains an outward form, as in the case of a number of Belgian associations where the Belgian non-Muslim committee members have become essentially 'sleeping partners', or where a hierarchical, family-based association continues its hierarchical ways behind the guise of an elected committee. In other situations, the desire to obtain public or trust funding has constrained informally constituted, charismatically led Sufi groups to adopt a formal structure. Of itself, this has been a contradiction with past practice, and it has granted the potential, at least, to committee members to challenge the charismatic leadership by resorting to the courts.

In Sweden and Denmark, one has seen quite direct effects on the very process of the formation of organisations produced by the nature of specific funding provisions. In Denmark, the free school legislation entitles any group of parents over a certain number to establish their own school with public funding. As a result, more than twenty such schools have been formed. But in Copenhagen, the largest of these schools has occasionally had the problem that a splinter group of parents has grown sufficiently large to break away and form its own new school. In Sweden, the government makes provision for state support for 'free church' associations. Again, there is a minimum size threshold which was a contributory factor in the splitting of the first Muslim federation in the early 1980s. Through additional splits and new initiatives there are now six Muslim federations.

In some ways more serious has been the effect that the conditions of public funding have had on the public language and the aims and goals of Muslim organisations. With the short-term exception of the Netherlands and the peculiar case of Belgium, the general attitude of public authorities in Europe has been that support for cultural and educational purposes is legitimate while that for religious purposes is not. The most obvious consequence of this is the spread of the concept of the 'Islamic cultural centre', a concept which, if it is found in the main parts of the Muslim world, has a completely different import. Programmes are prioritised and presented in such a way as to emphasise the preservation of the culture of origin, including language, arts and crafts, with religion taking the status of a footnote, at least in public presentation. One Turkish Muslim association in Denmark first constituted itself as a sports and cultural association, partly to encourage local authority funding and partly to avoid the attentions of the *Diyanet*, and then found that it could not obtain an entry permit for an imam because it was not a religious community.

The pressure imposed on Muslim organisations by European official, legal, political and bureaucratic expectations is such that Islam has to become an ethnic identity. Such a constraint may not be too serious a problem for Sikhs or Gujerati Hindus, but it is serious for Muslims throughout Europe, who come from a variety of ethnic backgrounds, even if in some countries they may have the same nationality of origin. It is also serious, and perhaps more so, in inadvertently imposing an ethnic restriction on Islam, which is as contradictory to its nature as a universal religion as it is to Christianity.

Questions to be asked

So far, this has been necessarily an impressionistic survey of the establishment and development of Muslim organisations, with an emphasis on the factors contributing to determining the directions they have taken. The second part of this chapter will seek to present basic information about the main movements and organisations of significance at national and regional levels in Europe, and each country chapter has sought to identify their places within the overall Muslim scene in that country. In the meantime, the purpose of the discussion so far has been to present sufficient background of a general nature to be able to identify the kinds of questions and issues which need to be addressed if one wishes to assess the nature of a particular organisation or movement, in terms of its internal processes as well as in terms of its relations to the countries of origin and of settlement.

First, one must look at the origins of the organisation or movement in question. Has it arisen primarily out of a local European situation, or is it in some way a branch or agency of a movement based in the country of origin or another Muslim area? Whatever its origins, has it retained those first links or has it subsequently changed allegiance?

Second, what is its theology, understood in the widest sense also of political and legal theology? There is a question here of relating the subject to the wider pattern of Islamic debate, both in relation to traditional Islamic trends and also in relation to the various 'modernistic' trends. The declarations and policy stances of the European branches need to be compared with their origins: do the various tendencies amend the mainstream views of their movement to accommodate the European milieu? To what extent do their spokesmen adapt to the 'ignorant' views of their European-based sympathisers so as to retain their allegiance? It is not unusual for groups of Muslims without advanced Islamic training to present Mu'tazilite views on the createdness of the Qur'an – is Mu'tazilism in this way sneaking in by the back door in Europe?

Third, what is the nature of the structure of the organisation? This has to be answered both in relation to the country of origin (in terms of formal to informal, hierarchical to consensual, charismatic to scholastic) and in relation to the country of settlement. On this latter point, it is not insignificant that since 1980 a number of West German mosque associations have changed legal status from *eingetragener Verein* (e.V) to *Stiftung*, where the first is a democratic association structure and the latter is controlled by the appointed trustees. A similar development has been taking place in the Netherlands, and both are associated with the increased influence of the Turkish *Diyanet* (DITIB) at the expense mainly of the *Süleymançi* movement (*Islamische Kulturzentren*).

Fourth, and related, is the crucial question of internal authority. This operates at two levels which are interrelated, namely Islamic and social. Anthropologists

would here distinguish between ascribed and earned authority. One of the problems of Muslim organisations in Europe is that, due to their being transplanted
out of an environment with continuity of tradition, leadership has usually to be
earned. Very few leaderships, collective or individual, can move into an ascribed
position; they can take over or be appointed, but to retain an effective position
they constantly have to earn and defend their gains. This means compromise
with the followers and the exploitation of all available resources to be able to
provide them with the services which they expect. This relates again to the
question of Islamic legitimacy. Organisations are in competition with each other
both for resources and for adherents, and a balance has to be found between
legitimisation by distribution of benefits (dependent on access to resources) and
legitimisation on Islamic grounds (Qur'an, consensus and/or line of succession).

Fifth, the purpose of amassing resources is to respond to needs by providing
programmes of activities. Most widely, this has tended to be instruction for the
young through the so-called Qur'an schools. Thus, a number of movements
which have met with little popular support in the country of origin have been
able to attract a wider circle of sympathisers, at least on a temporary basis, by
providing that service. Other activities are not insignificant: publishing, cultural
production, preaching (witness the work of the multinational *Jama'at-al-Tabligh*),
provision of halal food and burial, organisation of the *hajj*, sports clubs and *'id*
parties.

Sixth, what is the social base of recruitment? The vast majority of organisations still recruit primarily on an ethnic/national basis and many on a more
narrow base than that: clan, caste, region, craft, and so on. I have deliberately
not used the term class at this point, although it may become relevant with the
coming-of-age of the European-born generation and their children. One cannot
ignore, either, the small but growing number of professional associations,
over which there is a certain amount of competition by the larger, traditional
religious-political movements. Over the last two decades, a number of attempts
to start national Muslim youth movements have appeared both from young
people themselves and from the older organisations, and there is no doubt that
one aspect of the internal Muslim dynamics in Britain around the Rushdie affair
was the matter of control over such youth groups.

Seventh, there is the question of the personnel of an organisation. What
kind of people does an organisation seek to recruit for its salaried positions, if
such exist? Many mosques have only limited choice because they depend on
secondments either by the *Diyanet* or by a government agency from their own
country or from another country, such as Saudi Arabia (not necessarily of Saudi
Arabs). Other mosques have imported officials, especially in the early phases of
establishment, from their regions of origin and meeting the traditional criteria
of a village imam. The character of the particular person involved, the circumstances of recruitment and the nature of the importing organisation all combine

to determine the point at which a new appointee starts his functions: does he start from zero and have to earn every step of his way to respect and spokesmanship for his community? Is he dependent on the management committee which employs him, and how far does that expose him to exploitation and manipulation, ultimately with the threat of redundancy and expulsion under immigration regulations? Or has he come at the behest of a sending authority, whether this be a centralised structure like the *Diyanet* or the *Jama'at-i-Islami* or an inherited structure like a Sufi order or a Pakistani *pir*-based group? Recruitment by such processes has often meant that the personnel have little idea of the European urban environment in which they have to provide religious leadership and guidance; it has also often meant that they are undereducated simply in Islamic terms.

Eighth is the matter of the language or idiom in which a particular group expresses itself. This is probably the least researched area of all, since it requires an intimate knowledge not only of what is going on in Europe, both in terms of the internal communications of Muslim organisations and their presentations publicly both to their own community and the wider society, but also requires an extensive experience of those movements and communities' forms of expression in the countries of origin currently and historically. The comparison in time and geographical and cultural space is absolutely essential for any valid evaluation to be made. Areas which have to be given attention are the differences in spoken and written expressions of the organisation's aims and activities, requiring an analysis and comparison of expressions in the various languages used by the organisation concerned.

Ninth is the unspoken language, the symbols used by a given organisation and its followers. These symbols can take the form of pictorial expression, like the posters, illustrations, cartoons and diagrams which figure so widely in Muslim publications and buildings. Some of these are comparatively easy to interpret for the outsider, such as the persistent coincidence between Turkish-Ottoman history and Islamic slogans in many mosques in Germany – the absence of such historical symbolism in Pakistani mosques, where the national flag is also less prominently displayed, is a point worth exploring further. Others are much more difficult to interpret, including the beards of young men and the headscarves of women. The headscarf of the elderly peasant woman in Bavaria or Kashmir means something completely different from that of the young French Algerian or Dutch Muslim university graduate.

Tenth, and finally, is the question of effectiveness. This is very much a question of the perspective from which the matter is approached. European circles have expectations that at least some of these organisations are seeking to achieve improved circumstances for their communities. On the one hand, there may be very different perceptions of what is meant by improved circumstances – as in the area of education, where Europeans tend to see this linked to and dependent on educational 'integration', while many Muslims judge the question with reference to the preservation of Islam. On the other hand, the kinds of considerations which have been outlined earlier mean that for many organisations, effectiveness, for instance at achieving spoken or unspoken purposes, is related to questions of preserving legitimacy, authority and power. Whatever the public statements of purpose of, say, the Moroccan *Amicales* in France, for many their effectiveness will be judged by their ability to retain the influence of the Moroccan government over its émigrés. It is also often clear that the followers or members of a particular organisation may have a different perspective from the leadership. As the organisations are able to provide services desired by the community, their followings are larger than they would be if the organisations were more explicitly and exclusively devoted to the party programme.

Conclusions

In evaluating and analysing Muslim organisations and movements, we have to be aware of the biases and limitations of the observer, who is usually from outside the community – there are still few Muslim scholars in this field. I have suggested that our agendas and priorities for the organisations often tend to be different from theirs. Clearly, one also has to take into consideration the purpose of observation: is it a matter of extending and refining sociological or anthropological models, or is it policy-oriented, in which case in what kind of political context? The perspective of the observer – secular, Marxist, religious (and then which?), and so on – must also be considered.

But perhaps in an area like this, an even more important question regards the ability to see (determined by the equipment at the disposal of the observer) not only the acquired academic discipline, or the professional frameworks and categories of the social and educational practitioner, but also the inherited cultural patterns. Informal Sufi groups are virtually invisible to those who look only for formal organisations. The female half of community life is likely to be less visible because observers might be male as well as the organisations' spokespersons, and because the tools and models of the relevant academic disciplines have been developed by generations of male observers with access only to male society – a fatal weakness in relation to traditional Islamic cultures.

However, the ability to see is also affected by what the observed allows us to see. All the communities we are dealing with have long experience of some degree of European contact under empire – this is true to some degree also of the Turks. They learned to adapt the communal defence mechanisms, designed to minimise interference from their Ottoman, Mogul or other rulers, to mitigate the interference of British and French colonial and military officers. They learned how to manipulate their European collocutors, not always successfully, but often sufficiently to maintain some degree of autonomy. This experience is now being adapted and used in Europe itself. Thus, an older generation of Naqshbandi leaders in Britain, with some success at organising and obtaining public funding, turned out to have been non-commissioned officers in the British Indian army. One wonders how many of the observations which we make about Muslim communities, their processes, aspirations and organisations are coloured by this process.

This leads finally to the question of the role which Muslim organisations play in the integration or isolation of the Muslim community in Europe. One is tempted towards a conclusion that organisations, like the community as a whole, are tending in both directions. The continuing prevalence of imported leadership, priorities being set by factors outside Europe, the ambivalence of idiom and symbol all point towards, if not isolation, at least a strong degree of separateness. On the other hand, that same ambivalence of idiom and expression, changes in the nature and means of recruitment and, above all, the outer forms which organisations are adopting suggest a degree of adaptation to a new environment which indicates integration.

Indeed, it is possible to argue that developments around the Rushdie and 'headscarf' affairs in 1989 and cartoon crises of the twenty-first century (see Chapter 10) create a strong impression of a quite extensive integration at the organisational level. One part of the Muslim debates during those events was internal, directed at each other in a competition for legitimacy and support. But a significant part was concerned with communicating with the wider society. Certainly, what was being communicated did not often please that wider society, which responded negatively and wondered about Muslim separateness. But the organisations clearly thought it worth their while to engage in these controversies publicly and with stated wishes of the wider society, an attitude which puts them on a par with the majority of traditional European organisations.

An introduction to particular organisations

After this general introduction to the nature of Muslim organisations, and the kinds of questions to which observers may usefully pay attention, it makes some sense to present briefly and in general terms the major organisations and movements of the Muslim world which are represented in western Europe. This should be helpful in placing into the wider context those organisations and associations which were named and discussed in the earlier sections and chapters on individual countries.

1. South Asia
The context of Islamic movements originating in the Indian subcontinent was the decline of the Mogul empire during the eighteenth century and the subsequent expansion of, in particular, British control, culminating in the abolition of

Mogul rule and its replacement by British imperial rule in 1858 after the Indian Mutiny or the 'first war of Indian independence'.

An early Muslim response to Mogul decline had been concentrated among the *'ulama'*, in particular those of Delhi and Lucknow. The figure of Shah Waliyullah (1703–62) epitomises this first period, but various Sufi orders, which had played an important role at the Mogul court as well as in more popular guises under the leadership of *pirs* and centred on shrine pilgrimages, also played a leading part in preserving Islamic expression and developing responses to the decay of Muslim rule. It was also during this period, when the British East India Company was expanding a harshly exploitative domination over Bengal, that Islam became one of the prime means through which Bengali Muslims resisted British rule.

The foundations of the twentieth-century movements which have migrated to Europe are to be found in the second half of the nineteenth century, at the time when India fell under direct British rule. It is from this time that the Deobandi, Barelwi and *Ahl-i-Hadith* movements can be dated. Later, a new phase of organisational activity took place as Indian pressure for independence began to grow. Out of this and subsequent Pakistani politics appeared the *Jama'at-i-Islami*. Especially in the case of the earlier of these movements, their character was formed partly by opposition to the British, and therefore the need to show Islam as something both distinct and superior to what the British had to offer, and partly by controversy among each other, and therefore the need to show up the shortcomings and mistakes of their opponents.

The Deobandi movement. Deoband, a town some 100 miles north of Delhi, was a major centre of traditional Islamic learning during the Mogul empire. It had suffered economically from the Mogul decline and had been badly hit by the consequences of defeat in the Mutiny in 1857. Only after some interval did it regain prominence, but then as a centre of communications for post, telegraph and railways.

In 1866, a group of Muslim scholars around a man called Muhammad Qasim founded a college, *dar al-'ulum*, in the town. It differed from previous such colleges in that teaching took place around a fixed curriculum with annual examinations, much in the style introduced by the British. An informal system of branch colleges grew up around the main college in Deoband, often founded by graduates of Deoband. These colleges were financed mostly by annual contributions. In this way, they also differed from traditional colleges with their dependence on endowments (*waqfs*). The direction of the system was in the hands of a leading council, which was organised in such a way that it was difficult for one man or family to gain control of it.

The curriculum was centred on the study of Qur'an, Hadith, Shari'a, and logic and philosophy, but with the last two playing an increasingly subordinate role to the first two, the centrally Islamic sciences. Of these subjects it was, above all, the study of Hadith for which the college became famous. From the beginning, Urdu was the language of instruction, and Deoband became instrumental in spreading Urdu as the common language of Muslim learning throughout the subcontinent.

By the end of the nineteenth century, there were around forty colleges identified as Deobandi, and the network had become identified with a 'style', *maslak*, or tendency within Indian Islam. A century after the foundation of the first college in Deoband, nearly 9,000 schools were said to be in operation.

The Deobandi school has become identified with the more 'puritanical' tendencies in modern Indian Islam. This is due to its insistence on learning in Qur'an, Hadith and Shari'a. It is also, doubtless, due to the reputation it developed very early on for issuing legal opinions. With the decline of the official Islamic establishment, as the Mogul empire withered and died, Muslims across the subcontinent were desperate for guidance in all the ordinary matters of everyday ritual, practical and social life. The Deobandi *'ulama'*, in particular some of the early founding circle such as Rashid Ahmad and Muhammad Ya'qub, soon established a wide reputation as sources of authoritative legal opinions, or *fatawa*, in the Hanafi school of law. From 1911, these were recorded and published regularly.

However, the Deobandi *'ulama'* also had strong roots in the elite tradition of certain Sufi orders. Their emphasis was on the individual spiritual discipline, learned through individual instruction from a respected shaykh. This explicitly countered the 'Sufism of mediation' with its shrine-based popular cult, where *pirs* mediated divine favour and insight. The Deobandi shaykhs made common the previously unusual, but not unknown, practice of initiation into several of the great Sufi orders. Thus, most of the early founders were Chistis, but they were also initiated into orders such as the Qadiriyyah, Suhrawardiyyah and Naqshbandiyyah. In fact, the silent meditation of the Naqshbandiyyah tradition was strongly recommended for all Deobandi students.

The Ahl-i-Hadith. As the name suggests, this movement was noted for its insistence on the sound Hadith as the source for Qur'anic interpretation and the Shari'a. In this insistence, they rejected not only the traditional teachings and chains of authority of the Sufi orders, but also the authority of previous generations of scholars. In particular, this meant that the consensus of the classical schools of law was rejected. Such insistence on the text of Hadith laid the movement open to the charge that it lent too much weight to the individual responsibility of the scholar and implied rejection of anything but the most narrow interpretation of the *ijma'*, or consensus.

They shared with all the various movements the concentration on the person of the Prophet Muhammad, but they differed with most others in their insistence on the centrality of the Hadith. The Hadith were regarded as the direct channel of knowledge of the Prophet and his Sunna, or model way of life. In this way, the *Ahl-i-Hadith* considered that they had an immediate line of communication with the Prophet which differed from that of the Deobandis, where the line was mediated by the teacher-guide, or the Barelwis, where the role of the mediator-*pir* was important. While they did not reject the idea that certain Muslims had achieved special status as models, possibly as 'saints' (*wali*, pl. *awliya*'), they strongly rejected the practices associated with such people's graves, condemning even pilgrimage to the grave of the Prophet in Medina. All institutional forms of Sufism were rejected, and Sufism was restricted to a matter of private practice. The movement marked itself out from most other Muslim movements of the time by the centrality of serious Hadith scholarship. This meant that there was an emphasis on specialised scholarship, which served to concentrate the movement's following among the intellectual classes – it was already an elite movement from its inception in the mid-nineteenth century. As it was very soon attacked by most other movements, including the Deobandis and the Barelwis, the *Ahl-i-Hadith* took pride in underlining those particular practices which marked them out from the others, especially in the visibly different way in which they performed *salah* (ritual prayer). But they also stressed their claim to be related to key figures and movements in Islamic history: the Hadith scholars of the classical period who had brought the Hadith to the centre of the Islamic sciences, and the great teachers of the Islamic tradition, as well as links to the Wahhabi movement of their own time. In British India, the movement was often known as Wahhabi as opposed to Sunni, which essentially meant Hanafi.

The Barelwi movement. The context in which the Barelwi movement arose was common with the two groups already discussed. The *'ulama'* of the movement depended on popular support, in return for which they gave practical and religious guidance; they tended to avoid political activity. In many ways, they represented a reassertion of the more popular expressions of Sufi traditions, which had been denounced to varying degrees by the Deobandis and the 'Wahhabi' *Ahl-i-Hadith*. Consequently, most Barelwi polemics have been directed strongly against these two groups rather than against outsiders.

   The figure of Ahmad Riza Khan (1856–1921) stands as the founder. He came from a distinguished family of scholars and Sufi leaders which had settled in the city of Bareilly, about 150 miles east of Delhi. He is remembered by his followers as a child prodigy who recited poems in praise of the Prophet at the age of four and gave fatwas at the age of fourteen. But most importantly, he was renowned for his love of the Prophet, and in his speech and writing he clearly represents that tradition in Islamic piety which speaks of the 'light of Muhammad', and of the Prophet for whom the world had been created.

In this tradition, three elements are characteristic. The centrality of the Prophet is such that the Barelwi movement is accused by its opponents of treating Muhammad like a deity. Religious and teaching authority is emphatically mediated through the descendants of the Prophet, the *sayyids*, and the descendants of the great spiritual leaders, the saints and *pirs*. Lastly, associated with these aspects of piety and teaching are the popular festivals. Foremost among these is, of course, the celebration of the birth of the Prophet himself, the *mawlud*. This is a community-wide festival shared among all like-minded Muslims throughout the Islamic world. In addition, and reinforcing local identities within the Muslim community and in relation to surrounding non-Muslims, are the festivals associated with individual *pirs* at some local or regional centre of pilgrimage. Here are phenomena well-known from other parts of the Muslim world and from previous periods. Through the Barelwi movement, they find their particular North Indian expression.

Ahmad Riza Khan and his followers presented themselves as *ahl-i-sunnat wa-jama'at*. This referred to the common ground shared with other trends, namely the centrality of the Sunna, that is, the model of the Prophet as recorded in the Hadith. But it also referred to the people who held together on particular views; in other words, it gave authority to the practice of the community so long as it was not directly contradicted by an authoritative text. Clearly, many of the popular practices associated with saints' festivals, rites of passing and the like could thus be legitimised. In the arguments among these three groups, the use of fatwas was the favourite weapon, but none of them hesitated in using appeals to the British courts to support their claims in particular circumstances.

It is difficult to apply the term 'school' to the Barelwis, since much of their writing extols the person of Ahmad Riza Khan while dealing only minimally with the specific points of his teachings. His father had founded a *madrasa* (Islamic school) in Bareilly in 1872, but it soon fell under Deobandi control. This was a not uncommon occurrence, partly because the Deobandi network was more cohesive and, from the start, aimed at the training of *'ulama'*. But against the wide influence attained by the Deobandis through their growing networks of colleges, the Barelwis were able to rely on the support of the rural village structures in the United Provinces and the Punjab.

Tablighi-jama'at. This movement, known in its Arabic form as *Jama'at-al-Tabligh*, could be described as the active pietism of the Deobandi movement. Founded in 1927 by a leading Deobandi, Muhammad Ilyas (1885–1944), the movement insists on an individual internalisation of the faith combined with external performance of the religious duties. Only through the example of individual piety and good action will others be drawn to revive their Islam or become Muslim, and only through such revival of Islamic piety at the individual level will Islamic society be restored.

The movement's dominant activity is preaching and inviting to Islam (*tabligh*). Members will often commit themselves to spending some months 'on the road' travelling from place to place preaching on the way. Such groups of temporarily itinerant preachers may spend some days based in a mosque holding public meetings, before they move on. They emphasise the need to set a good example in social behaviour and, combined with the individual pietism, this has given the *Jama'at-al-Tabligh* its generally political quietist character.

Such political quietism, forged together with active preaching, may be one reason why the movement has succeeded in gaining a following across the ethnic and geographical divisions of the Muslim world. Spreading out from northern India, the *Jama'at-al-Tabligh* has found a large following in Malaysia, Indonesia and Singapore, as well as in North Africa, particularly in Algeria. From India and Pakistan, the movement spread with migration to Britain, where it is organised in close conjunction with the Deobandi network, its European regional headquarters being in Dewsbury, Yorkshire. From Algeria, it spread into France under the name *Foi et Pratique* in the early 1970s, although it was only during the 1980s that the movement began to grow to the extent that it has become a major factor in French Islam.

Jama'at-i-Islami. The *Jama'at-i-Islami* is closely associated with the career of its founder, Abu al-A'la Mawdudi (1903–79). His ideas were developed in the late 1930s, at a time when British India was looking towards independence, which for Muslims would have meant continuing as a minority only under Hindu rather than British rule.

Mawdudi took a thoroughly anti-secular line, insisting that Muslims should be aiming for an Islamic state governed by Islamic ideology founded on the Qur'an and Sunna, and implemented by people committed to that ideology. This put him in opposition both to the independent democracy proposed by Congress and to the Pakistan plan, since this latter was, in his view, a plan for a Muslim rather than an Islamic state. At this stage, Mawdudi's programme consisted primarily in calling on Muslims to rid themselves of everything to do with secularism, the West or Hindu culture.

As the Pakistan plan began to gain popularity among Indian Muslims, Mawdudi founded the *Jama'at-i-Islami* in 1941 as a political party to have a stronger voice in the processes moving towards independence. In 1947, together with thousands of other Indian Muslims, he migrated to the new state of Pakistan, created out of partition and independence.

The situation after 1947 provided a fertile ground for Mawdudi's ideas and his party. Stressing fundamental Islamic principles with a strong tendency towards a literalist interpretation of Qur'an and Hadith, his writings and the policy of the *Jama'at* were particularly attractive to the *muhajirs*, those Urdu-speaking Indian Muslims who had gone through the trauma of migration and settlement in a new country whose identity was proclaimed to be Muslim but which so often appeared to fall short of Islamic ideals. It was to be expected that Mawdudi and the *Jama'at* were to be particularly active during the 1950s and 1960s in issues which were related to the Islamic identity of the state of Pakistan: the place of the Ahmadiyya, the nature of the constitution and the role of Shari'a in legislation, to mention just the main ones. As a political party, however, it was also clear that the *Jama'at* had to operate within a political system in which its main support was to be found among the *muhajirs* and, as time went by, among young university and college graduates. The movement's policies and structures did not make it popular either among the urban professionals or among the rural masses.

Through the Pakistan years, Mawdudi continued a prolific writing career, and many of his books and pamphlets became best-sellers in translations throughout the Middle East and the rest of the Muslim world. As his ideas developed, they often came to complement those of Sayyid Qutb in Egypt. They shared a rejection of anything which was perceived as an external intellectual or cultural import into the pristine Islam of the Prophetic period in Medina. Mawdudi differed from Qutb in the centrality which he gave to the Islamic state, as distinct from the Islamic society. The state should rule according to God's revelation and law, and only those who understand this are entitled to implement it. At the same time, the Muslims individually and collectively have a bounden duty to be the guardians of Islamic morality in the individual and collective social, economic and political life. One sees here a combination of the Kharijite emphasis on moral as well as doctrinal purity, and Ibn Taymiyyah's insistence on the public individual and collective responsibility of 'encouraging the good and indicting the evil'. This last aspect in particular, combined with Mawdudi's strong opposition to 'foreign' influences in Islam, especially Sufi and popular religious practices, lies behind a basic empathy shared by the *Jama'at*, Wahhabi tendencies, and elements of the Muslim Brotherhood.

During the 1971 war between India and Pakistan over the revolt of East Pakistan and the creation of Bangladesh, the *Jama'at* had firmly committed itself to the continuing unity of Pakistan. In consequence, it was discredited in Bangladesh after the war and had strengthened its opposition to the government of Pakistan which had lost the war. By the late 1970s, the *Jama'at* was strongly against the Bhutto government and, after Mawdudi's death, it was one of the key supporters of the military regime of Zia al-Haq during its early years. During 2002–8, *Jama'at* cooperated with other Islamist parties in a coalition called *Muttahida Majlis-i 'Amal* (United Council of Action) and tried to gain more influence, but the coalition failed due to internal antagonism. The party also exists in India and in Bangladesh. While it has been very marginal in India, it has temporarily had some success in Bangladesh but has also been banned. Presently, since 2013, it is banned.

In its organised form, the *Jama'at* has had little success outside Muslim communities of Indian subcontinental origin. But its acute sense of political opportunity has meant that *Jama'at*-related organisations in Britain have had success in achieving a public profile which far outstrips their popular support within the community.

Ahmadiyya movement. Two related groups are referred to as Ahmadiyya. To complicate matters further, there are several other Ahmadiyya groups across the world, not least Sufi groups. But the two groups that originate from the area that is now Pakistan both sprang from the teaching of charismatic Muslim Mirza Ghulam Ahmad (1835–1908). Early on in his life, Ghulam Ahmad engaged in religious studies, both under the supervision of others, but also on his own. In 1989, at the age of fifty-four, he founded the Ahmadiyya movement. At that point, Ghulam Ahmad already had followers who had pledged him loyalty. He had spent the previous decades studying, but also engaging in debates with Christian missionaries defending Islam. The two groups, often referred to as the Qadian and the Lahori (labels the Ahmadiyyas themselves do not endorse), interpret the legacy and claim of Ghulam Ahmad differently. Both agree that he was a *mujaddid* (reformer) but the Qadian branch goes further, interpreting Ghulam Ahmad's use of *nabi* (prophet) about himself literally and not allegorically as the Lahoris. These claims of Ghulam Ahmad, together with others – of being the Mahdi and Messiah with special reference to the return of Jesus Christ – had already caused non-Ahmadis to question his Muslimness during his life, and he was proclaimed to have strayed from Islam by several religious scholars. The Qadian branch, the larger of the two, has been led by a caliph since the death of Ghulam Ahmad, yet another usage of words that irritate other Muslims. Both branches are strictly pacifist and are known to be actively engaged in missionary work, spreading their message through all conceivable media. In Pakistan, the Ahmadiyya movement was declared non-Muslim in the constitution of 1974, increasing already severe persecution. Ten years later it became illegal to propagate the Ahmadi faith: doing so could lead to blasphemy charges. Also internationally, the movement has been declared non-Muslim, not least in 1974 by the Muslim World League issuing a declaration, signed by 140 delegates from 120 countries, declaring 'Qadianism' to be out the fold of Islam.

Nevertheless, Ahmadiyya has successfully spread throughout the world and is known in most places as engaged in dialogue and missionary work, not least through publications, but also a wide variety of ambitious charity work. London is the headquarters in Europe, but Ahmadis live all over Europe and are often among the first (self-defined) Muslims to have arrived in different countries.

2. The Arab world – East

As it relates to Europe, the Arab world has to be considered in two parts. The three North African countries of Tunisia, Algeria and Morocco have their own particular history and characteristics as regards Islamic movements and organisations, and they will be dealt with individually later. The eastern part of the Arab world, above all Egypt and Saudi Arabia, is also relevant, in two ways. On the one hand, developments there during the nineteenth and the first half of the twentieth century have been one of the factors influencing developments further west. On the other hand, certain Islamic movements based in the region have established themselves in Europe through influence and conversion rather than through immigration.

The rise of new Islamic movements in the Arab world has taken place in two stages over the last three centuries. In the first stage, there was a reaction against perceived shortcomings, deviation and decline within the Muslim world. This was an internal Islamic discourse which took little or no notice of the signs of encroaching European influence, and to that extent it has its parallels in eighteenth-century India. Most of the Arab world – certainly the Fertile Crescent and Egypt – was under Ottoman rule during this period, and the rebellion against the perceived decline took place away from the urban centres of economic and political power.

The Wahhabis. The most notable of the movements which arose at this time was that of the Wahhabis in Arabia. Its founder, Muhammad ibn 'Abd al-Wahhab (1703–91), had studied in Basra and travelled around Iraq. What he had seen there of popular Muslim practice, allied with Sufi traditions, clashed profoundly with the strict Hanbali upbringing and training which he had experienced in his home in the Najd of central Arabia. Returning to his home district, he preached with renewed fervour the doctrine of *tawhid*, insisting on the uniqueness and oneness of God. Basing himself on the teachings of the great thirteenth-century Hanbali scholar Ibn Taymiyyah, Ibn 'Abd al-Wahhab rejected the traditional consensus (*ijma'*) of the scholars and called for Islamic teaching to be based solely on Qur'an and Sunna, as recorded in the Hadith. A strong element of his teaching was the obligation to 'impose the good and indict the evil' (*al-amr bi'l-ma'ruf wa'l-nahy 'an al-munkar*).

This teaching amounted to a call for not only religious revival but also the return of Islam in a Bedouin society which appears to have left Islam in all but name. In 1744, the great breakthrough came when the head of one of the leading chiefly families in the Najd, Al Sa'ud, entered into an alliance with Ibn 'Abd al-Wahhab. Soon, the movement dominated Arabia and threatened the interest of the Ottoman empire in the region. When Mecca fell to the Wahhabis at the end of the century, the Ottoman sultan's claim to be the protector of the holy places was challenged. In 1818, an Egyptian military expedition defeated the Wahhabis and returned Mecca to Ottoman control, which was only lost again in 1916 during the Arab revolt.

Through the nineteenth century, the Wahhabis remained confined to their immediate base in the Najd, but in the turmoil following the collapse of the Ottoman empire at the end of the First World War, they succeeded in reestablishing a dominant role in the peninsula, taking over Mecca and Medina in 1924. In 1932, 'Abd al-'Aziz ibn Sa'ud was proclaimed king of Saudi Arabia.

The new state was soon to face the profound challenge of western influence when oil was discovered in 1933. The militant Wahhabi elements, gathered in semi-military encampments, were eager to spread the message and were creating problems for the government along the border with British-controlled Iraq. At the same time, the government wanted the income promised by the oil industry, but that brought with it modern technology and communications with the wider world.

This tension has faced the Saudi state ever since. On the one hand, the traditional Wahhabi element retains its appeal in wide circles, although the military encampments were crushed during the 1930s. In their place, it has developed institutions and structures which lend it power, especially in some universities and colleges and in the network of mosques. It has sympathy within parts of the large royal family. On the other hand, there are factions in government and the royal family, in other universities and among the educated classes, who see a necessity to adapt the 'purity' of eighteenth-century Wahhabi teaching to changed circumstances.

The Saudi government maintains a number of organisations which have actual or potential influence among Muslims in Europe. The Ministry of Islamic Affairs, Pious Endowments, Mission and Guidance (*wizara-l-shu'un al-islamiyya wa'l-awqaf wa'l-da'wa wa-irshad*) employs and seconds imams to mosques around Europe, particularly in Britain. But the numbers are at the level of a few dozen rather than the large figures (for example, 100 for Britain) which have sometimes been quoted in the press. More important is the Muslim World League (*Rabitat al-'Alam al-Islami*). Almost all its funds come from Saudi Arabia, its main office is in Mecca, and its general secretary is a minister of the crown. While this places the League within the Wahhabi ambit, it does not mean that it necessarily adheres to a strictly traditional Wahhabi line. In fact, the League replicates much of the internal Saudi discourse between those who insist on a conservative and strict Wahhabi tradition and those who have a wider horizon; there has, in fact, been a certain shift from the former to the latter since the 1980s. Another organisation, working close to the League, is the World Assembly of Muslim Youth (WAMY) (*al-nadwa al-'alamiyya li'l-shabab al-islami*). It has headquarters in Saudi Arabia but might as well be called a Muslim brotherhood organisation. It has UN non-governmental organisation status and does charity work, issues publications and organises conferences. WAMY has a very active UK branch.

The Salafiyyah. The second phase of the development of Islamic movements in the Arab world in modern times has seen the appearance of much more numerous tendencies, representing a conscious reaction to European encroachments. In fact, they share in varying degrees a perceived common origin in the seminal figures Jamal al-Din al-Afghani (1839–97), Muhammad 'Abduh (1849–1905) and Rashid Rida (1865–1935). Al-Afghani stressed the necessity of Muslims working together politically to resist the encroaching western powers, and his life was dominated by political action. 'Abduh collaborated very closely with al-Afghani, especially during their common exile in France, but he was a man of learning rather than of action. He was one of the prime movers in the early reforms of Al-Azhar University in Cairo, and as Chief Mufti of Egypt he issued a series of fatwas bringing the application of Islamic law into a closer relationship with current conditions. He started a major Qur'an commentary, called *al-Manar*, which was taken over and completed by Rida. Rashid Rida provided the intellectual foundations for much of the theological, legal and political thinking which had gone before, and continued during the 1920s as the Muslim world sought to come to terms with Turkey's abolition of the caliphate and the apparently complete success of Britain and France in taking over the Arab world. Central to Rida's ideas were a return to and revival of the ideals and practices of the first generation of Muslims, the *salaf*, whence the term *Salafiyyah* by which Rida and his followers are often known.

The Muslim Brotherhood. A significant outcome of the work of Rashid Rida has been the movement commonly known as the Muslim Brotherhood or Brethren (*al-Ikhwan al-Muslimun*). It was founded in 1928 by Hasan al-Banna (1906–49), and while Rida was not a member, the movement had his sympathies and for a long time looked to him almost as its mentor. The Brotherhood represented a desire to develop individual and social self-reliance among Muslims in the face of westernisation, European political dominance and the British military presence. Its success in Egypt rested on a combination of an appeal to Islamic roots, Muslim dignity and widespread social and educational work in the towns and villages. Its individual members and sections were often in the forefront of political demonstrations, and occasionally guerrilla-style activity, against the foreign occupier.

Hasan al-Banna and his founder colleagues were men of action, so the ideas of the early Brotherhood are to be found in the texts of speeches and pamphlets rather than in systematic and detailed exposition of theory. It is really only with the appearance of Sayyid Qutb (1906–66) that the Brotherhood acquired an ideological foundation. Qutb started his career as a journalist and civil servant with no particular commitment to Islam, but that changed after a two-year study period in the United States. He returned to Egypt to start a prolific period of writing committed to the reinstatement of Islam at the centre of political and social life. His analysis was, in many ways, more radical than anything which had previously been proposed – perhaps with the exception of the revolutionary Kharijites after the first Muslim civil war in 656–61! Anything introduced into Muslim life which did not have sanction in the life of the community during the time of the Prophet Muhammad was corrupting of Islamic principles, and represented *jahiliyyah* or pre-Islamic ignorance. The only way forward was to withdraw from such a society, to perform a new *hijrah*, and to enter into a struggle, a jihad, against it. The process of identifying the *jahiliyyah* society, of identifying its disbelief, is *takfir*.

Sayyid Qutb's major political test came in 1954, when the Free Officers' leadership, in the person of Jamal 'Abd al-Nasir, sought to obtain his support. He rejected the overtures and spent most of the following years in prison, until he was executed for alleged involvement in a Brotherhood-inspired attempted revolt. His ideas, however, have remained the inspiration for a complex of groups and factions which have moved to more radical political stances than the more conservative older generation of Brotherhood leaders.

The writings of Qutb spread the popularity of the Brotherhood into the rest of the eastern Arab world, far beyond the small groups which had appeared in places like Jordan and Syria during its first generation. The post-Qutb Brotherhood was the prime mover and planner in the Islamic uprising in Syria during the early 1980s, and the ideas of Qutb have been absorbed into the Palestinian Islamic resistance movement, Hamas.

In Egypt, the Brotherhood was long barred from national politics and found alternative ways to be active instead. A wide engagement in civil society, unions and media made the Brotherhood influential in society and experienced in poli- tics, and from the 1990s active members of the Brotherhood started successfully to run for the People's Assembly in Egypt, either for other parties or as independ- ent candidates. This was tolerated up until the revolution in 2011. During the period, the Brotherhood constituted a social conservative force in the Assembly but more importantly gained experience of everyday pragmatic politics. After registering a political party and winning the first election after the revolution, the Muslim Brotherhood ran Egypt for a year but was forced from power in a military coup in 2013. Currently the Brotherhood is persecuted in Egypt.

The intellectual challenges of Brotherhood ideology since Qutb have also been the main factor in the creation of students' Islamic societies in Europe. In some cases, especially in Britain, it was students from the Muslim world, study- ing at European universities, who founded such societies and formed their main active support. In West Germany, groups of such students and political exiles joined together with German converts to form the Islamic Centres of Munich and Aachen, both with traditionally strong Brotherhood connections or, at least, sympathies. Munich was initially reputed to be particularly close to the Egyptian Brotherhood, while Aachen was one of the main exile refuges of the Syrian branch, to the extent that some observers attributed to it, probably in exaggerated terms, the role of coordinator of the Islamic uprising in Syria during the three or four years up to 1982.

One of the most profiled leaders of the Brotherhood, Sa'id Ramadan, escaped arrest in the 1950s by moving to Switzerland. There he set up the Islamic Center of Geneva that was to become an important base for the Brotherhood in Europe. In 1982, in Munich, the International Organization of the Muslim Brotherhood (IOMB) was established. Instrumental in this was the Egyptian Mustafa Mashhur, one of the most powerful Brotherhood leaders, who was head of the Brotherhood from 1996 until his death in 2002. IOMB coordinates activities globally, keeping Egypt at the centre of the organisation.

Another important organisation, not run by the Brotherhood but inspired and connected to it, is the Federation of Islamic Organisations in Europe (FIOE) formed in 1989. FIOE has encouraging its members to establish Islamic schools to give intellectual support to European Muslims. The Federation was central in the founding in 1997 of the European Council for Fatwa and Research headed by Yusuf al-Qaradawi and Faysal Mawlawi. Its ambition is to guide European Muslims to a pious life in harmony both with Islamic law and European political, social and legal conditions.

The Salafi trend. The Salafis are not to be confused with the *Salafiyyah* mentioned above. Both names refer to *al-salaf*, the term for a Muslim belonging to the three first generations of believers. European Salafism is not an organisation; rather it is a revivalist trend with many faces. Locally, Salafism may consist of loose networks or, at times, take on a sect-like guise. Salafism started to spread in Europe in the 1990s; inspiration came from visiting scholars, not least from Saudi Arabia, belonging to the oppositional *Sahwa* movement calling for a conservative turn of Saudi society. At the heart of *Salafi manhaj* (method) lies a literalist reading of the Qur'an and Sunna. While salafis generally do not engage in European national politics, they do promote lifestyle politics, wanting to distinguish themselves and claim their right to resist and reject majority society values and instead follow what they perceive as the true values of Islam. Inspiration is taken from a wide range of Muslim thinkers. A minority of Salafis actively promote jihadist ideas in Europe.

3. The Arab world – West
The historical experience of the Maghreb, that is the countries from Libya through Tunisia and Algeria to Morocco, was substantially different from that

of the eastern Mediterranean Arab world, especially in the colonial and post-colonial phases. Here, the story is not one primarily of identifiable religious movements, as in the instance of India or Turkey. Rather, we are dealing with the relationships between Muslims and the colonial power and with the independence movements.

Morocco. Political authority in Morocco has traditionally rested on the legitimacy conferred by claims of descent from the Prophet Muhammad, and within that by adherence to the families of shaykhs of the Sufi orders centred on their shrines. The central urban and cultivated areas have been ruled by dynasties of sharifs, claiming descent from the Prophet, who were able to extend their control over the less accessible surrounding areas through alliances with Sufi orders and their regional charismatic leaders. For a long time, a policy of exclusion of the European world was maintained, but this became impossible after the French occupation of Algeria. Through the nineteenth century, the Moroccan sultans had to play a balancing act among the various European interests, mainly French, Spanish and British, until finally in 1912 a French protectorate was accepted to avoid a complete dismemberment, with a smaller area of the Rif in the north coming under Spanish protection.

A few attempts at introducing the rationalistic *salafiyyah* teachings were met with resistance by the traditional Islamic leaderships, and the French protectorate was effective in ensuring that further *salafiyyah* infiltration was restricted initially. French policy relied on strengthening the traditional elites, especially in the mountainous Berber regions, a policy which further strengthened the religious elites in those areas. With a settlement policy similar to that practised in Algeria but refined to reflect the lessons learned there, the tensions between indigenous populations and the hundreds of thousands of settlers inevitably had religious overtones. These were emphasised when, in 1921, a rebellion broke out in the Spanish zone, led by Muhammad ibn 'Abd al-Karim. Although acknowledging the sultanate of the Alawi Sharif Yusuf, ibn 'Abd al-Karim spoke for a reformist Islam which was strongly opposed to the power of both sharifs and shaykhs. In 1926, his republic of the Rif was finally defeated by joint Spanish-French action.

During the 1920s, *salafiyyah* ideas again gained strength and support, especially in the towns, and above all in Fez. *Salafiyyah* groups were instrumental in setting up a series of 'free schools', which became the base for a network of opposition to the French and to the Sufi orders, especially the Tijaniyyah, who were regarded as being in collaboration with the French. By the early 1930s, this network and its leaders and supporters were known as the National Action Bloc and were seeking to mobilise the support of the sultan. During the economic crisis of the mid-1930s, the Bloc found itself leading a protest of popular Muslim frustration. Although its leaders were arrested and exiled, the religious nature of the Moroccan nationalist movement had been established. A few years later, after French defeat by Germany, the exiled leaders returned to help form Istiqlal, the independence movement under the leadership of 'Allal al-Fasi. The movement's attempts to get the support of Sultan Muhammad V were beginning to succeed – so much so that by the early 1950s he had in effect become the leader of the nationalist movement, thus both confirming its religious nature and lending it his inherited legitimacy. When the country became independent in 1956, it had been achieved in a way which emphasised the legitimacy of the traditional ruler and which had to a certain extent discredited the political authority of the Sufi orders. As a result, the authority of the king as the Islamic leader for Moroccans has also remained important for émigrés in Europe. For decades, Moroccan Islamists have tried to establish a political party but have either not gained legal status or have had no success in elections. But in the elections of 27 September 2002, the Justice and Development Party (*Hizb al-'Adala wa'l-Tanmiyya*) became the third largest party. In later elections (2007, 2011), the party continued to be successful and after the 2011 election, when the party entered into a coalition, Abdelilah Benkirane, the leader of the party, became prime minister of Morocco.

Because of the restrictive nature of Moroccan politics over time, several Moroccan Islamic activists have emigrated to European countries, not least the Netherlands, Spain and France. For example, several leading members of the Justice and Charity Gathering (*Jama'at al-'Adl wa'l-Ihsan*), headed by long time Islamist and spiritual leader Sheikh Abdesslam Yassine (1928–2012), have been in forced or voluntary exile. The movement hold the ambivalent status of 'tolerated' by Moroccan authorities due to its social work and its outspoken rejection of violence, thought to counter more revolutionary groups.

Algeria. The date traditionally given for the French conquest of Algeria is 1830, but initially French rule was restricted to the main cities on the coast, while a precarious balance of power was retained with the forces of the amir 'Abd al-Qadir in the hinterland. Resistance to the French from 'Abd al-Qadir and the Bey of Constantine was expressed in Islamic terms. By 1840, resistance had been crushed and the foundations were being laid for the structures of French Algeria and the tensions which ultimately broke out over a century later in the war of independence.

Central to these tensions were the questions of land-ownership and the place of French settlers. The number of settlers had already reached over 100,000 during the 1830s, and during the 1840s they began to spread out of the cities, taking over lands which had been Ottoman state land as well as the lands belonging to the religious endowments (*waqfs* or *habus*). In the following decade, various government measures also allowed the distribution of tribal lands into the ownership of French settlers. The settlers' ambitions were, however, obstructed by the military authorities with their concern for security and order. The settlers' demands therefore grew for incorporation of Algeria into metropolitan France. A first recognition of this came with the French republican constitution of 1848.

The rest of the century was dominated on the French side by a constant tension between the French military and civilian authorities on the one hand and, on the other, regular revolts by native Algerians, often under tribal leaders claiming to be sharifs with power-bases in the Sufi orders. From the beginning, therefore, there was a strong identification of Islam with Algerian opposition to French rule. Measures announced in 1864 by Napoleon III confirmed Algeria as French territory and offered French citizenship to all Algerians. But a condition of this offer was that they would become subject to French civil law rather than traditional Islamic law. As a result, a measure intended to improve the position of Algerians in relation to settlers only served to underline the perception of Muslim Algerian being opposed to French non-Muslim.

After the discrediting of the French army during the Franco-Prussian war, the settlers gained the upper hand. The last major Muslim rebellion was crushed ruthlessly in 1871–2, and the whole of the economic, financial, educational and judicial structure of Algeria was now based on a suppression of Arab-Islamic identity and the priority rights of the settlers. This was reinforced by, on the one hand, French control of the Islamic official structures and recognition only of those religious officials who accepted the authority of the colonial administration and, on the other hand, sometimes aggressive measures undertaken by certain church leaders to strengthen Christianity.

In the decade before the First World War, Algerian Muslim opposition again began to grow, given voice by the *'ulama'*. The two specific causes were the government's project of producing a reformed code of Islamic family law, the so-called Code Morand, which was rejected by the religious scholars, and the plan from 1907 to conscript Algerians into the army. Around the latter point, a small group of Francophone and Francophile young Algerians, called the *évolué*, constructed a set of demands for full political assimilation of Algerian Muslims as French citizens, together with the abolition of the various forms of institutional discrimination. After the war, in which 25,000 Algerians lost their lives serving in the French army, attempts in Paris to reward the Algerian support by radical changes in the government of Algeria were thwarted by the power of the settlers. The programme of the *évolué*, expressed by people like Ben Djelloul and Farhat 'Abbas, attracted French liberals, but any governor in Algiers who sympathised with them could expect soon to be recalled. Ultimately, the *évolué* were rendered irrelevant because of their lack of support on the French side and the absence of roots on the Muslim side.

The beginnings of more serious opposition were laid during the 1920s. On the one hand, Arab nationalism with a nostalgic Islamic element attracted support among the thousands of Algerian workers in France with the foundation in 1926 of the *Étoile Nord-Africain*. After a period of imprisonment and exile, its founder Messali al-Hajj was allowed back into Algeria in 1933, where he founded a mass nationalist movement. On the other hand, the ideas of the *salafiyyah* movement were being noticed, especially through its activities in Morocco. Around the key figure of 'Abd al-Hamid Ibn Badis, an Association of Algerian *'ulama'* was founded in 1931. The message of the Algerian *salafiyyahs* was that Islam was a religion of progress and dignity, that it was not Islam which had caused the backwardness of Algerian Muslims – the common message of the French *mission civilatrice* – but French policies. Following the Moroccan model, the Association established a network of its own schools. As this Islamic revival took hold, it coincided with the centenary celebrations of the French conquest, celebrations which glorified the colonial history and the Christian heritage of North Africa before Islam, all of which served to underline again the absence of common interests between Algerian Muslims and French settlers. The final blow to any remnants of Algerian hopes for support in Paris against the interests of the settlers came in 1938 when the Senate, under settler pressure, threw out a bill to extend citizenship rights to certain classes of Algerian Muslims.

During the Second World War, the nationalist movements developed hopes of negotiating for an independent, or at least autonomous, Algeria, perhaps with the help of the United States. But demonstrations and uprisings were brutally suppressed in 1945, and three years later an assembly created for Algeria only further served to disillusion those with any hopes of independence by peaceful means.

Ibn Badis had died in 1940, and after that the *'ulama'* lost their influence in political developments. As the struggle for independence began to move a decade later, they gradually moved their support behind the *Front de Libération Nationale* (FLN), which thus represented both the nationalist and Islamic trends.

After independence in 1962, an industrialisation of the country started not least around the extraction of oil. The country also began to reclaim Arabic as a main language for education and thus needed educated teachers. Many Egyptian teachers, of whom some were Muslim Brotherhood supporters looking for a way out of Egypt, took the opportunity and some inspired the creation of Algerian Islamic opposition. During the 1980s, internal Islamic political activities grew, culminating in the formation of the Islamic Salvation Front (FIS, *al-jabha al-islamiyya li'l-inqadh*) in 1989. The party, which sought to establish an Islamic state through the ballot box, had tremendous success in local elections of 1990 and it started to prepare for the coming national election. However, the sitting government suppressed the national election. The conflicting interests of FIS and the government took the country into chaos and civil war for much of the 1990s. Several sympathisers and activists ended up in Europe during the war and some FIS war propaganda was printed and spread from, among other places, a small print shop south of Stockholm.

Tunisia. The rivalry of French and Italian interests in Tunisia grew during the nineteenth century until, in 1881, the resident French consul was able to bring in French troops and establish a protectorate. Despite encouragement, French settlement was slow and hardly affected private lands. The fact of the protectorate also meant that there was a less obviously confrontational relationship between Tunisians and French, even when the Catholic church engaged in conversion programmes. It has also been suggested that the French administrators had learned at least some of the lessons of their mistakes in Algeria. Just prior to the establishment of the protectorate, Tunisia had been ruled by a Muslim reformist prime minister, Khayr al-Din Pasha, and most of the politically conscious of Tunis looked to him as a model, thus bridging the Islamic and westernising tendencies for a time.

In 1911–12, incidents in Tunis served to break the status quo when protests were crushed by the French. There were no *évolués* on the Algerian model to distract the subsequent development of a nationalist movement with assimilationist policies. The leadership of the united anti-colonial movement of the Destour Party, started in 1920, came from a well-to-do urban background with close links with the religious classes, and their programme was very similar to that of Khayr al-Din. With the absence of a sharp divide in the educational system, Islamic schools continued to thrive and were supplemented by French-style schools, in which Arabic was given a serious place and which attracted the sons of people from humble backgrounds. By the 1930s, the graduates of these schools were mixing and competing for careers and political influence with the children of the old urban elites. Out of this mixture came the leadership of the new Destour movement, the Neo-Destour.

The Neo-Destour hardly differed from its predecessor in its aims, only in its methods. In fact, Habib Bourghiba resigned from the Destour Party to set up the rival in 1934, when he was censured for organising demonstrations in support of a fatwa that Muslims who had become French citizens could no longer be regarded as Muslims and could not therefore have a place in a Muslim cemetery.

In 1922, the government of the protectorate had been handed to a Grand Council with a French and a Tunisian chamber, and French policy from then on remained that Franco-Tunisian cooperation meant French involvement in government. This was a position which Paris maintained until the early 1950s. By then, Bourghiba's Neo-Destour Party had escalated demands for full independence, which was achieved, via a 1955 agreement to limited autonomy, in March 1956, and soon afterwards the old monarchy was abolished. Through this period, Bourghiba's readiness to consider a temporary autonomy agreement led to a break with more explicitly Islamic sections of his party with a power-base in the trade unions. The leaders were imprisoned and, in one case, assassinated, while Bourghiba was able to appeal more popularly with his adoption of the title 'the great *mujahid*'. However, by the 1970s this appeal began to weaken, as he got older and was not able to live up to his earlier promises, thus leaving the field open to a renewed interest in Islamic movements.

The most famous Islamic political movement is *Harakat al-Nahda* (The Renaissance Movement) led by Rashid al-Ghannushi. His personal story illustrates the history of Islamic movements in Tunisia. Since the early 1970s, al-Ghannushi had tried to gain influence through different Islamic organisations, and from 1981 he was part of a group trying to register an Islamic political party. It was to take another thirty years before this ambition came true. During that time, al-Ghannoushi was in prison twice, but also twice pardoned, and spent two decades in exile in Great Britain. *An-Nahda* was officially formed in December 1988, but was preceded by several other organisations with similar goals and the same leaders. After the revolution in 2011, *an-Nahda* finally gained formal recognition as a political party with al-Ghannoushi as its president, and became the largest party in the elections later that year. It formed a coalition government with two secular parties but running the country proved a difficult task. In 2014, *an-Nahda* left the government to defuse a looming political crisis.

Several other leading critics of Tunisian politics have lived in exile in Europe, particularly in France, and *an-Nahda* sympathisers were instrumental in the formation of, for example, the Federation of Islamic Organisations in Europe mentioned above.

4. Turkey

Of the major Muslim powers, the Ottoman empire had had the longest experience of Europe. Its history, before the conquest of Syria and Egypt in 1516–17, had been as much tied to its position in the Balkans as in Anatolia. For several centuries, it was a major European power in constant tension with the Habsburg and the Russian empires. Its position, in its own perception, was traditionally one of superiority, but through the eighteenth century that superiority weakened. By the end of the century there was a clear feeling in the Ottoman establishment that the European powers had caught up.

The administrative and military reforms by which Istanbul sought to meet the challenge in the early part of the nineteenth century, occasionally at some danger to the throne itself, were insufficient to stop a steady retreat from the Balkans or the loss of North Africa. The success of the nationalist movement which led to the establishment of an independent Greece was a signpost for subsequent developments, marking as it did both the growing strength of nationalist movements within the empire and the increasing readiness of the other European powers to interfere in the internal affairs of the state, which came to be known as 'the sick man of Europe'. Further internal constitutional reforms were the price that the empire had to pay for British and French support against, especially, Russian pressures.

By the beginning of the twentieth century, the Ottoman empire had, to all intents and purposes, been reduced to a Turkish-Arab state. Continuing nation-alist demands from the remaining minorities, combined with the beginnings of a specifically Arab nationalism in the Syrian and Iraqi provinces, contributed to an ever-stronger Turkish identity being asserted at the administrative and mili-tary centre in Istanbul. Against this background, the Ottoman empire collapsed in defeat during the First World War. Only the resolute action of Turkish mili-tary officers around General Mustafa Kemal (Atatürk) prevented the complete occupation of Anatolia and succeeded in preserving the territory which became modern Turkey in 1920.

Led by Mustafa Kemal Atatürk, the new government and its supporters, especially in the military, represented a full commitment to the incorporation of Turkey within the European cultural and political sphere. This was not to deny the Islamic tradition of Turkey, but this tradition had to be privatised. The laicism of Kemalist Turkey, deeply infused with anti-clericalism, owed much to the intellectual heritage of France, while economic policy and social organisa-tion reflected the fast-growing partnership between Berlin and Istanbul before and during the First World War.

During the 1920s, laicism was pushed through with the abolition of the caliphate, the replacement of Islamic law with European codes, the complete separation of religion from the state, and the Latinisation of the Turkish alpha-bet and the 'cleansing' of the language of Arabic and Persian vocabulary. Over the following decades, the military, the financial and industrial leadership in the cities, and the state-trained teachers became the main bearers of what came to be known as Kemalism.

On the surface, the Kemalist reforms appeared to be completely successful, but underneath, away from the large urban centres of power, Islamic tradition continued to flourish. The major change was that the scholarly Islam of the *'ulama'* had been seriously weakened. This effectively destroyed the learned dis-cipline through which the *'ulama'* had in the past counterbalanced the popular religious tendencies to which local village *hojjas* (religious leaders) were otherwise exposed. This left the field open for Sufi traditions, especially the networks of the Naqshbandis and the more esoteric Bektashis, and for new movements.

From the late 1930s, and gathering pace through the 1950s, it was realised in the Kemalist establishment that some form of accommodation with Islam had to be reached, and there was a retreat from the extreme laicism of the Atatürk reforms. The government recognised so-called *Imam Hatip* colleges which pro-duced officials for local mosques, although it was not until much later that their graduation certificate was recognised for entrance to the theological faculties of the universities. A Department for Religious Affairs (*Diyanet*) was created in the Prime Minister's office.

During the two decades leading up to the military coup in September 1980, the army and the government became increasingly nervous about the growing attraction of left-wing movements and ideologies, which tended to be branded communist. To combat this, careful contacts with movements and groups representing traditional Islamic tendencies were taken up, and they were allowed a more active part in politics through involvement in accepted political parties. This trend has been strengthened in the years since the coup, with the expansion of the role of the *Diyanet*, strengthened connections with the Arab world, especially Saudi Arabia, and a practice of coopting certain of the Islamic movements, previously confined to the underground.

During the last two decades, Islamic parties have been increasingly success-ful in elections. After the last three elections (2002, 2007, 2011), the Justice and Development Party (AKP, *Adalet ve Kalkınma Partisi*) has run the country. The political program of AKP has inspired several Islamic political movements in the Arab world.

The Süleymançis. It was inevitable that there should be some form of Islamic reaction in the face of the disestablishment of Islam and its institutions and its relegation to the private sphere. It was out of the network of the Naqshbandi Sufi order that the first major step was taken to preserve and spread Islam in the new situation. Süleyman Hilmi Tunahan (1888–1959) was the son of a shaykh of the order. He had studied in Istanbul and qualified as an Islamic judge (*qadi*) under the old regime. His father had passed on the leadership of his branch of the order to him, and there were soon stories circulating of various ways in which divine favour towards him had been manifested.

Soon after the establishment of the republic, Shaykh Süleyman started founding Qur'an schools in the villages and small towns of Anatolia. These schools quickly found widespread support among the local populations, but at the same time they were, rightly, perceived as rivals by the expanding network of state schools. In 1933, Süleyman was arrested for the first time. As his move-ment spread, he was regarded as a growing threat by the Kemalist state as well as, increasingly, a saintly figure by his followers. At one time, he was said to have been proclaimed the Mahdi, and his followers often describe him as the 'Seal of the Saints'.

After the Second World War, as the Turkish state eased back from its previ-ously inflexible laicism, Süleyman's son-in-law Kemal Kacar took over a major expansion of the Qur'an schools, which were presented as the bearers of a pure, uncompromising Islam, in contrast to the *Imam Hatip* schools set up by the state in an attempt to encourage a politically quietist form of preaching. The *Süleymançi* movement thus came to be identified with radical extremism. During the mid-1960s, it started cooperating with Süleyman Demirel's Justice Party, on whose ticket it won three seats in the parliamentary elections of 1977.

The *Süleymançis* were the first major Turkish Islamic movement to become established among Turkish émigrés in Europe using the name Islamic Cultural

Centres (*Islamische Kulturzentren*). With their centre in Cologne, they soon came
to dominate the Turkish Islamic scene in West Germany, and from there they
spread their network to wherever there were Turkish immigrant communities.
After the 1980 coup, however, they found themselves retreating steadily in
the face of a concerted *Diyanet* policy of spreading its control, also centred, for
European purposes, in Cologne and cooperating quietly with the *Milli Görüş*. A
decade later, they were faced with accusations of being heretics, a charge based
on the high place allocated to Süleyman Hilmi Tunahan linked with the strong
Sufi tradition of the core cadres.

During the 1980s and 1990s, the movement grew and opened up to society
under the leadership of Kemal Kacar; an estimation of members in Turkey in
the early 1990s suggested more than 2 million. In 2000, Ahmet Arif Denizoglun,
a grandson of Tunahan and once a member of parliament for the Welfare Party
(*Refah Partisi*), inherited the leadership. Denizoglun has chosen to be less opened
than Kacar and has encouraged members to engage in educating youth rather
than to engage in dialogue with the surrounding society.

The Nurcu. The *Jama'at al-Nur* (Association of Light) was founded by Badi' al-
Zaman Nursi (d. 1960). He was educated in the traditional Islamic sciences
during the last decades of the Ottoman empire and became known as a politically active Muslim 'modernist'. In the years immediately after the First World
War, he cooperated with Kemal Atatürk and was apparently seen by the latter
as one of his main Muslim allies. But quite quickly, Nursi seems to have become
disillusioned by Kemal's laicist policy. His withdrawal from active politics took
him into a programme of personal piety, where Islamic traditions of personal
spirituality were fundamental. This meant emphasising the individual's Islamic
identity and personal commitment, a concept which was felt by the laicist state
to be a threat. As early as 1925, Nursi experienced his first internal exile.

Nursi's major work, *Risale-i Nur*, has become the key text for his followers
and the schools and colleges, many informal and some formal, which the
movement maintains throughout the world. The stress on personal spirituality and piety has been particularly successful, on the one hand in attracting
support among educated and entrepreneurial Turks, and on the other hand
among individuals in many other countries, especially the United States. It
is a movement which is both open to the outside world and missionary in its
attitude. Like the *Jamaat-al-Tabligh*, the Nurcu seek to avoid political involvement and conflict.

Milli Görüş. This movement of the 'national view' combined an orthodox Islam
with Turkish nationalism. Its Islamic content meant that there was for a long
time a tense relationship with the Turkish state, but as the government during
the 1970s accepted Islamic movements as a counterweight to increasingly radical

left-wing politics, a close alliance grew up between the National Salvation Party (MSP) and the *Milli Görüş*. After the 1980 coup, the party was banned, but this was no new experience to the *Milli Görüş* who had got used to having to organise themselves informally and under various pseudonyms, often incorporating the terms 'culture' and 'solidarity'. As the military government handed over to its civilian successors led by Turgut Özal, one effectively witnessed the success of the MSP, the pre-1980 party in which the new prime minister, later president, has been active.

Within the *Milli Görüş* movement, especially in Germany, the Iranian revolution sparked a momentary crisis, as a radical minority led by Cemalettin Kaplan split off in a pro-Iranian faction. But the increasingly constructive relationship with the Turkish state became the dominant factor during the 1980s. The result was a usually friendly and cooperative relationship between the *Diyanet* agency in Germany, DITIB and the *Milli Görüş* such that it became not unusual to find that imams appointed by the *Diyanet* have basically *Milli Görüş* sympathies, even when they were not functioning in the few independent *Milli Görüş* mosques.

Milli Görüş has remained an important organisation in Europe but has, since the mid-1990s, lost political power and relevance in Turkey, much due to the success of first the Welfare Party and then the AKP.

The Gülen movement or *Hizmet*. Fethullah Gülen is a religious scholar turned social activist who coordinates and guides a movement (not an organisation) that has representatives and sympathisers all over Turkey and Europe – globally actually. In Europe, Gülen enthusiasts open schools, dialogue centres and arrange conferences to spread its message. During his youth, Gülen was inspired and changed by reading Nursi's *Risale-i Nur*. He deduced from it that social activism was the way to change society for the better, hence the Turkish name *Hizmet*, 'the service'. Engaging in social aid, education and activism for free speech without at the same time propagating Islam but rather showing the effects of an Islamic worldview through action, has proved an efficient way of getting recruits for the movement's message and inner circles. When the Welfare Party and then AKP gained power it was supported by Gülen and many AKP politicians were in fact part of the Gülen movement. In connection with a corruption scandal in 2013 exposing several AKP politicians, Gülen supporters were blamed for the leak and accused of trying to take control of Turkey. Since then, relations between AKP and the Gülen movement have deteriorated to the point of open hostility.

Alevi. A few words need to be said about the Alevis of Turkey (not to be confused with the Syrian community of the same name, *'alawi*, more traditionally called Nusayris). It is a community which has tended to be mistrusted both by Sunni orthodoxy and by the Turkish state, and it has therefore usually kept a low profile. This also means that the extent of its following in Turkey or among Turkish communities in Europe can only be guessed at – occasional claims that Alevis make up as much as a quarter of the Turkish population cannot be checked. A substantial proportion of Alevis are Kurds, and this is a further reason for the tense relationship with the Turkish state.

As the name suggests, the community has a strong reverence for the person of Ali, the cousin and son-in-law of the Prophet, although they would not go so far as to call themselves Shi'ites. Traditional Sunni rites are hardly practised, and many Alevi villages do not even have mosques, instead they have a *cem evi*, literary house of gathering. Sunni institutions have been replaced by the rites of the Bektashi Sufi tradition, with some influence also from the Mevlevi tradition. The teachings and writings of the two great medieval mystics Hajji Bektash and Jalal al-Din Rumi are held in particularly high regard. It has been suggested that the Alevis represent the popular remnant of the Bektashi order, once one of the most powerful in the Ottoman empire, and one which the reformers of the nineteenth and twentieth centuries particularly sought to weaken, in part because of its close links with the Janissary regiments. Alevis have migrated to Europe in large numbers, especially to Germany. Since 2004, a split has occurred among Alevis. A fraction called Ishikism claims to represent true Alevism and rewrites the history of Alevism.

CHAPTER 10

European Muslims in a new Europe?

Coming into Europe, Muslims have been part of the far larger phenomenon of post-1945 labour immigration, which has led to the settlement of significant ethnic minority groups throughout the region. As they have settled, Muslims have raised challenges to their surroundings as well as been challenged themselves. There has been a complex of adjustments, not always easy, which both sides have had to make in the details of daily life. But the increasingly permanent Muslim presence and Muslims' interaction with their surroundings are raising deeper questions and challenges to both sides, issues which relate to individual and collective senses of identity and which therefore affect and will continue to affect basic patterns of corporate and public life in western Europe.

It became common during the 1980s, especially in educational and religious circles, to talk of a Europe which was becoming 'multicultural'. As a description of the situation in some city districts, the term had some justification, but behind it lay, on the one hand, an optimism as regards the degree of change which had been achieved and, on the other hand, the affirmation of a common European myth of a pre-existent monocultural society.

Historically, of course, Europe had for centuries been multicultural. What commonly goes under the simplistic heading of European – or even Western – culture is a product of Hellenistic, Roman, Middle Eastern and Germanic inter-mixing with previous cultures. No modern European nation can claim to be other than the product of cultural and human intermarriage. Britain had its Celtic, Norse, Saxon and Norman immigrations further enriched by more recent Dutch, Huguenot, Jewish, Italian, Polish and Ukrainian influxes. All other European countries can draw up similar lists – even before the list is expanded to include the Caribbean, Arab, Turkish, Pakistani, Indian, Vietnamese or other migrations which are the direct background to the new presence of Muslims in Europe.

Advocates of a multicultural Europe often appeal to such histories in support of their case. Such appeals can obviously be useful as an educational tool, but their usefulness as a description of realities is doubtful – and it is realities which must be dealt with before dealing positively with futures. These realities can be briefly summed up under three headings: the liberal myth of a multicultural Europe; the social reality of a multicultural Europe; and the unreality of cultural encounter in Europe.

The liberal myth of a multicultural Europe

The multicultural history of Europe has, as already indicated, often been exemplified in the continuous immigration experience of the various countries. The history of European culture can be written in terms of a constant process of intellectual, artistic, spiritual and technological cross-fertilisation. A substantial portion of this process has been mediated by the movement of people, individually and collectively. The movement of Dutch artisans and farmers into parts of Britain, Scandinavia and elsewhere is but one of the better-known examples of such more recent migrations.

European intellectual history is one unending chain of ideas on the move. But there is an important sense in which the late eighteenth, nineteenth and early twentieth centuries have become a watershed separating the past from the present. The success of the concept of nation, made concrete in the nation state, entailed a qualitative change in the traditional processes in two interrelated fashions. First, the work of the nineteenth-century romantic movements coalesced with nationalism to create a mythical history of the nation and its cultural roots. This new history stressed a myth of the common heritage with the purpose of creating a common present. This tendency found possibly its most articulate expression in Germany in both philosophical and artistic terms, but virtually all European countries developed their particular manner of expressing the cohesion of the nation. Second, the very success of the concept of nation involved creating an ideological identity which, whatever its variety of cultural sources, presented a common culture as an essential distinguishing characteristic of the nation. This last point leads directly into the second reality.

The social reality of a multicultural Europe

The rewriting of national histories and the invention of national cultures were not as successful as they appeared at the time. What was achieved was to some extent only superficial. European countries remained multicultural but in a now radically different form. The new national culture could be identified with a new dominant national class, which emerged in the context of the economic and political changes associated with the Industrial Revolution. The multicultural nature of Europe was now one increasingly related to class. The new national class – certainly not monolithic, but sharing a wide spectrum of common assumptions all the same – controlled governmental and private institutions, the arts, the media, political patronage, education and, significantly, the national language. The way of life, the attitudes and preconceptions and the forms of self-expression of the non-dominant sectors of society were truly subcultures. This applied both to regional cultures and to the cultures of the working classes. It is only slowly that this situation has changed since the 1960s. Regional accents have become more legitimate in the broadcast media and elsewhere, but in most countries they remain part of the staple diet of comedy, and there remain situations in which a strong regional accent may be regarded as inappropriate, if not a distinct disadvantage. The educational system remains primarily the forum for the transmission of the national culture in fact, whatever educationists may say and regardless of many attempts to break the mould.

The ethnic minority communities which have arisen out of the recent period of immigration to Europe have in one sense integrated reasonably successfully in these terms. They have simply taken the place of further subcultures underneath the dominant national culture. The problem is, of course, that there are qualitative differences between these new and the existing subcultures. Most importantly, because they have not shared the European history of the last few centuries from the inside, they do not recognise the leadership or superiority of the national culture, even though they may recognise the political, economic and social dominance of the classes which are the upholders of that culture. Indeed, they may – as do clearly major proportions of those ethnic minority groups who are Muslims – look to quite different quarters for their cultural reference points; to Turkey, Pakistan and Algeria, or to Iran, Saudi Arabia or Egypt – all places outside Europe, and all places whose cultural histories can be described in terms of processes similar to those of Europe, but whose experiences of Europe have been from the outside and primarily as an adversary.

So is Europe multicultural in the sense which is usually intended? In a study published as part of the 1985 Swann Report in Britain, Professor John Rex answered with an emphatic negative. What he meant was that in Britain there was not a number of cultural traditions with more or less equal access to the instruments of political, economic, social and cultural power. Thirty years have passed since and a number of legal adjustments to national codes have been made to accommodate aspects of migrants' cultures including religions. In several countries, the rules regarding naturalisation have been eased, new categories for the recognition of minority religions have been created, the education system has created space for minority religions and authorities have increased their cooperation with Muslim representatives. At the same time, hatred and suspicion against Muslims and Islam have grown immensely over the last fifteen years. Integration has happened in some areas but not all, and certainly not in an all-together predictable, linear fashion.

The unreality of cultural encounter in Europe

Simply stating the situation in these terms raises questions which lead directly to the third reality, or rather the continuing unreality, of cultural encounter in Europe. The increasing European practice of distinguishing between multicultural, as a description of situations, and intercultural, as a description of processes, is useful in this context. For while it may be justified to describe certain urban districts as multicultural, it is hardly justified to apply the term intercultural.

All the evidence available indicates that cultural encounter is strictly limited. Individual friendships can develop in the most unexpected circumstances, but the extent to which they have an effect on the wider social network has usually been minimal. However, it must be recorded that it is precisely such individual friendships among young people which provided a motivation for the spontaneous anti-racist campaigns which have swept across Europe since the mid-1980s. Some of the cultural encounter which takes place is at the level of folklore, food and occasionally religion, although this last is fraught with its own special difficulties.

Where the major part of the cultural encounter takes place is with the children of the immigrants, in the so-called second generation. At the collective level, this can be seen in the variety of responses among young people to the differing expectations and opportunities offered by the parental and host cultures. A few have become almost totally 'westernised' in their way of life and attitudes. At the other end of the scale, some have either totally accepted the parental models or have chosen to identify with the orthodoxies of their parents' religion. All manner of paths in between the two extremes are being followed by the majority. It is seldom a matter of conscious choice, rather a process of continual negotiation between individual personality and circumstances. At the individual level, the encounter can be seen as a psychological response which, in a few, entails coping with almost irreconcilable desires and demands, while in most the bargaining among possible behavioural options is surprisingly successful. Some develop critical skills honed by the experience of balancing different worldviews and demands, allowing them to see society through bifocal glasses when creating art and writing critical scholarship.

What characterises the vast majority of such encounters is, however, that the flow of information and experience is mostly one-way. It is the minority groups who are having to adapt their way of life, their attitudes and their language to the European environment. When the talk is of integration or assimilation, it is applied to the minority group – it is not the Swiss, Dutch or German who is going to integrate with the minority.

There are two sides to this. For purely numerical reasons, it is inevitable that the minority is more likely to be drawn into the majority than the reverse – what one might call a sociological law of gravity. But the likelihood becomes a certainty in the context of the existing power relationships. It is the bearers of the native European national culture who also control the instruments of political, economic and social power. The monocultural myth of the national culture predisposes it against a multicultural model, not to mention a model in which religion plays a significant role. Such a combination of power and *Weltanschauung* is almost irresistible. Any adaptation of lifestyles, attitudes and thought patterns must take place among the minority groups and only minimally, if at all, among the majority. The cultural and religious traditions and preferences of the minorities tend to be tolerated so long as they do not impinge on the life of the majority. The natural tendency of newly-arrived communities to strengthen their internal links is reinforced by the majority community's tendency to minimise links with them, with the result that they easily become neutralised by encapsulation – they are *treated* as foreign bodies and therefore they *are* foreign bodies.

What remains of cultural encounter has often been limited. There is the front line of the streets, the bars, the discos and coffee houses. There is the sterile meeting across the cash point in 'ethnic' shops. Above all, there is the direct encounter of the minority communities with the instruments of majority power: the officials of local, regional and national government, police, social security, schools, healthcare, and so on.

This analysis may seem too categorical, and there are, of course, variations and gradations both within the ethnic minority groups and in the majority. But as regards the Muslim minorities, it is important to keep in mind that one is here in contact with a process which, both at the level of political and economic power and at the level of culture, started before the immigrations. It is a process which had already started during the period of European expansion. In one sense, what is happening today in Europe is the fulfilment of one particular aspect of imperialism, namely the subjugation of colonial peoples into the economic necessities and cultural thought patterns of the owners of the national cultures of Europe and, more widely, the West.

Within the majority European communities there have been, as we have seen in previous chapters, institutions, movements and individuals which have sought to break this pattern of subjugation. Occasionally, they have had some success, at least in raising issues into the public debate, as in the case of the anti-racist campaigns in France organised since the mid-1980s. But the prejudice and racism against which they have struggled have hardly weakened, let alone disappeared. Attempts at constructive progress have more often been, at best, isolated by the bureaucracies in which the attempts have been made or, at worst, prohibited. At various stages, some political parties and churches have taken up the cause of fighting against racism and xenophobia, either in general terms or in the context of specific political projects, such as the Nationality Act 1981 in Britain or the more recent revision of the German law on immigration and the rights of foreigners. The EU has initiated several anti-racist projects and further put pressure on member states to revise and strengthen anti-discrimination legislation leading to substantial legal changes in the first decade of the twenty-first century.

Characteristic of most of the debate and campaigning within the European majority communities was for long the essentially secular analysis of the situation. The grounds for campaigning were the human rights documents of the United Nations and the Council of Europe; in the case of the churches and individual Christians, these grounds have themselves been based on their Christian belief, of course. The analysis of the context tended, however, to ignore the religious dimension of the immigrant and ethnic minority communities. Even church bodies, such as the Brussels-based Churches' Committee for Migrants in Europe, were remarkably slow to recognise that a significant proportion of the people they were dealing with were Muslim and that this fact might be of some relevance to their work. It was not until the mid-1980s that a recognition of the Islamic dimension of community and ethnic relations began to spread beyond small specialist cadres in the churches.

At about the same time, a small but growing number of academic sociologists, especially in France, Britain and Scandinavia, began to take a serious interest in the Muslim dimension of the minority communities. In Denmark, the government-sponsored research councils funded a series of projects under the general title 'Islam in the world today' running from 1982 to 1990. The second half of the period was explicitly devoted to researching and documenting the situation of Islam in Denmark. In 1986, the work of a few Swedish scholars led to the convening of a European conference on 'The new Islamic presence in Europe'. In France and Britain, noted sociologists have turned their attention to Muslim communities. A small collaborative project across Europe was sponsored by the European Science Foundation in the mid-1980s, and in 1990 the Leiden University Foundation made Muslims in Europe a major component in its centenary conference. These were the timid beginnings of a development in the university sector which took off during the 1990s. Across the disciplines, research into communities of Muslim background, and increasingly into Muslim communities as such, became a major growth area both nationally and in transnational research settings.

There is little doubt that such developments were essentially brought about by Muslims themselves. An early assumption, in both political and sociological circles, had been that the immigrants were leaving their religion behind. This seemed, on the face of it, a reasonable assumption to make, given the almost complete absence of religious expression among the men who came for temporary work without their families. When religious expression then began to make its mark as a result of family reunion, the assumption was often that this was a transitory phase while the immigrant communities adapted and assimilated to their new context. There was an almost evolutionary view that, as Muslims and other religious communities settled, they would quickly pass through the same development which Europeans had passed through over the previous several centuries. Muslims would become, if not secularised, at least like most North European Christians in confining their religious life to a small private niche.

This last assumption was not necessarily completely mistaken. Clearly, the Muslim community leaderships as well as many of the immigrant generation, the parents of young Muslims brought up in Europe, are afraid of this very scenario. There is no doubt that many young people of Muslim background across the continent are drifting away from Islam. Equally, it is clear that many are developing new forms of expressing their Islam, which they consider more appropriate to the European context. Often, community leaders and parents, each from their own perspective, regard such developments as equally disquieting, both in themselves and because they are seen as a loss of control over the younger generation.

At the very end of the 1980s, all the tensions indicated above broke out into the open for the first time. On the one hand, the affair of Salman Rushdie's *The Satanic Verses* raised questions not only about the role of religion in public life in general, but also about the role of Islam and Muslims in a Christian and post-Christian Europe. On the other hand, the 'headscarves affair' in France posed quite directly the questions of relations between religion and the secular state. Behind the complex debate and the political manoeuvrings lay tensions between the older and the younger generations of Muslims, between orthodox urban-based and traditional village expressions of Islam, not to mention tensions among various Muslim movements both inside and outside Europe. The 'affairs' exposed tensions between ideological secularists in the political and cultural establishments of Europe, the bearers of the culture of the nation state, and those who saw religion as having an active and critical role to play in public life. Above all, issues of the education of children were central: were they to be educated into a national culture, or did parents have the right to determine the nature of their children's education?

The 'Rushdie affair'

The essential elements in the events surrounding the protests against Salman Rushdie's book *The Satanic Verses* are comparatively straightforward. At the end of September 1988, Viking Penguin published the book despite advice from their reader in India, a professor and novelist of Sikh origin, that the book would cause trouble. During early October, the newly formed UK Action Committee on Islamic Affairs, with the particular initiative of the Islamic Foundation, Leicester, circulated copies of the offending passages to the governments of Muslim countries asking for action. Other groups, including the Union of Muslim Organisations, asked for the author to be prosecuted. In mid-December, a group of Muslim ambassadors protested to the Home Office (Ministry of the Interior), asking unsuccessfully for action to be taken for the book to be withdrawn. Until this point, the Muslim campaign had shown no success and had attracted little attention outside very limited circles.

In Britain, the public only became aware that something was going on when a copy of the book was publicly burned during a demonstration in Bradford on 14 January 1989. A heated debate in the media followed, which was exacerbated a month later when on 14 February Ayatollah Khomeini issued a fatwa (a religious ruling) to the effect that Rushdie had insulted the Prophet and Islam and that, as a self-confessed apostate, he should be killed. There was a reward on his head. This introduced a radically new dimension into the affair, leading to international repercussions. Britain and Iran broke off diplomatic relations at the beginning of March, and the Organisation of the Islamic Conference called for all possible action within the law to be taken against the book and its author. After the Iranian fatwa, Rushdie had to go into hiding for his own safety. Demonstrations of various kinds continued to attract media headlines. Discussions about possible legal remedies centred on libel and blasphemy law and culminated in a decision of the High Court in April 1990 that blasphemy law could not apply to Islam.

In the rest of Europe, public attention was only attracted as a result of the Iranian fatwa. A few demonstrations took place in some European cities. As a result, in the Netherlands, the government instituted a dialogue with the main Muslim organisations. In France, initial demonstrations calling for the death of Rushdie were soon replaced by a lively press debate about Islam, laicism and religious freedom. In other European countries, the debate was revived as translations of *The Satanic Verses* were announced. Italy was quickest off the mark. In Sweden, strong Muslim protests aroused some Swedish resentment about the 'ingratitude' of the Muslim community, which had been 'so favourably' treated, and the first anti-Muslim speech in parliament was held that year making references to the Rushdie affair. In Norway, the debate on the extent of religious freedom, previously aroused by plans to build a mosque in Oslo, was briefly revived. Everywhere, the effect of the pressure on Muslims after the fatwa and of their campaigns to prevent publication of the book was to provoke a degree of cooperation among Muslim groups previously unknown. Among the 'host community', there was tension between those who sought to identify all Muslims with Iran and those, mostly from within the churches and anti-racist groups, who wished to present a more differentiated picture. But essentially the affair lasted only a few months in public (for Salman Rushdie the issue is on-going), soon to be replaced in France by the 'headscarves affair'.

There is no doubt that behind this crisis lay a complex of factors of a political and social nature, which most observers have had little trouble in identifying. It was noticeable during the early phase of the demonstrations across Europe that Pakistani groups were particularly prominent, while the affair aroused hardly any response among the bulk of North Africans. The role of immigrant communities in Europe as a base for political opposition activities in Turkey before the military coup of September 1980 has been well attested. It seems apparent that a similar process was taking place between Pakistan and the Pakistani émigré communities in Europe in this instance. The return of Benazir Bhutto as opposition leader in Pakistan was greatly aided by the boost she found among Pakistani groups in Britain. It is likewise probable that the Rushdie affair and the Pakistani British campaign were helpful to Islamic groups opposing the government of Benazir Bhutto.

Within the political processes of the Muslim communities in Britain, the affair was likewise a significant tool. During the early months of the campaign, several different groups were presenting themselves as champions of the Muslim cause in rivalry with each other rather than in cooperation. Later, the creation of the UK Islamic Party was regarded by many as an attempt by a group consisting mainly of European converts to Islam to gain political advantage out of the affair. The affair also came as a welcome opportunity to existing Muslim organisations in Britain to reassert their influence over younger people who had shown a distinct tendency to drift away from traditional structures and set up their own informal and increasingly formal youth groups.

However correct such explanations of the complexities and causes of events may be, they really only relate to processes and not to the underlying issues. As many Muslims of all kinds of backgrounds said and wrote at the time, there was a deep revulsion at the insult to Islam, and especially to the person of the Prophet, contained in the book. The incident of the Satanic Verses is well known from scholarly writing and classical Islamic sources. As some Muslims have often pointed out, in a general attack against 'orientalism', most western scholars have shown little sympathy towards Islam and have sometimes been extremely critical of quite fundamental concepts and texts. But this has not provoked a reaction of the kind one has seen against Salman Rushdie. The issue was the sense of insult and revulsion at the language used about Muhammad and the description of events in his life.

In view of this, it should have come as no surprise that there was a particularly strong popular reaction against the book in places like Bradford. The Muslim community in Bradford is overwhelmingly from Kashmiri and Punjabi village backgrounds, with hardly any professionals among the older generation. The Barelwi tendency, with its great veneration for the person of Muhammad, permeates Bradford Islam, and the community was therefore collectively more prepared to register the insult claimed to be contained in the book. The virtual absence of a group of professionals in the local community leadership meant that it had little guidance as to how public actions might be perceived by the wider society.

The fundamental context of the affair was one in which a deep lack of mutual comprehension was central. On the part of some Muslim organisations, there was a serious lack of understanding of how statements and actions would be heard and interpreted by the wider society. In Britain, most significantly, those

Muslims who organised the burning of Rushdie's book were only marginally aware of the significance of book-burning in European history, with its associations of Inquisition and the more recent Nazi period in Germany.

Even deeper, however, was the lack of comprehension of Muslim concerns on the part of Europeans. The extent to which European society, and especially the political and literary sectors, had become distanced from religious priorities was exemplified in the way in which freedom of speech was held forth as an absolute. It was particularly telling that this could be done in this situation with little apparent sense of inconsistency, when compared with a general acceptance of some degree of limitation on freedom of expression in areas such as race relations, pornography, personal libel and national security.

Muslims could justifiably claim that their concerns, in this case their anger over the Rushdie book, were being measured by criteria different from those applied in other instances. It particularly hurt when the British Home Secretary, in a speech to the Muslim community in Birmingham, called on them to stay within the law in their protests – this to a community which had a record of being among the most law-abiding in the country. It was felt that public pronouncements by politicians and literary figures applied standards to the Muslim community which were not being applied to others, and that Islam and Muslims could be subjected to abuse without fear of being condemned as racist: Muslims felt that they were 'fair game' for attack. Certainly, those who attacked Islam and Muslims in sometimes quite extreme terms were not prepared to differentiate in any way among various Muslim tendencies. Furthermore, at the time, British legislation did not protect from discrimination on grounds of religious conviction, which it does today through the Equality Act 2010, and the now repealed seldom-used blasphemy law did not cover Islam. It was a particular complaint among Muslims in France, Germany and the Netherlands that observers refused to listen to many Muslims' own quite sharp statements against Khomeini's fatwa of death to Salman Rushdie.

In the British case, there was a further aspect which preceded the Rushdie affair but which led almost inexorably into it. The debate over education and the Muslim place in the education system had become increasingly vocal and politicised during the 1980s. Demands for Muslim voluntary aided schools (discussed in Chapter 4), had been growing and were the only point on which the Swann commission report *Education for All* had failed to agree. Despite Muslim arguments with aspects of the report, the general thrust of the inclusion of all minority groups as equal and full participants in the educational process was welcoming and welcomed. However, the report coincided with, and perhaps sharpened, a reaction among many 'white' parents against the concepts of anti-racist and multicultural education as they had been propounded by some politicians and many educationists. The reaction was typically most marked in areas where the ethnic minority school population was growing. The success of the Bradford Council of Mosques in helping to achieve the dismissal of a head teacher who had written and spoken against anti-racist and multicultural education not only encouraged the Council to engage in further campaigning leading to its active role in the Rushdie affair, but it also fed the fears of white parents.

In effect, soon after the optimism of the Swann Report, the educational arena was becoming a battleground. This was reflected in the political debates which accompanied the passing of the Education Reform Act 1988. In the discussions on religious education and school worship, the emphasis on a broadly and mainly Christian approach suggested to Muslims and others that they were marginal, a perception ironically strengthened by the facility for making exceptions when a school had a mainly ethnic minority population. The very groups which had campaigned strongly in the House of Lords for this change were the same groups which set about encouraging schools with a high proportion of ethnic and religious minority pupils to leave the control of local education authorities and to become self-governing with direct central government funding.

At the same time, central and local government and most of the educational establishment had set its mind firmly against any approval of Muslim voluntary aided schools. This was a stand which Muslims could only regard as discriminatory. The fact that the Labour Party in its policy review during 1989–90 chose to favour the establishment of such schools was welcomed, but at the same time regarded as political opportunism, as the decision was made at the height of the Rushdie affair.

The issues raised by this complex situation exposed the weaknesses of much of liberal Britain. In particular, the so-called 'race relations industry' initially found itself at a loss as to how to help alleviate the communal divides which were being exposed. The academic and ethnic relations structures had long operated on a basis of the divide between 'white' and 'black' Britain, the latter including people of both Afro-Caribbean and South Asian origin, regardless of what these people might think of themselves. The fact that the Turkish Cypriots of East London had always rejected their being lumped together with other 'blacks' had not altered anything, nor had the evidence of conflict between Afro-Caribbean and South Asian in the urban disturbances of 1981 and 1985, especially in Birmingham where cooperation between the two groups on the local Community Relations Council became extremely difficult as a consequence. Increasingly, Muslims, as well as Hindus and Sikhs, were rejecting the label 'black' and with it much of the sense of a shared interest with the Afro-Caribbean communities. Only as a result of the Rushdie affair was the pressure for such differentiation recognised, while the academic sociologists grudgingly began to consider that there might be a question to discuss.

Perhaps another factor which may help to explain why Muslims were especially active in Britain is the fact that most Muslims in Britain are British citizens. They had been told by their own leaders and by the political establishment of the country that they were citizens with equal rights and obligations towards their country. The experiences of young British Muslims trying to find work during the economic depression of the early 1980s, in the face of often blatant racial discrimination, were combined with the growing sense of the whole community that their alleged equal status was in practice more imaginary than real. The result had to be a frustration which was bound to find expression in one form or another.

An effect of the affair in Britain was to bring to the fore those Muslim organisations and spokespersons who were prepared to take on the media directly and in terms which could be understood by journalists with little or no conception of the wider background or context. As a result, media attention was focused not only on Bradford, where the main initiative had been centred, but also on a few groups or individuals. It is sometimes suggested that the media preferred the provocative stance.

This would certainly be true of the manner in which Dr Kalim Siddiqi of the Muslim Institute in London gained attention. Dr Siddiqi did not formally 'represent' anyone but himself, although he probably voiced the anger and frustrations of many Muslims, especially the younger educated ones. Through the 1980s, he had identified himself with the cause of Iran. He supported Khomeini's fatwa and on one occasion almost got himself prosecuted for incitement to murder. In 1990, his campaigning culminated in the publication in July of a 'Muslim Manifesto' which set out an agenda for Muslim action to attain a satisfactory status within British structures. Press reporting exposed the deep gulf of understanding because, while the press announced that Dr Siddiqi had called for a separate Muslim political entity with its own parliament, the context of the manifesto's use of the word 'parliament', in quotation marks, clearly referred to some form of joint representative council of all Muslims, on the lines of the Board of Deputies of British Jews.

In a similar manner, the press made much of a group with the title of 'Women against Fundamentalism', formed during the Rushdie affair. Based around the Ealing area in West London, its few members of Muslim background were voices welcomed by the press as speaking not only against the Muslim campaign to ban the book but also, by implication, against any form of committed Islam which broke with a secularist concept of the place of religion in society.

The 'headscarves affair'

In France, the affair of 1989 blew up in September, at the beginning of the school year. Three girls at a secondary school in the town of Creil insisted on wearing headscarves in school in contravention of a new school rule. They were escorted home by a teacher to explain the rule to their parents. Two of the girls were then kept away from school for a time. Having hit the national press headlines, the political debate and pressures started with at first contradictory reactions from various parts of the regional and national governments. In the first instance, the affair was concluded when the *Conseil d'État*, to which President Mitterrand had referred the matter, issued a statement in general terms to the effect that the principles of the public education system had perhaps not been observed fully by various parties in the case, and that these principles should be observed fully. It was a statement which neatly avoided any reference to headscarves or to Islam.

In the event, this was not the end of the matter, although the situation at the school in Creil had resolved itself. In response to the continuing political pressures, especially the activities of the *Front National*, led by Jean-Marie Le Pen, the government in March 1990 adopted three measures. It formed a High Commission on Integration, a commission to consider Islam in France, and it presented a national plan to combat racism.

As could be expected, the reasons for the incident which sparked off the affair soon became irrelevant. The college in Creil had for some years been faced with the question of what to do about a number of Jewish pupils who regularly absented themselves from school on Saturdays and during the first ten days or so of the school year in September. Having taken the decision to tolerate this no longer, the administration felt it appropriate to enforce a ban on overt expressions of religious practice on all religions – thence the ban on headscarves.

In fact, this ban was fully within the tradition of the public sector education system in France. It has been within the state schools that the republican and laicist tradition of French identity has been enshrined for a century. In the past, those who have not wanted to take part in this tradition have usually been Roman Catholic, and for them the Catholic network of 'free' schools was available. The laicist and republican tradition of the state school was regarded as an environment which could contribute positively to the integration of children of immigrants from North Africa into mainstream French culture.

This laicist and republican tradition was one of the factors which contributed to the headscarves affair becoming a national issue so quickly, while a similar case in Britain a few months later remained low-key. The year 1989 was of great symbolic importance in France, as the country was celebrating the bicentenary of the 1789 revolution. At one level it was a national celebration, but it was clearly a celebration of a particular kind of France: republican and anti-clerical France. While the latter of these two aspects, closely linked with the laicist tradition, was not emphasised during the celebration, it was nevertheless present, as evidenced by a somewhat ambivalent attitude to the celebrations in some Roman Catholic circles and, from outside the church, to the participation of the church in the celebrations.

The refusal of the girls of Creil to attend school without their headscarves was seen as a symbol of the challenge to the republican and laicist identity of France. In fact, it was not the only occasion during the year in which this identity and immigrant concerns clashed. In the town of Montfermeil, the mayor refused to admit the children of newly arrived immigrants to nursery classes, while in Lyons the city council refused permission to build a mosque. In Marseilles, when the mayor announced his support for the construction of a new central mosque, he was widely attacked from across the political spectrum, although the local bishop expressed his qualified support for the project.

Another reason why the headscarves affair assumed such importance was that at the same time as France was celebrating a tradition which many felt to be under threat from the growing ethnic minority communities, the country was also experiencing direct challenges abroad, primarily in the Muslim world. French hostages were being held in Beirut, and the government had again attempted an unsuccessful intervention in the Lebanese war. Events in North Africa were constantly threatening to pull France into cross-border disputes, while in Algeria the growth of the Islamic Salvation Front (FIS) was causing severe uncertainty. There had for some years been increasing talk in French media and academic circles about the spread of Islamic 'fundamentalism' (*intégrisme*) in France as posing a threat to social stability. The headscarves affair was popularly seen as evidence that *intégrisme* had finally infiltrated from North Africa into France. Le Pen, his *Front National* and more extreme racist tendencies had a field day.

During this period and in this context, there was a common French perception that Muslim extremists of various provenances were making France their battlefield. In fact, their agendas were more Middle Eastern and anti-imperialist than explicitly and exclusively Islamic, as witness the fact that several of the Arab 'terrorists' allegedly supported by Iran and brought to trial in the late 1980s in France were Lebanese with typically Lebanese Christian names, usually of Arab Orthodox (Patriarchate of Antioch) origin!

However, the sense of worry was strong enough among French officials for them to seek actively to encourage some sort of supreme Muslim council for the country. Enough Muslim leaders and organisations were, in the same manner, sufficiently worried to agree to take part in such a government-sponsored initiative. In November 1989, the minister of the interior invited six Muslims to form a *Conseil de réflexion sur l'Islam en France*. The six original members, three French and three foreign, coopted a further three French and six foreign Muslims. Clearly, the French government hoped that they might in this way help to create a supreme representative body of Islam in France which could encourage 'moderate' voices and marginalise 'extremists'. In 2015, eight EU states have actively created national councils to represent Muslims.

From 11 September 2001 to the new Iraq war

The terrorist attack on the World Trade Center in New York had an impact on the situation of Muslims in Europe of a magnitude which easily bears comparison with that of the 'affairs' of 1989. The suddenness of the event made the impact immediate and sharply public in a way which had not been experienced in 1989. Within twenty-four hours, physical attacks on people and premises considered to be Muslim were being reported in some countries and verbal attacks in all. Women's headscarves were torn off, individuals of 'Muslim' appearance were struck, spat at or verbally abused. Windows were smashed and walls covered in graffiti. But the attackers often betrayed their ignorance by attacking targets they thought were Muslim but were not. Sikh men, in particular, were assumed to be Muslim, presumably because their turbans reminded people of the pictures they had seen from the Taliban's Afghanistan. Only in France were the full beards of some Muslim men seen as an indicator of Islam. Otherwise, people with dark skin colour and buildings associated with 'foreign' religions were also labelled as Muslim. In Rome, children threw stones at a Syrian Orthodox archbishop!

But after such initial reactions, responses began to vary in different European countries. It seems clear that the main factor in such variation was the directions taken by politicians, the media and civil institutions such as churches in their responses. In many places tempers calmed, and while public debate could still be tense, direct attacks decreased in frequency or stopped altogether. This was the case in countries like Austria, Belgium, Britain, Finland, Germany and Portugal. In all these cases leading opinion formers, including government and political leaders, took public initiatives to distinguish between the perpetrators of the New York attacks and Islam and Muslims generally. In Britain, the prime minister and other party leaders met with Muslim representatives, and the Archbishop of Canterbury in cooperation with Tony Blair hosted an international Christian–Muslim seminar the following January. When Lady Thatcher, former Conservative prime minister, complained that Muslim leaders had not condemned the attack loudly and often enough, she was disowned by her party leaders. In Austria, President Thomas Klestil invited Christian, Muslim and Jewish leaders together to reaffirm the necessity of dialogue, a move which was supported by Catholic bishops. In Germany, an annual Day of the Open Mosque, set for 3 October to coincide with the national holiday marking German reunion, met with a massive positive response and was used by politicians and church leaders to emphasise the distinction between Islam and terrorism. In Belgium, all political parties, except for the right-wing *Vlaams Blok*, signed a common declaration of mutual respect.

Italy and Denmark were different. In the former, Islam had already become a subject for bitter debate a year earlier with the publication by Oriana Fallaci of a virulently anti-Muslim book. This had helped to set a public debate whose tone was generally against Islam and Muslims, in which the negative statements of certain politicians, bishops and newspaper editors far outweighed the numerous attempts by others, including statements from the Vatican and high-profile

Christian–Muslim meetings in Rome and Florence, to prevent the spread of prejudice and misunderstanding. This negative public atmosphere was then strengthened and to an extent legitimised by the statement made in Berlin in the late autumn of 2001 by Prime Minister Berlusconi that western Christian culture was 'superior' to Islamic – even if he did later claim that his statement had been 'taken out of context'.

In Denmark, a general election campaign had just started when the World Trade Center was hit, a campaign in which immigration and asylum already were key issues. The attack moved these questions to the top of the political agenda, and most parties adopted defensive positions to avoid losing votes, while the prime minister cancelled a meeting with Muslim representatives, the first-ever such meeting planned. The result of the election in November brought in a markedly right-of-centre minority coalition which depended on the extreme-right Danish People's Party to give it a majority vote in parliament. Among the earliest measures were cuts in public funding to organisations working with ethnic minorities and interreligious relations and the introduction of draconian new immigration and asylum legislation.

A significant factor in the public atmosphere regarding Islam and Muslims was the nature of media presentations and discussion. The balance of opinion and the way in which stories were presented in both the print and broadcast media appeared to correlate reasonably well with attitudes in local communities to local Muslims and their institutions. Certainly, in both Denmark and Italy there were very few media voices which were not explicitly or implicitly anti-Muslim and tending to identify the domestic Muslim community with the activities of groups like al-Qaʻida and the Taliban. In Denmark, it could be very difficult to argue that not all Muslims were like the noisy, but essentially harmless, young people from *Hizb al-Tahrir*. In countries like Britain, France, the Netherlands, Sweden and, to a lesser extent, Germany, media opinion tended to be much more open and evenly balanced. The debate was undoubtedly lively, sometimes bordering on the libellous and insulting, but the Muslim communities found as many friends as they found opponents. In the case of Britain and France, there is little doubt that the major issues had already been subjected to hard discussion a dozen years earlier at the time of the Rushdie and headscarf affairs, and the discussion had, in a sense, moved on. These issues had not previously been given a similar airing in countries like Denmark and Italy, so everything was compacted into the intense reaction in response to the September 11th events.

The responses to 11 September 2001 coincided with a period when, in certain countries, the political far right was again experiencing a resurgence. This was most notable in France and the Netherlands, where elections took place during the first half of 2002. When the Socialist vote collapsed in the first round of the French presidential election, it was the *Front National* leader,

Jean-Marie Le Pen, who emerged as the competitor to Jacques Chirac, himself right-of-centre in the second round. In the event, all parties of the left and centre combined to freeze out Le Pen, but in the process it had become clear that the racist dimensions of *Front National* ideology had moved markedly towards a targeting of Islam and Muslims as the main threat. The target was the same in the astounding, even if only temporary, popular following achieved in the Netherlands by Pym Fortuyn's entry first into Rotterdam local politics and then into the general election campaign of 2002, during which he was murdered by an animal rights activist. Although his new party soon collapsed after its successful entry into parliament, its appearance had unsettled the accustomed political processes. Equally significantly, it had undermined the myth that the Dutch were somehow more tolerant and less racist and xenophobic than most other European nations. As also in Denmark and France, complaining about Islam and Muslims and presenting them as a major threat to national tradition and cohesion had become legitimate. In the coming years, populist, nationalist parties sprouted all over Europe using a similar scapegoating of Islam and Muslims for everything from bad national economics to crime.

A concept which had entered the media debate in the late 1990s, and which the responses to the September 11th attacks pushed to the fore, was that of 'Islamophobia'. The term had been used very occasionally during the 1990s but gained prominence in the UK when in 1997 the anti-racist research and lobbying group the Runnymede Trust published its report *Islamophobia: A Challenge for Us All*. The report, drawn up by a commission chaired by a senior university academic and including Christian, Muslim and Jewish members, concluded that distrust, fear and even hatred of Islam and Muslims was pervasive in British society and was particularly being reinforced by media stereotypes and sensationalism. The response to the report was mixed, rejected out of hand by some newspapers and analysts and more or less grudgingly acknowledged by others. The report's publication coincided with the foundation of the Muslim Council of Britain, which quickly took up the recommendations as its own. The MCB, and very soon after more specialised organisations such as FAIR (Forum Against Islamophobia and Racism), actively approached newspapers when they were considered to be engaging in Islamophobia.

But the concept of Islamophobia, while it very quickly entered public discussion across all of Europe, did not remain uncontested. Many academics, while accepting that there was some substance to the accusations, were concerned about the definitions of Islamophobia suggested by the report. They felt that the definitions were of a nature that could open anyone engaging critically with aspects of Islam to accusations of Islamophobia. Some argued strongly that the phobia was not against Islam, which was an abstract, but against some Muslims or Muslim movements as people and social and cultural realities, in vain suggesting the term 'Muslimphobia' as a better alternative. On the other hand, major

Muslim organisations and personalities across Europe rejected the concept. While they acknowledged that public antipathy towards Islam and Muslims was widespread, and often associated with deeply rooted forms of racism, they resisted the implications, as they saw it, of Islam and Muslims being cast in a role of victimhood. As some put it, they did not want to see 'Islamophobia' become a new anti-semitism. However, almost two decades later, the concept is firmly established in European anti-racist environments, among Muslim organisations, and to a certain extent in state policies. For example, the Swedish state organises and finances anti-discrimination campaigns using the word, and the Crime Prevention Board has produced statistics on Islamophobic motivated crimes since 2006. Within academia, the discussion about a proper definition goes on. Some prefer the term anti-Muslim prejudice, but what is described is essentially the same.

Headscarves – again

In the meantime the question of headscarves had not disappeared. In France, since the original 'affair', it has reappeared as a major national issue on at least three occasions. Revised instructions from the government in the mid-1990s, in essence upheld by the *Conseil d'État*, left it to school heads to decide what might constitute the legally unacceptable 'ostentatious' wearing of religious symbols. The association of the headscarf with Islamic 'fundamentalism', of a kind identified in the public mind with violent Islamic resistance to the military dictatorship of Algeria, did not temper public paranoia, especially when the violence apparently spilled over into bombs in the Paris Métro. By early 2004, the National Assembly had approved a law banning the wearing of all forms of religiously 'ostentatious' dress, and in September 2010 a specific ban on 'face covering in public places' was introduced. Both bans were formulated in general language but much of the discussion when preparing the laws circled around female Muslim covering.

In the late 1990s, the question suddenly hit Denmark, when a couple of major retailers announced that their staff uniform policy could not allow the wearing of a headscarf. Extensive public protest, supported by most trade unions, government ministers and the majority of the retail trade, forced a retreat on the part of the two companies which had originally provoked the debate. However, in another case in late 2003, an appeal court upheld an employer's right to ban headscarves being worn by staff dealing with the public. In May 2008, a law was passed forbidding the wearing of religious attire of any sort by specifically Danish judges when practicing law, this to uphold the idea of a neutral and fair juridical system.

In Britain, the earlier House of Lords decision upholding the right of a Sikh boy to wear a turban under the terms of the Race Relations Act meant that the lower courts regularly upheld the rights of Muslim female employees to wear headscarves, so long as they were of ethnic minority background. Only with the introduction of a European directive against religious discrimination in employment in December 2003 was it possible to liberate this issue from the racial and ethnic constraints of the Race Relations Act. These cases tended to attract greater significance in reports outside the country than they did inside.

In Germany, the headscarf became an issue when the Constitutional Court had to deal with the case of a female Muslim teacher who insisted on wearing a headscarf to work. In the late summer of 2003, the court decided that her employer did not have the right to prevent her. However, the basis of the decision was that the federal state concerned had taken this decision without any foundation in existing state law, rather than with reference to constitutional principles. The response on the part of a number of states was immediately to draw up legislation banning the wearing of headscarves by teachers. After a decade of debates, the German Federal Constitutional Court ruled the ban unconstitutional, discriminatory and not compatible with the idea of freedom of religion in March 2015. In the German case, of course, the context of the public debate was conditioned not only by responses to the 11 September 2001 attacks in New York and Washington, but also by reference to the debate taking place in Turkey over the wearing of the headscarf by public employees and, above all, by university students.

The European Court of Human Rights (ECHR) in Strasbourg could conceivably extend its restrictive understanding of the role of Islam in the public domain, as applied to its support for the Turkish banning of the Refah Party, to a more general application of Article 9 of the Convention relating to freedom of religion. However, if it in due course were to take a more liberal view, it is difficult to imagine how the French measures to legislate against the headscarf in public institutions could survive a legal challenge to Strasbourg. But the ECHR seldom confronts member states, especially not in matters involving religion. For example, in 2014, the French ban on face covering in public was found not to violate any basic rights. Even if some laws regarding covering may be expected to be comparatively short-lived, their impact on a constructive Muslim integration in Europe is likely to have a negative impact far beyond their practical implications.

Drawing Muhammad and violence

In Denmark, following the complaints by a Danish author, Kåre Bluitgen, about his difficulties finding an artist willing to illustrate his biography on Islam's final prophet, Muhammad, the daily *Jyllands-Posten* published in September 2005 twelve cartoons portraying Muhammad in an attempt to stand up against artistic self-censorship. The cartoons were hastily drawn and for the most part harmless. Some made fun of the initiative. A couple of the drawings directly associated Muhammad with terrorism, criminality, female oppression, even giving him a demonic appearance. At first little happened. Most significantly, a week after the publication, a group of Danish imams and mosque leaders asked *Jyllands-Posten* to apologise for some of the cartoons, but *Jyllands-Posten* ignored them. *Islamisk Trossamfund* (the Islamic Society) in Copenhagen contacted Prime Minister Anders Fogh Rasmusen to complain about the treatment of Muslims in Denmark and soon after eleven embassies of Muslim countries sent a letter to the prime minster requesting a meeting about the situation. The requests were declined stating that the authorities did not restrain the media. The embassies reported home and the Danish imams turned to contacts abroad for support. The consequent reactions were not foreseen by anyone. Soon, Denmark became vilified in preaching across the Muslim world, the Arab League condemned the Danish government, and the Organisation of the Islamic Conference initiated a boycott of Danish products and cultural events. Protests were held in at least thirty different countries. Street protests culminated in violence and in Beirut the Danish consulate was torched on 5 February 2006. As often before, protests were used to express discontent with local politics turning the demonstrations into clashes between demonstrators and police in, for example, Afghanistan and Pakistan. At the same time, others rallied to the support of *Jyllands-Posten* and 'free speech'. Several newspapers reprinted the cartoons, among them French satirical magazine *Charlie Hebdo* adding a cartoon of their own on 8 February 2006. Several death threats against the cartoonists were issued – both locally in Denmark and by Islamist leaders in the Middle East.

While supporters of *Jyllands-Posten* tended to frame the conflict in words like free speech, censorship, and the presumed prohibition of images in Islamic tradition, the critics were of two kinds, referring to completely different set of ideas. Anti-racists criticised the daily for being overtly racist in its treatment of immigrants generally and Muslims specifically. Muslim critics referred to *sabb an-nabi* (insulting the prophet). In fact, insulting the prophet is considered graver than insulting God, since God can defend himself whereas Muhammad is dead. Thus, he needs to be defended, and many rose to the occasion. Muslims rarely claimed the depiction as such as a major problem. When Danish author Bluitgen finally published his respectfully illustrated biography of Muhammad it caused no commotion.

The cartoon crisis has not ended. Through the Internet, the cartons have spread and become tools in Islam-hatred all over the world. They have also become symbols. For those who argue for limitless freedom of speech, the reproduction of the images is a way not to fold under Muslim pressure. For violent extremist Muslims, the cartoonists and the papers that have reproduced them have become token targets, for example mentioned on al-Qaʻida magazine

Inspire's most wanted lists 2013. On the same list one finds Swedish post-modern artist Lars Vilks and French satire magazine *Charlie Hebdo*.

Lars Vilks claimed his original intent in 2007 was to dare a gallery to show images drawn by Vilks of Muhammad as a 'roundabout dog'. The gallery had asked Vilks for composition on the theme 'The dog in art'. Vilks who, allegedly, thought the fuss about the Danish cartoons had dissipated wanted to provoke by combining the most popular art expression in Sweden (round-about dogs) with the least used (Muhammad). A roundabout dog is a home-crafted statue of any material of an animal – not necessarily a dog – illegally placed in a roundabout for the fun of it. Some dogs become popular and are allowed to stay for quite a while. The drawings were first accepted and then withdrawn before the opening for security reasons. When this was repeated at another more established institute, a debate on self-censorship started in Swedish papers and, on 18 August 2007, several papers published one of the drawings.

Reactions were not as widespread as to the previous cartoon crisis, but severe enough. The emerging organisation, the Islamic State in Iraq, put a price on Vilks' head, and since then he has lived with security police protection, and survived at least two serious attempts to his life. But this crisis confirmed the positions taken earlier on.

The brutal murder of artists and staff of *Charlie Hebdo* on 7 January 2015 played out the pattern again. Publications were met with threats and then attacks, discussions on freedom of speech contrasted with those on racism and blasphemy followed suit.

Together with other acts of violence in, for example, New York (11 September 2001), Madrid (11 March 2004), London (7 July 2005), Stockholm (11 December 2010) and Copenhagen (14–15 February 2015) when the per-petrators proudly have announced that their deed was done to defend Islam, because of Muslim beliefs, or to protect Muslims in Muslim countries from 'Western' armies, a strong notion of radicalised Muslims as a security problem started to take hold among European politicians.

Many reports and much scholarly work have been devoted to either trying to prevent and contain Muslim radicalism or point out the negative effects of excessive surveillance. Continuous threats from radical Islamist groups like IS (Islamic State) do not help the moderating voices. The polarisation between Muslims and non-Muslims in western Europe and the stigmatisation of Muslims are in fact worse in 2015 than fifteen years ago. At the same time, Muslim integration in the labour market and in schooling is better functioning today than fifteen years ago in many European countries, and one finds more coop-eration between non-Muslim and Muslim civil society organisations, between churches and mosque organisations and between governments and Muslim representatives.

Conclusion: Muslim and/or European?

As we have seen, the settlement of Muslim communities of significant size has inevitably raised challenges to traditions, both Muslim and European. Given sheer power relationships – political, economic, cultural, demographic – it is to be expected that it is the Muslim minorities which have to carry the weight of adapting. Traditional institutions, such as the mosque, and those of more recent origins, such as particular movements and organisations, have changed and are continuing to change to respond to circumstances and needs different from those of the past.

The character of this adaptation is strongly influenced by two particular overlapping factors. On the one hand is the ethnic and cultural variety among the Muslims in Europe. They have come from many different parts of the Muslim world and are mixing in European cities. With them, the immigrant generation brought the whole of their cultural baggage with all its variety from different countries, regions, even villages. In the alien context, each has often defended a particular tradition as being Islamic and found that the neighbour was defending a different tradition in the same terms. It was necessary to abandon exclusive claims to Islamic legitimacy without abandoning Islamic legitimacy as such. It became necessary to identify those aspects of the way of life which were culturally relative and to categorise them apart from the central Islamic core which must remain absolute.

On the other hand is the generation of young Muslims born or grown up in Europe. These people have been through a European system of education and have experienced the wider society – positively as well as negatively – and are consciously undertaking the analysis of Islam and its cultural expression necessary for Islam to remain meaningful to them and to their children in turn.

These young people are beginning to form the core of the next generation of leadership of Muslim groups and organisations. They are also becoming increasingly articulate in expressing forms of Islamic practice and priorities relevant to their European situation. It is, however, clear that they are not anywhere near being a numerical majority. Against their growing influence is weighted the experience of a majority of young Muslims, who have not been successful in education and who are growing up into unemployment and other forms of social marginalisation. In Britain, the most concrete example of this is to be found in the phenomenon of Asian youth gangs in conflict with their parents, with community leaders, and with the police. In Parisian suburbs, the uprisings in 2005 and 2007 are further examples of alienation and frustration.

Such developments are not only the effects of educational and social neglect, at best, or discrimination at worst. They are also closely related to the continuing problem of racism in European society. This takes different forms in different countries. In Britain particularly, it is closely associated with skin colour. This is clearly also an element in mainland Europe, but there racism often takes on a more general anti-foreign character – xenophobia. Racism and xenophobia include as one significant component an anti-Islamic element, which tends to be expressed in many different ways and picks on specific attributes or customs like food, dress, family relations, language and ritual. Often these may be genuinely linked to one particular Muslim group, but they are then generalised as being applicable and characteristic of all and are mobilised in a denigratory fashion as insulting slogans and 'reasons' for hatred.

The collapse of the communist system in eastern Europe in the period 1989–92 has provided a context which has strengthened racist and xenophobic trends. The problems associated with the unification of the two parts of Germany are clearly part of the background to a series of violent incidents across the country, which included arson and murder attacks against Turks during 1992 and 1993. Furthermore, during the first decade of the twenty-first century, the neo-Nazi cell National Socialist Underground murdered eight Turks. On the other hand, such developments were not reflected in regional elections, where radical right wing parties consistently failed to win seats. Generally, there has been a growth in racist and xenophobic violence, but the translation of this into changes in the balance of electoral power has been very uneven. In 2009, the street protest movement the English Defence League (EDF) was set up, its prime target being the alleged Islamisation of Britain. The EDF does not shy away from promoting violence and actively engaging in it. Other national defence leagues were formed and soon followed suit. For example, all Nordic countries have one. But as pointed out earlier, nationalist, populist, but not explicitly racist, parties have done remarkably well in elections in most European countries in the last decade or so.

As symbolised in the wars in Bosnia Herzegovina and, to a lesser extent, in Kosovo, the communist collapse has also contributed to making Muslims again feel more insecure. Islam is in some quarters presented as 'the new enemy' in a new 'clash of civilisations'. Events in Bosnia and the Caucasus are interpreted in many Muslim quarters as evidence of a renewal of an aggressive Christendom, often perceived as a continuation of the Crusades. The failure of western governments to react as decisively to these developments as they did to the Iraqi invasion of Kuwait in 1990 is adduced as proof. On the other hand, the events of 11 September 2001 and international responses to them, especially in Afghanistan and Iraq, have been seen by a small minority of Muslims as a restitution against those earlier events, while they have left many others feeling under increased pressure.

The international situation combines with local developments to encourage the revival of age old memories of a Christian–Muslim frontier. But today that mythical frontier no longer runs along the Mediterranean basin; it spreads through the cities of Europe – or at least it has the potential to do so, if European institutions misunderstand and mishandle the situation.

It is the European context which will be the major influence on how Muslims perceive their place and contribution. This is the case in the various practical issues described throughout previous chapters. But it goes much deeper, as events since the late 1980s up to the present have highlighted. The question, in the last analysis, must be how far European society is also prepared to adapt.

A plural society in which all participants are respected, where everybody's constructive contribution is valued, and where all feel accepted, is a model for which there is arguably no precedent, although historians of the Islamic world may wish to point to the Ottoman empire and Islamic Spain at certain periods, as may also historians of certain periods of the Habsburg empire. Models may be suggested, but they cannot be imposed. Many of the ethnic minority communities, including Muslims, traditionally place an emphasis on collective identity and communal solidarity which may seem to contradict the modern European cult, at least superficially, of the individual personality. So, models of plurality may range from a collectivist 'community of communities' to an individualist ideal of personal religious and cultural freedom of movement.

Different people have different ways of doing things, and in a plural society there must be more room for such differences than the traditional nation-state-culture unity allows. Justice can have several faces. It must be possible to open up the options for different forms of family life, different kinds of business relations, different educational priorities, different views on health, and different approaches to religious and social organisation.

However, the threat of social disintegration as a consequence cannot be ignored. Differences and plurality, especially of a religious kind, have historically been more destructive than constructive. Differences have to find a place within an overall political, social and legal consensus. In Europe, we have tended to find this consensus in overarching institutional frameworks and in a basic core of common cultural content and national identity. This kind of consensus need not be the only kind. It is equally possible to imagine a socially cohesive consensus founded on modes of intercultural and interreligious relations. What could hold the various communities together is a combination of welcoming acceptance of positive differences and a commitment to mutual respect. This would need a change of attitudes on all sides, a readiness to subject all our human absolutes to the goal of peaceful coexistence.

In a European recognition of the permanence of the Muslim presence comes a challenge to European self-understanding. In the constant process of saying to the new minorities, 'You cannot do this' or 'This is not possible', the response is often, 'Why not?' Often, the European answer to the 'Why not?' uncritically reflects inherited solutions and modes of action which can be changed. Concepts such as nation, constitution, laicism, secularism, established church, and so on, are the products of history. They have evolved from the past into the present, and there is no reason why they cannot continue to evolve into the future. The danger is that they are exploited to restrict and delimit the scope for the self-development of Muslim or other minorities rather than used constructively so as to make space. So long as this continues to be the case, professions of support for cultural and religious plurality risk being taken for hypocrisy.

A note on statistics

It is evident throughout this book, as it is obvious to observers in any way acquainted with the subject, that one of the most uncertain aspects of this study is the nature of the statistical data. This uncertainty is founded on two points, namely the categories used in official statistics and, more fundamentally, on the problem of definition.

The increasingly secular character of the state in western Europe over the last century or so has meant that the collection of statistics for all kinds of purposes coincided with a period when the role of religion was coming to be perceived as an increasingly private affair. The state had no right or no interest in collecting information from the citizens about their religious adherence or activity. So it is that only in very few instances do government censuses include a question on religion: in the Federal Republic of Germany, the Netherlands, Switzerland and Northern Ireland. As the minimum period between censuses tends to be ten years, their usefulness is minimal. The absolute laicist nature of the French state precludes any official religious data at all, while in Britain religious data is haphazardly available in some government departments and not in others, although a question on religion was included for the first time in the 2001 census. For reasons of laws of association, it is however possible to obtain some information on the numbers of members of Muslim organisations in, for example, Norway and Sweden.

However, the basic dilemma remains one of definition. In sum, statistics on Muslims in Europe are not comparable in nature and quality with those on Christians and Jews. The latter two long-established communities have forms of organisation and membership which allow the observer to identify – however differently from one country to the next – those sections of the population which have some form of relationship with a religion of adherence, through registered baptism or confirmation, or regularly kept data on church attendance. This is clearly not the case with Muslims. As the various country chapters make clear, this book, like most other recent and current work on Muslims in western Europe, operates on the assumption that anyone who comes from a Muslim cultural background and is not explicitly Christian, or of some other non-Muslim religion, is Muslim. This is why so many of the statistics presented throughout are based on nationality or country of birth. But it is therefore also, strictly speaking, a nonsense to say, as is often done, that Islam is the second-largest religion after Catholicism in, for example, France: like is simply not being compared with like.

Having emphasised this weakness, it is also necessary to point out that there remains a justification for continuing the use of this definition in this book. One of the theses of the present study is that the communities of Muslim origin in western Europe are still very much in the process of settling down, a process which will continue not only as the children of immigrants grow up and establish their own families, but also as their children in turn mature and grow to find a place. As events of recent years have increasingly underlined, Islam is a very important element in this process. So, as we observe – and take part in – this gradual settlement, integration and definition of Islam in the Europe of the future, we are dealing overwhelmingly with the communities for whom Islam is an immediate option of personal identity and social belonging, and that must be all those who share a Muslim cultural heritage.

Bibliography

Introduction

When the first two editions of this book were published during the 1990s a major feature of the title was the Biographical Essay at the end. Information about Muslims in Europe was scattered in working papers, a large variety of scholarly journals, newsletters, or obscurely published work by individual researchers in all different European languages. *Muslims in western Europe* brought these together for the benefit of many scholars and students eager to learn.

Today, the situation is quite different. 'Islam in Europe' is an established field of research with a wide variety of actors from different disciplines. The number of books and articles is immense. Just typing 'Islam in Europe' in a library database or an on-line book store will retrieve hundreds of titles, several of them actually called exactly 'Islam in Europe'. If articles are included there are several thousand titles. Online encyclopaedias like Wikipedia are often amazingly resourceful (even though not always correct), giving the reader the possibility to following links to scholarly work, governmental statistics, and journalism as well as to web pages run by Muslim organisations. Search engines will provide links to texts, photographs and films enabling everyone to follow the inauguration of an Italian mosque in Agrigent in 2015, view images from inside a Swedish mosque in Trollhättan or read qualitative journalism on the spread of the Gülen movement in Germany. Thus, a biographical essay is not *needed* anymore.

In 2015, the major feature of the book is to be able to bring together, in a concise fashion, the research of decades and synthesise it to a manageable text. Due to its essayistic character, the book does not make many references in the main text, and there is a risk of loosing the connection to the scholarly works it is based on. For this reason the biographical information is kept but the essay is reduced to a thematic literature list with a few additions. If the reader feels this is a great loss, we refer the reader to earlier editions of the book.

General works

Abedin, S. Z. and Z. Sardar (eds), *Muslim minorities in the West* (London: Grey Seal, 1995).
Allievi, S. and J. S. Nielsen (eds), *Muslim networks and transnational communities in and across Europe* (Leiden: Brill, 2003).

AlSayyad, N. and M. Castells (eds), *Muslim Europe or Euro-Islam: politics, culture and citizenship in an age of globalisation* (Lanham: Lexington Books, 2002).

Amghar, S. *et al.* (eds), *European Islam: challenges for society and public policy* (Brussels: Centre for European Policy Studies, 2007).

Blaschke, J. *et al.* (eds), *Muslims in Europe: a bibliography* (Berlin: Parabolis, 2002).

Castles, S., *Here for good: Western Europe's new ethnic minorities* (London: Pluto Press, 1984).

Castles, S. and G. Kosack, *Immigrant workers and class structures in Western Europe* (London: Oxford University Press, 1973).

Cesari, J. (ed.), *Muslims in the West after 9/11: religion, politics and law* (London and New York: Routledge, 2010).

Cesari, J. (ed.), *The Oxford handbook of European Islam* (Oxford: Oxford University Press, 2015).

Dassetto, F. (ed.), *Paroles de l'Islam: individus, sociétés et discours dans l'islam européen contemporain* (Paris: Maisonneuve, 2000).

Dassetto, F. and A. Bastenier, *Europa: nuova frontiera dell'Islam* (Rome: Edizioni Lavoro, 1988).

Dassetto, F. and Y. Conrad (eds), *Musulmans en Europe occidentale: Bibliographie commentée* (Paris: L'Harmattan, 1996).

Ferrari, S., *L'islam in Europa: lo statuto giuridico delle communità musulmane* (Bologna: Il Mulino, 1996).

Ferrari, S. and A. Bradney (eds), *Islam and European legal systems* (Aldershot: Ashgate, 2000).

Fetzer, J. S. and J. C. Soper, *Muslims and the state in Britain, France, and Germany* (Cambridge: Cambridge University Press, 2005).

Gerholm, T. and Y. G. Lithman (eds), *The new Islamic presence in Europe* (London and New York: Mansell, 1988).

Haddad, Y. Y. (ed.), *Muslims in the West: from sojourners to citizens* (Oxford: Oxford University Press, 2002).

Haddad, Y. Y. and I. Qurqmaz, 'Muslims in the West: a select bibliography', *Islam and Christian-Muslim Relations*, vol. 11 (2000), pp. 5–49.

Höfert, A. and A. Salvatore (eds), *Between Europe and Islam: shaping modernity in a transcultural space* (Brussels: Peter Lang, 1999).

Hunter, S. (ed.), *Islam in Europe: the new social, cultural and political landscape* (Westport: Greenwood, 2001).

Hunter, S. T. (ed.), *Islam, Europe's second religion: the new social, cultural, and political landscape* (London: Praeger, 2002).

Johnstone, P., 'A decade of European churches and Islam', *Research Papers: Muslims in Europe*, no. 38 (June 1988).

van Koningsveld, P. S. and W. Shadid (eds), *The integration of Islam and Hinduism in Western Europe* (Kampen: Kok Pharos, 1991).

Laurence, J., *The emancipation of Europe's Muslims: the state's role in minority integration* (Princeton and Oxford: Princeton University Press, 2012).

Maréchal, B. (ed.), *L'Islam et les musulmans dans l'Europe élargie: Radioscopie* (Louvain-la-Neuve: Academia Bruylant, 2002).

Maréchal, B., *The Muslim Brothers in Europe: roots and discourse* (Leiden: Brill, 2008).

Maréchal, B., S. Allievi, F. Dassetto and J. Nielsen (eds), *Muslims in the enlarged Europe* (Leiden: Brill, 2003).

Martin Muñoz, G. (ed.), *Islam, modernism and the West* (London: I. B. Tauris, 1999).

Morsy, M. (ed.), *L'Islam en Europe à l'Epoque moderne* (Paris: Sindbad, 1985).

Nielsen, J. S., 'State, religion and laicite: The western European experience', in G. Speelman *et al.* (eds), *Muslims and Christians in Europe: Breaking new ground (Essays in honour of Jan Slomp)* (Kampen: Kok, 1993), pp. 90–9.

Nielsen, J. S., 'Christian–Muslim relations in Western Europe', *Islamochristiana*, 21 (1995), pp. 121–31.

Nielsen, J. S. *et al.* (eds), *Yearbook of Muslims in Europe*. Vols 1–6 (Leiden: Brill, 2009–2014).

Nonneman, G., T. Niblock and B. Szajkowski (eds), *Muslim communities in Europe* (Reading: Ithaca, 1996).

Peter, F. and R. Ortega (eds), *Islamic movements of Europe: public religion and Islamophobia in the modern world* (London and New York: I. B. Tauris, 2014).

Power, J., *Migrant workers in Western Europe and the United States* (Oxford: Pergamon, 1979).

Rath, J., R. Penninx, K. Groenendijk and A. Meyer, *Western Europe and its Islam* (Leiden: Brill, 2001).

Shadid, W. A. R. and P. S. van Koningsveld (eds), *Religious freedom and the position of Islam in Western Europe* (Kampen: Kok, 1995).

Shadid, W. A. R. and P. S. van Koningsveld (eds), *Religious freedom and the neutrality of the state: the position of Islam in the European Union* (Leuven: Peeters, 2002).

Shadid, W. A. R. and P. S. van Koningsveld (eds), *Intercultural relations and religious authorities: Muslims in the European Union* (Leuven: Peeters, 2002).

Sinno, A. H. (ed.), *Muslims in western politics* (Bloomington and Indianapolis: Indiana University Press, 2009).

Vertovec, S. and C. Peach (eds), *Islam in Europe: the politics of religion and community* (London: Macmillan, 1997).

1. A brief history

Abdullah, M. S., *Geschichte des Islams in Deutschland* (Graz: Styria, 1981).

Ageron, C.-R., 'L'immigration maghrébine en France: un survol historique', in M. Morsy (ed.), *L'Islam en Europe à l'Epoque moderne* (Paris: Sindbad, 1985), pp. 201–22.

Ally, M. M., 'The growth and organisation of the Muslim community in Britain', *Research Papers* (from Selly Oak, University of Birmingham), no. 1 (March 1979).

Balic, S., *Die Muslims im Donauraum* (Vienna: Moslemischer Sozialdienst, 1971).

Eherecht, Familienrecht und Erbrecht der Mohamedaner nach dem hanefitischen Ritus (Vienna: Kaiserlich-königliche Hof- und Staatsdruckerei, 1883). [The German codification of Islamic family law.]

Gillette, A. and A. Sayad, *L'immigration algérienne en France*, 2nd edn (Paris: Éditions Entente, 1984).

Rose, E. J. B., *Colour and citizenship: A report on British race relations* (London: Oxford University Press, 1969), pp. 65–90.

2. France

Amiraux, V., 'CFCM: a French touch?', *ISIM Newsletter*, no. 12 (June 2003), pp. 24–5.

Andezian, S., 'Pratiques féminines de l'Islam en France', *Archives des sciences sociales des religion*, vol. 55 (1983), pp. 53–66.

Boyer, A., *L'Institut Musulman de la Mosquée de Paris* (Paris: CHEAM, 1992).

Cesari, J., *Etre musulman en France aujourd'hui* (Paris: Hachette, 1997).

Cesari, J., *Musulmans et républicains: les jeunes, l'islam et la France* (Brussels: Editions Complexe, 1998).

Costa-Lascoux, J. and E. Témime, *Les algériens en France: Genèse et devenir d'une migration* (Paris: Publised, 1985).

Etienne, B., *L'Islamisme radical* (Paris: Hachette, 1987).

Frégosi, F. (ed.), *La formation des cadres religieux musulmans en France – approaches socio-juridiques* (Paris: l'Harmattan, 1998).

Geisser, V., *Ethnicité républicain: les elites d'origine maghrébine dans le système politique français* (Paris: Presse de Sciences Po, 1997).

Hargreaves, A. G., *Immigration, 'race' and ethnicity in contemporary France* (London: Routledge, 1995).

Kepel, G., *Les banlieues de l'Islam* (Paris: Seuil, 1987).

Legrain, J.-F., 'Aspects de la présence musulmane en France', *Dossiers du S. R. I.* (Paris), no. 2 (September 1986).

Leveau, R. and G. Kepel (eds), *Les musulmans dans la société française* (Paris: Fondation nationale des sciences politiques, 1988).

Rocher, L. and F. Charquoui, *D'une foi à l'autre: les conversion à l'Islam en occident* (Paris: Seuil, 1986).

Sellam, S., *L'Islam et les musulmans en France* (Paris: Editions Tougui, 1987).

Ternisien, X., *La France des mosques* (Paris: Albin Michel, 2002).

Thépaut, F. (ed.), *L'Islam en France* (Paris: CIEMM, 1978).

Wihtol de Wenden, C., 'La vie associative des Harkis', *Migration sociétés*, vol. 1, no. 5–6 (October–December 1989), pp. 9–26.

Wihtol de Wenden, C. and René Mouriaux, 'French trade unionism and Islam', *Research Papers: Muslims in Europe*, no. 36 (December 1987).

Wisniewski, J., *Etrangers en France: Des chiffres et des hommes* (Paris: Hommes et migration, 1986).

3. Germany

Abadan-Unat, N. (ed.), *Turkish workers in Europe 1960–1975* (Leiden: Brill, 1976).

Amiraux, V., *Acteurs de l'Islam entre Allemagne et Turquie: parcours militants et experiences reli-gieuses* (Paris: L'Harmattan, 2001).

Bentzin, A., 'Islamic TV programmes as a forum of a religious discourse', in S. Allievi and J. S. Nielsen (eds), *Muslim networks and transnational communities in and across Europe* (Leiden: Brill, 2003).

Blaschke, J., 'Islam und Politik unter türkische Arbeitsmigranten', *Jahrbuch zur Geschichte und Gesellschaft des Vorderen und Mittleren Orients, 1984* (Berlin: Express, 1985), pp. 295–366.

Deutsche Welle, *Einwanderungsland, Vielvölkerstaat oder was sonst? Die Bundesrepublik und ihre Ausländer* (Cologne: Deutsche Welle, 1982).

Elsass, C., *Identität: Veränderungen kultureller Eigenarten im Zusammenleben von Türken und Deutschen* (Hamburg: EBV-Rissen, 1983).

Feindt-Riggers, N. and U. Steinbach, *Islamische Organisationen in Deutschland: eine aktuelle Bestandsaufnahme und Analyse* (Hamburg: Deutsches Orient Institut, 1997).

Freund, W. S., *Integration oder Rückkehr? Grundfragen der Ausländerpolitik* (Neustadt: Arca Verlag, 1980).

Al-Hamarneh, A. and J. Thielmann (eds), *Islam and Muslims in Germany* (Leiden: Brill, 2008).

Heitmeyer, W., J. Müller and H. Schröder, *Verlockender Fundamentalismus: türkische Jugendliche in Deutschland* (Frankfurt a/ M: Suhrkamp, 1997).

Hoffman, B. *et al.*, *Graue Wölfe, Koranschulen, Idealistenvereine* (Cologne: Pahl-Rugenstein, 1981).

Katsoulis, H., *Bürger zweiter Klasse: Ausländer in der Bundesrepublik* (Frankfurt: Campus Verlag, 1978).

Lähnemann, J. (ed.), *Erziehung zur Kulturbegegnung* (Hamburg: EBV-Rissen, 1986).

Leitlinien der Landesregierung Nordrhein-Westfalen zur Ausländerpolitik (Düsseldorf: Ministerium für Arbeit, Gesundheit und Soziales des Landes Nord-Rhein-Westfalen, 1980).

Miteinander leben: Ausländerpolitik in Berlin (West Berlin: Senator für Gesundheit, Soziales und Familie, 1982).

Schiffauer, W., *Die Gottesmänner: türkische Islamisten in Deutschland: eine Studie in religiöser Evidenz* (Frankfurt a/M: Suhrkamp, 2000).

Spuler-Stegemann, U., *Muslime in Deutschland – nebeneinander oder miteinander?* (Freiburg: Herder, 1998).

4. United Kingdom

Ansari, K. H., *The infidel within: the history of Muslims in Britain from 1800 to the present* (London: C. Hurst, 2004).

Anwar, M., *The myth of return* (London: Heinemann, 1979).

Anwar, M., 'Muslims in Britain: 1991 census and other statistical sources', *CSIC Papers: Europe*, no. 9 (September 1993).

Anwar, M., *Between cultures: continuity and change in the lives of young Asians* (London: Routledge, 1998).

Basit, T., *Eastern values – western milieu: identities and aspirations of adolescent British Muslim girls* (Aldershot: Ashgate, 1997).

Bradney, A. G. D., 'Separate schools, ethnic minorities and the law', *New Community*, vol. 13, no. 3 (Spring 1987), pp. 412–20.

Brown, C., *Black and white Britain* (London: Heinemann, 1984).

Charlton, R. and R. Kaye, 'The politics of religious slaughter: an ethno-religious case study', *New Community*, vol. 12, no. 3 (Winter 1985–6), pp. 490–503.

Gilliat-Ray, S., *Muslims in Britain: an Introduction* (Cambridge: Cambridge University Press, 2010).

Halliday, F., *Arabs in Exile: Yemeni migrants in urban Britain* (London: I. B. Tauris, 1992).

Hopkins, P. and R. Gale (eds), *Muslims in Britain: race, place and identities* (Edinburgh: Edinburgh University Press, 2009).

Jacobson, J., *Islam in transition: religion and identity among British Pakistani youth* (London: Routledge, 1998).

Johnson, R. O., '"Race", religion and ethnicity: Religious observance in the West Midlands', *Ethnic and Racial Studies*, vol. 8 (1985), pp. 426–38.

Joly, D. and J. S. Nielsen, *Muslims in Britain: An annotated bibliography 1960–84* (Coventry: University of Warwick, Centre for Research in Ethnic Relations, 1985).

Lewis, P., *Islamic Britain: Religion, politics and identity among British Muslims* (London: I. B. Tauris, 1994).

Maan, B., *The New Scots: The story of Asians in Scotland* (Edinburgh: John Donald, 1992).

Modood, T., *Britain's ethnic minorities: diversity and disadvantage* (London: Policy Studies Institute, 1997).

Nielsen, J. S., 'A survey of British local authority response to Muslim needs', *Research Papers: Muslims in Europe*, no. 30/31 (June–September 1986).

Nielsen, J. S., 'Other religions', in L. M. Barley *et al.*, *Reviews of United Kingdom statistical sources*. Vol. 20: *Religion* (London: Pergamon Press, 1987), pp. 563–621.

Nielsen, J. S., 'Muslims in English schools', *Journal: Institute of Muslim Minority Affairs*, vol. 10, no. 1 (January 1989), pp. 223–45.

Nielsen J. S., 'Muslims, the state and the public domain in Britain', in R. Bonney, F. Bosbach and T. Brockmann (eds), *Religion and politics in Britain and Germany* (Munich: K. G. Saur, 2001), pp. 145–54.

Religions in the UK: a multi-faith directory (Derby: University of Derby, 1997).

Robinson, F., *Varieties of South Asian Islam* (Coventry: University of Warwick, Centre for Research in Ethnic Relations, 1988).

Saifullah-Khan, V., 'Pakistani women in Britain', *New Community*, vol. 3, nos 1–2 (Summer 1976), pp. 99–108.

Shaw, A., *A Pakistani community in Britain* (Oxford: Blackwell, 1988).

Vertovec, S., *Annotated bibliography of academic publications regarding Islam and Muslims in the United Kingdom, 1985–1992* (Coventry: University of Warwick, Centre for Research in Ethnic Relations, 1993).

Werbner, P., *The migration process: gifts and offerings among British Pakistanis* (Oxford: Berg, 1990).

5. The Netherlands and Belgium

Bagley, C., *The Dutch plural society* (London: Oxford University Press, 1973).

van Bakelen, F. A., *De status van de imaam in het Nederlandse arbeidsrecht* (Groningen: RIMO, 1985).

Bakker, E. S. J. and L. J. Tap, *Islamitische slagerijen in Nederland* (Utrecht: OKU, 1985).

Butt, W. M., *The life of Pakistanis in the Netherlands* (Amsterdam: University of Amsterdam, 1990).

Carlier, J. Y. and M. Verwilghen, *Musulmans en Belgique: Un statut juridique spécifique?* (Brussels: Academia, 1989).

Dassetto, F. (ed.), *Facettes de l'islam belge* (Louvain-la-Neuve: Academia Bruylant, 1997).

Dassetto, F. and A. Bastenier, *L'Islam transplanté* (Antwerp: Editions EPO, 1984).

Dassetto, F. and A. Bastenier, *Medias u Akbar: Confrontations autour d'une manifestation* (Louvain: CIACO, 1987).

Destrée, A. *et al.* (eds), *Acculturation ou double culture: La spécificité des enfants musulmans en Belgique* (Brussels: Centre pour l'étude des problèmes du monde musulman contemporain, 1982).

Documentatie: Christelijke scholen en moslem-leerlingen (Leusden: Raad van Kerken in Nederland, 1983).

Lesthaeghe, R. (ed.), *Communities and generations: Turkish and Moroccan populations in Belgium* (Brussels: NIDI-CBGS Publications, 2000).

Panafit, L., *Quand le droit écrit l'islam: l'intégration juridique de l'islam en Belgique* (Brussels: Bruylant, 1999).

Reesink, P., 'Chrétiens et musulmans aux Pays-Bas', *Se Comprendre*, no. 89/08 (17 July 1989).

Religieuze voorzieningen voor etnische minderheden in Nederland (Rijswijk: Ministerie van Welzijn, Volksgezondheid en Cultuur, 1983).

Shadid, W. and P. S. van Koningsveld, *Moslims in Nederland: Minderheden en religie in een multiculturele samenleving* (Alphen aan de Rijn: Samson Staflev, 1990).

Shadid, W. and P. S. van Koningsveld, *Islam in Dutch society* (Kampen: Kok Pharos, 1992).

Slomp, J., 'Islam in Nederland', in J. Waardenburg (ed.), *Islam: Norm, ideaal en werkelijkheid* (Weesp: Het Wereldvenster, 1984), pp. 419–42.

Sunier, T., 'Muslim migrants, Muslim citizens: Islam and Dutch society', *The Netherlands Journal of Social Sciences*, vol. 35, no. 1 (1999), pp. 69–82.

Wagtendonk, K. (ed.), *Islam in Nederland, Islam op school* (Muiderberg: Coutinho, 1987).

6. The Nordic countries

Ahlberg, N., *New challenges – old strategies: themes of variation and conflict among Pakistani Muslims in Norway* (Helsinki: Finnish Anthropological Society,1990).

Alwall, J., *Muslim rights and plights: the religious liberty situation of a minority in Sweden* (Lund: Lund University Press, 1998).

Bajaj, K. and H. S. Laursen, *Pakistanske kvinder i Danmark* (Esbjerg: Sydjysk universitets-forlag, 1988).

Berglund, J., *Teaching Islam: Islamic religious education at three Muslim schools in Sweden* (Uppsala: Uppsala University, 2009).

Betænkning om udenlandske arbejderes sociale og samfundsmæssige tilpasning her i landet (Copenhagen: Socialministeriet, 1975).

Dindler, S. and A. Olesen (eds), *Muslimsk indvandrerkultur i Danmark* (Århus: Århus Universitetsforlag, 1989).

Engelbrektson, U.-B., *The force of tradition: Turkish migrants at home and abroad* (Gothenburg: Gothenburg Studies in Social Anthropology, 1978).

Ferdinand, K. and B. Selmer (eds), *Islam: Familie og samfund* (Århus: Århus Universitetsforlag, 1984).

Hatlehol, O. and J. Opsal, 'Ikke-kristne religioner i Norge', in H. Nordhoug (ed.), *Naar tro møter tro* (Oslo: Verbum, 1990), pp. 114–19.

Larsson, G. (ed.), *Islam in the Nordic and Baltic countries* (London and New York: Routledge, 2009).

Larsson, G. and Å. Sander, *Islam and Muslims in Sweden: integration or fragmentation? A contextual study* (Berlin: LIT Verlag, 2007).

Lithman, Y. G., 'Social relations and cultural continuities: Muslim immigrants and their social networks', in T. Gerholm and Y. G. Lithman (eds), *The new Islamic presence in Europe* (London and New York: Mansell, 1988), pp. 239–63.

Muslim i Sverige (Norrköping: Statens indvandrarverk, 1981).

Muslimer og kristne ansigt til ansigt (Copenhagen: IKS, 2001).

Naguib, S.-A., 'The Northern way: Muslim communities in Norway' in Y. Y. Haddad and J. I. Smith (eds), *Muslim minorities in the West* (Walnut Creek: Altamira, 2002), pp. 161–74.

Olesen, A., *Islam og undervisning i Danmark* (Århus: Århus Universitetsforlag, 1987).

Sachs, L., *Evil eye or bacteria: Turkish migrant women and Swedish health care* (Stockholm: Stockholm Studies in Social Anthropology, 1983).

Sakaranaho, T., *Religious freedom, multiculturalism, Islam: cross-reading Finland and Ireland* (Leiden: Brill, 2006).

Sander, Å., *Islam and Muslims in Sweden* (Gothenburg: University of Gothenburg, Institutionen för filosofi, 1989).

Sander, Å., 'The road from musalla to mosque: Some reflections on the process of integration and institutionalization of Islam in Sweden', in P. S. van Koningsveld and

W. Shadid (eds), *The integration of Islam and Hinduism in Western Europe* (Kampen: Kok Pharos, 1991), pp. 62–88.

Undervisning af fremmedsprogede elever i folkeskolen: en redegørelse (Copenhagen: Undervisningsministeriet, 1981).

7. Southern Europe

Aguer, B., 'Résurgence de l'Islam en Espagne', *Revue Européenne des Migrations Internationales*, vol. 7, no. 3 (1991), pp. 59–74.

Allemann, F., 'Muslime in der Schweiz', *CIBEDO-Dokumentation*, no. 27 (April 1986).

Allievi, S. and F. Dassetto, *Il retorno dell'Islam* (Rome: Edizioni Lavoro, 1993).

Arat, K., 'Der Islam in Österreich', *CIBEDO*, vol. 1, no. 4 (1987), pp. 97–119.

Basset, J.-C., 'Musulmans en Romandie', *Repères*, no. 4 (1982), pp. 41–6.

Ferrari, S. (ed.), *Musulmani in Italia: la condizione giuridica delle communità islamiche* (Bologna: Mulino, 2000).

Lasoda, T., 'La ley de extranjeria y la situacion de los Marroquies en Espana', *Encuentro Islamo–Christiano*, no. 165 (March 1986).

Moreras, J., *Musulmanes en Barcelona: espacios y dinàmicas communitarias* (Barcelona: Cidop, 2000).

Saint-Blancat, C., (ed.), *L'islam in Italia: una presenze plurale* (Rome: Lovoro, 1999).

Strobl, A., *Islam in Österreich: eine religionssoziologische Untersuchung* (Frankfurt a/M: Peter Lang, 1997).

Tassello, G., 'L'Italie, pays d'immigration', *Dossier migrations* (September–October 1981).

Tassello, G., 'L'Italie, pays d'immigration', *Hommes et migrations*, no. 1083 (15 July 1985), pp. 15–21.

Tiesler, N. C., 'No bad news from the European margin: the new Islamic presence in Portugal', *Islam and Christian–Muslim Relations*, vol. 12, no. 1 (January 2001), pp. 71–91.

8. Family, law and culture

Aldeeb, S. *et al.* (eds), *Le droit musulman de la famille et la succession à l'épreuve des ordres juridiques occidentaux* (Zurich: Institute Suisse de droit compare, 1999).

Allievi, S., *Les convertis à l'Islam: les nouveaux musulmans d'Europe* (Paris: L'Harmattan, 1998).

van Amersfoort, H., 'Ethnic residential patterns in Dutch cities: Class, race or culture?', in T. Gerholm and Y. G. Lithman (eds), *The new Islamic presence in Europe* (London and New York: Mansell, 1988), pp. 219–38.

Anwar, M., *Young Muslims in a multicultural society* (Leicester: The Islamic Foundation, 1982).

Buskens, L., 'Marokkaans familierecht in Nederland', in idem, *Islamitisch recht en familiebe-trekkingen in Marokko* (Amsterdam: Bulaaq, 1999), pp. 536–60.

Coulson, N. J., *A history of Islamic law* (Edinburgh: Edinburgh University Press, 1964 and reprints).

Foblets, M.-C., *Familles – Islam – Europe: le droit confronté au changement* (Paris: L'Harmattan,1996).

El-Husseini, R., 'Le droit international privé français et la repudiation islamique', *Revue critique de droit international privé* (1999), pp. 427–68.

Kastoryano, R., *Quelle identité pour l'Europe? Le multiculturalisme à l'épreuve* (Paris: Presse de Science Po, 1998).

Köse, A., *Conversion to Islam: a study of native British converts* (London: Kegan Paul, 1996).

Leveau, R. (ed.), *Islam(s) en Europe: approches d'un nouveau pluralisme culturel européen* (Berlin: Centre Marc Bloch, 1998).

Modood, T., *Britain's ethnic minorities: diversity and disadvantage* (London: Policy Studies Institute, 1997).

Nielsen, J. S., 'Islam and Islamic law in the United Kingdom', *Recht van de Islam*, vol. 10 (1992), pp. 92–9.

Pearl, D., *Family law and the immigrant communities* (Bristol: Jordans, 1986).

Poston, L., *Islamic Da'wah in the West: Muslim missionary activity and the dynamics of conversion to Islam* (New York: Oxford University Press, 1992).

Poulter, S. M., *English law and ethnic minority customs* (London: Butterworth, 1986).

Ramadan, T., *To be a European Muslim* (Markfield: Islamic Foundation, 1999).

Ritter, S., *Moslims in de Nederlandse rechtspraak* (Kampen: Kok, 1988).

Rosen, L., *The Anthropology of Justice* (Cambridge: Cambridge University Press, 1989).

Rude-Antoine, E., 'L'héritage et les familles maghrébines en France', *Hommes et migrations*, no. 1097 (15 November 1986), pp. 34–42.

Rude-Antoine, E., *La vie des familles: les immigrés, la loi et la coutume* (Paris: O. Jacob, 1997).

Sayad, A., 'L'Islam et immigration en France: Les effets de l'immigration sur l'Islam', in M. Morsy (ed.), *L'Islam en Europe à l'Epoque moderne* (Paris: Sindbad, 1985), pp. 239–76.

Schacht, J., *An introduction to Islamic law* (Oxford: Oxford University Press, 1964).

Schiffauer, W., 'Migration and religiousness', in T. Gerholm and Y. G. Lithman (eds), *The new Islamic presence in Europe* (London and New York: Mansell, 1988), pp. 146–58.

Schmied, M., *Familienkonflikte zwischen Scharia und bürgerlichem Recht* (Frankfurt a/M: Peter Lang, 1999).

Smith, D. J., *The facts of racial disadvantage* (London: Political and Economic Planning,1976).

Taverne, M., *Le droit familial maghrébin (Algérie-Maroc-Tunisie) et son application en Belgique* (Brussels: F. Larcier, 1981)

Thomä-Venske, H., *Islam und Integration* (Hamburg: EBV-Rissen, 1981).

Weische-Alexa, P., *Sozial-kulturelle Probleme junger Türkinnen in der Bundesrepublik Deutschland* (Cologne: the author, 1977).

Wolf-Almanasreh, R. *et al.*, *Mein Partner oder meine Partnerin kommt aus einen anderen Land: Inter-ethnische Ehen und Lebensgemeinschaften* (Frankfurt: IAF, 1986).

9. Muslim organisations

Abun-Nasr, J. M., *A history of the Maghrib in the Islamic period* (Cambridge: Cambridge University Press, 1987).

Ageron, C. R., *Politiques coloniales au Maghreb* (Paris: PUF, 1972).

Ageron, C. R., *Histoire de l'Algérie contemporaine* (Paris: PUF, 1979).

Ahmad, A., *An intellectual history of Islam in India* (Edinburgh: Edinburgh University Press, 1969).

Anwarul Haq, M., *The faith movement of Mawlana Muhammad Ilyas* (London: Allen and Unwin, 1972).

Bennoune, M., *The making of contemporary Algeria, 1830–1987* (Cambridge: Cambridge University Press, 1988).

Binder, L., *Religion and politics in Pakistan* (Berkeley: University of California Press, 1961).

Birge, J. K., *The Bektashi order of dervishes* (Hartford: Hartford Seminary Press, 1937).

Blaschke, J. and M. van Bruinessen, *Islam und Politik in der Türkei* (Berlin: Parabolis, 1989).

Blaschke, J., 'Islam und Politik unter türkischer Arbeitsmigranten', *Jahrbuch zur Geschichte und Gesellschaft des Vorderen und Mittleren Orients, 1984* (Berlin: Express, 1985), pp. 295–366.

Carré, O. and G. Michaud, *Les frères musulmans: Egypte et Syrie* (1928–82) (Paris: Gallimard, 1983).

Dumont, P., 'Disciples of the light: The Nurju movement in Turkey', *Central Asian Survey*, vol. 5, no. 2 (1986), pp. 33–60.

Dunn, R. E., *Resistance in the desert: Moroccan responses to French imperialism 1881–1912* (London: Croom Helm, 1977).

Erbakan, N., *Milli Görüş* (Istanbul: Dergah Yayinlari, 1975).

Gellner, E., *Saints of the Atlas* (Chicago: Chicago University Press, 1969.

Gellner, E., 'Doctor and saint', in N. Keddie (ed.), *Scholars, saints and sufis* (Berkeley: University of California Press, 1972), pp. 307–26.

Gellner, E., *Muslim society* (Cambridge: Cambridge University Press, 1981).

Gökalp, A., *Têtes rouges et bouches noires* (Paris: Société d'Ethnographie, 1980).

Green, A. H., *The Tunisian ulama 1873–1915* (Leiden: Brill, 1978).

Habib, J. S., *Ibn Sa'ud's warriors of Islam* (Leiden: Brill, 1978).

Halstead, J. P., *Rebirth of a nation: The origins and rise of Moroccan nationalism, 1912–1944* (Cambridge, MA: Harvard University Press, 1967).

Hardy, P., *The Muslims of British India* (Cambridge: Cambridge University Press, 1972).

Hourani, A., *Arabic thought in the liberal age 1798–1939* (London: Oxford University Press, 1962).

Husseini, I. M., *The Moslem Brethren* (Beirut: Khayat, 1956).

Kehl-Bodrogi, K., *Die Kizilbas-Aleviten* (Berlin: Klaus Schwartz Verlag, 1988).

Kepel, G., *Les Banlieues de l'Islam* (Paris: Seuil, 1987).

Kreiser, K., 'Die Religionspolitik der Türkei im Jahre 1985', in J. Lähnemann (ed.), *Erziehung zur Kulturbegegnung* (Hamburg: EBV-Rissen, 1986), pp. 216–29.

Laroui, A., *Histoire du Magreb* (Paris: Maspéro, 1976).

Laroui, A., *Les origines sociales et culturelles du nationalisme marocain (1830–1912)* (Paris: Maspéro, 1977).

Lewis, B., *The emergence of modern Turkey* (London: Oxford University Press, 1961).

Makdisi, G., *The rise of colleges* (Edinburgh: Edinburgh University Press, 1981).

Makdisi, G., *The rise of humanism in classical Islam and the Christian West* (Edinburgh: Edinburgh University Press, 1990).

Mardin, S., *Religion and social change in modern Turkey – The case of Bediüzzaman Said Nursi* (New York: State University of New York Press, 1989).

Merad, A., *Le réformisme musulman en Algérie, 1920–1962* (The Hague: Mouton, 1967).

Metcalfe, B., *Islamic revival in British India, 1860–1900* (Princeton: Princeton University Press, 1982).

Mitchell, R. F., *The society of the Muslim Brethren* (Oxford: Oxford University Press, 1969).

Pedersen, L., *Newer Islamic movements in western Europe* (Aldershot: Ashgate, 1999).

Piscatori, J. (ed.), *Islam in the political process* (Cambridge: Cambridge University Press, 1983).

Rex, J. *et al.* (eds), *Immigrant associations in Europe* (Aldershot: Gower, 1987).

Salem, N., *Habib Bourguiba, Islam and the creation of Tunisia* (London: Croom Helm, 1984).

Seufert, G. and J. Waardenburg (eds), *Turkish Islam and Europe* (Stuttgart: Steiner, 1999).

Sivan, E., *Radical Islam, medieval theology and modern politics* (New Haven: Yale University Press, 1985).

Tamimi, A. S., *Rachid Ghannouchi: a democrat within Islamism* (New York: Oxford University Press, 2001).

Toprak, B., 'Politicisation of Islam in a secular state: the National Salvation Party in Turkey', in S. A. Arjomand (ed.), *From nationalism to revolutionary Islam* (London: Macmillan, 1984), pp. 119–33.

Trimingham, J. S., *The Sufi orders in Islam* (Oxford: Oxford University Press, 1971).

Troll, C. W. (ed.), *Muslim shrines in India* (Oxford: Oxford University Press, 1989).

Yapp, M. E., *The making of the modern Near East 1792–1923* (London: Longman, 1987).

Yapp, M. E., *The Near East since the First World War* (London: Longman, 1991).

Al-Yassini, A., *Religion and state in the Kingdom of Saudi Arabia* (Boulder: Westview, 1985).

Ziadeh, N., *Origins of nationalism in Tunisia* (Beirut: Khayat, 1969).

10. European Muslims in a new Europe?

Allam, M., *Bin Laden in Italia: viaggio nell'islam radicale* (Milan: Mondadori, 2002).

Allen, C. and J. S. Nielsen, *Summary report on Islamophobia in the EU after 11 September 2001* (Vienna: European Monitoring Centre on Racism and Xenophobia, 2002).

Bousetta, H. (ed.), *Rompre le silence: 11 septembre 2001–11 septembre 2002. Une prise de position citoyenne d'intellectuels belges d'origine maghrébine* (Brussels: Labor, 2002).

Laïdi, A. and A. Salam, *Le jihad en Europe: les filières du terrorisme islamiste* (Paris: Seuil, 2002).

Muslim Council of Britain, *The quest for sanity: reflections on September 11 and the aftermath* (London: Muslim Council of Britain, 2002).

Roy, O., *Les illusions du 11 septembre: le débat stratégique face au 11 septembre* (Paris: Seuil, 2002).

The Runnymede Trust, *Islamophobia: a challenge for us all* (London: Runnymede Trust, 1997).

Index